Issues of Impurity in Early Judaism

Itero

Reprints in the Service of the Scholarly Community
www.ehs.se/itero

Series Editor
Thomas Kazen

No. 4

Thomas Kazen

Issues of Impurity in
Early Judaism

Enskilda Högskolan Stockholm

Itero – Reprints in the Service of the Scholarly Community

Books still in demand should not get out of print, and with today's techniques there is no defence. With the reprint series *Itero*, the Biblical Studies department at Stockholm School of Theology would like to make books available for free online and at a very low cost in print. Part of the background is the fact that several faculty members have published their studies in series that were cancelled. With the publishing market in constant flux, series migrate, and volumes still in demand can suddenly become unavailable. This is unsatisfactory. In collaboration with the authors, we are now republishing a number of such volumes and we will consider publishing other out-of-print titles, for which authors hold the copyright. This is entirely a non-profit project. Files may be downloaded at *www.ehs.se/itero* and books can be bought through most major internet bookshops.

University College Stockholm – Stockholm School of Theology

University College Stockholm (Enskilda Högskolan Stockholm) is a major Swedish provider of education in Human Rights and Democracy, as well as in Theology/Religious Studies. EHS offers Bachelor's Master's and Doctoral programmes. The university college was founded in 1993 through a merger of educational institutions with roots dating back to 1866. *Stockholm School of Theology* is the common designation for the two theological departments: Religious Studies and Theology, and Eastern Christian Studies. *Stockholm School of Human Rights and Democracy* is the designation for the programmes in Human Rights and Democracy.

© 2010 Thomas Kazen. © 2021 Thomas Kazen & Enskilda Högskolan Stockholm.
Reprint edition. Previously published by Eisenbrauns.

ISBN: 978-91-8890-616-8

Cover design by Carl Johan Berglund. Typeset in EB Garamond.
Printed by BoD – Books on Demand, Norderstedt, Germany.

Stockholm School of Theology
University College Stockholm
Åkeshovsvägen 29, 168 39 Bromma, Sweden
www.ehs.se

Preface to the Itero Reprint Edition

This collection of articles was originally published by Eisenbrauns in 2010. Just like my dissertation, *Jesus and Purity* Halakhah, it suddenly went out of print when the ConBNT series changed home. The interest in ritual purity seems not to go away and new scholars continuously enter the scene, so it is reasonable for the book to remain available.

Since this collection was first published, I have continued to write on the topic and a dozen articles and papers from the last decade were recently published as *Impurity and Purification in Early Judaism and the Jesus Tradition* (SBL Press, 2021). Together, these two volumes represent my continuous work on purity issues through two decades. The reader of both volumes will see how my views have gradually evolved and matured somewhat through the years – at least that is what I hope! While some people think that ritual purity is a tedious topic, I still find it fascinating.

Bromma in November 2021

Thomas Kazen

Preface to the 2010 edition

When in the late 1990's my *Doktorvater* Kari Syreeni suggested that purity might still be an open slot for one who wished to write a dissertation within the field of Historical Jesus studies, I was not immediately convinced that the task would be interesting enough or even worthwhile. Today I would not for a moment regret the choice of subject, although one sometimes has to suffer comments from friends and family about the reasons for such an interest in all that yucky stuff. Those issues that in my earliest outlines of *Jesus and Purity* Halakhah were supposed to be covered within 30–40 pages, to provide "background" (my apologies both for the bias and for being so naïve!), were to become the bulk of my dissertation in 2002.

While *Jesus and Purity* aimed to present an unfolding argument, the present volume does not aspire at such coherence. It consists of a number of articles and papers on various issues, some of which have been previously published and others not. Chapters 1, 2, 5, 6 and 8 were written for this volume; chapter 2 was previously read as a paper at the "Workshop on Ritual in Early Judaism and Early Christianity: Texts and Practices" in Helsinki, August 26–29, 2009, arranged by the Helsinki Collegium for Advanced Studies and the Nordic Network for the Study of Early Christianity in Its Greco-Roman Context; chapter 8 is based on my response to John P. Meier at a review session on his recent book, *A Marginal Jew*, vol. 4: *Law and Love*, at the SBL Annual Meeting in New Orleans, November 20–24, 2009.

Chapter 3 has been published previously in *Revue Biblique* 114 (2007): 348–371. Chapter 4 was recently published in *Dead Sea Discoveries* 17 (2010): 53–87. Chapter 7 is based on an excursus in *Jesus and Purity* and has been published separately in *Svensk Exegetisk Årsbok* 71 (2006): 131–144. I am grateful to the publishers for granting permission to republish these items.

I am also grateful to my employer, Stockholm School of Theology, for providing ample time for research. Without such conditions, this book would not have been written. Research for various articles and papers in this volume has received additional sponsorship from Helge Ax:son Johnson's foundation and SKY's stipendiary fund.

This book is dedicated to my youngest son, Johannes. He will not understand why and he will most probably never read it, since he thinks that the issues herein are pretty strange and altogether beside the point. Since he is now taller and stronger than I am, I can no longer have a gainsay. And I am not immune to the viewpoint that there are other things in life, too, such as onewheeling on a 36" or on a 6' giraffe unicycle and playing virtuoso baroque music on treble recorders. Well, music we can play together, but this is my way of onewheeling. I hope that I am keeping my balance all right!

Märsta in August 2010

Thomas Kazen

Contents

Notes

Transliteration of Hebrew words follows a simplified model. References to my dissertation *Jesus and Purity* Halakhah are to the original 2002 edition, but a corrected reprint edition (Eisenbrauns, 2010) is now available. The pagination is virtually the same.

Chapter 1

Introduction: Impurity in the Second Temple Period

Introduction

"Purity broke out in Israel," said Rabbi Simeon ben Eleazar, at least according to the *Tosefta*.[1] The common rendering is close to mistranslation, as some scholars remind us of,[2] at least if taken to mean a sudden explosion of purity practices rather than a continuous spread and development of a paradigm.

Alluding to this saying, one could perhaps suggest that there has been a "burst" of interest in purity issues with a particular focus on the Second Temple period, or interest has at least become more widespread than before, during the last decades.[3] This has partly to do with an increased engagement in the study of ritual and an emphasis on physical, tangible, or bodily aspects of religion. It is also, in my view, a natural result of the continuous re-evaluation of, and negotiation between, early Judaism and early Christianity in all their diversity as well as their interrelationship. Hence purity is now being studied from a number of viewpoints, taking into account the variety of movements and contexts present during the Second Temple period.

In view of this, would it not be appropriate with a systematic discussion of purity during the Second Temple period, neither as "background" for New Testament studies, nor for Rabbinic studies, but in its own right? The present volume is *not* that book and I am not sure that the time is yet ripe for such a comprehensive work. We are still exploring the diversity of Early Judaism: Is Philo describing Hellenistic diaspora practices or do his texts have a bearing on

---

[1] *t. Šabb.* 1:14.
[2] Miller 2007, 222 and n. 47.
[3] Meier provides a compact bibliography from 1906 to 2006 in a single footnote to his recent chapter on "Jesus and Purity Laws" (2009, 415–426). The note covers eleven full pages, ten of which refer to publications since 1975. Although a number of entries have their main focus on the historical Jesus and/or gospel studies, the list is nevertheless impressive, without claiming to be complete, and witnesses to a growing interest in purity issues. There is no reason to repeat this work. Since then (and also including entries not in Meier) one could mention Wahlen 2004; Philip 2006; Werrett 2007; Schwartz, Wright and Meshel (eds.) 2008; Ellens 2008; Furstenberg 2008; Haber 2008; Lockett 2008; Noam 2008; Adler 2008; 2009; Achenbach 2009; Meier 2009; Avemarie 2010; Noam 2010.

the wider issue? Is Josephus close to actual practice in Palestine or not providing any useful information at all? Can we speak of a purity "system" in Qumran
or do we only have disconnected pieces of information from a variety of
sources? Do gospel texts count as evidence for early Jewish practices or are
they mostly to be seen as late apologetic disinformation? In what way, if any,
can rabbinic texts be used in outlining first century CE practice? And how do
we handle archaeological evidence, which is most concrete but does not speak
with its own voice?

This book does not answer those questions either, but it does touch upon
some of them, and is one contribution among many to the ongoing discussion.
There is in several of the chapters a certain emphasis on two questions, discharge impurity and hand-washing before meals, but other issues are also dealt
with, such as corpse impurity and the question of common denominators or
underlying explanations for the diverse use of impurity language.

Another thing that this book does not provide is a general overview of the
purity "system," nor is there any attempt to write a comprehensive history of
research. For such overviews the reader is referred to other publications;[4] the
present work discusses details and interpretations, but presupposes a general
knowledge.

Pre-exilic purity

If purity "spread" we should be excused for looking for an origin, but of purity
practices during the First Temple period we know very little. The Deuteronomistic History contains a few references to impure conditions, which should be
taken into account, although these books were not edited and completed until
the exilic and post-exilic periods.[5] When David does not turn up at the banquet
(1 Sam 20:26), King Saul assumes that something has happened to him so that
he is not clean.[6] One thinks easily of semen-emission, although this is not
spelled out and no term for "unclean" is actually being used. In 2 Sam 11:4,
however, Bathsheba is said to have sanctified herself from her impurity

---

[4] See for example Sanders 1990. 134–151, 29–42; Harrington 1993, 28–43; 2004, 7–44; Klawans 2000, 3–20; Kazen 2002, 1–7; or encyclopaedia articles like those in *Encyclopaedia Judaica*, s.v. Purity and Impurity, Ritual (EH); *Anchor Bible Dictionary*, s.v. Unclean and Clean
(Wright; Hübner); or *The New Interpreter's Bible Dictionary*, s.v. Clean and Unclean (Harrington). For a classification of various ancient as well as scholarly approaches to understanding the
concept of purity and impurity that is brief but rich with references, see Noam 2010, 67–69.
[5] For a recent work on the Deuteronomistic History, see Römer 2005.
[6] מקרה הוא בלתי טהור הוא כי־לא תהור

(*tum'ah*), which has been understood as her menstrual period, but could just as well refer to impurity contracted by intercourse.[7]

When David curses Joab for the murder of Abner, the discharger (*zav*) and the "leper" (*metzora'*) belong to those categories that he wishes Joab's house never to lack (2 Sam 3:29). These conditions are not specified as impure, but rather included in a list of possible punishments. Naaman, the Syrian "leprous" commander, is healed by the prophet Elisha by immersing seven times in the Jordan (2 Kgs 5). Although Naaman is repeatedly said to become clean (*taher*) by washing,[8] the emphasis is on healing as restoration, and neither he, nor Gehazi, who receives Naaman's "leprosy" (*tzara'at*) in return for his greed, is called impure. Similarly, the skin-diseased four men who discover the sudden flight of the Aramean army (2 Kgs 7: 3–20) are never called unclean. It is noteworthy, however, that they are portrayed as spending the night outside of the city gate, even under such circumstances as a siege. King Azariah is said to have been struck by the Lord so that he became "leprous" and had to live in a separate house (2 Kgs 15:1–7). This happened in spite of the fact that he was supposed to have been a just king – except for not taking away the *bamot*. (This causes the Chronicler, who talks of him as Uzziah, reserving the name Azariah for his opponent, the priest, to describe his pride and attempt to offer incense in the temple, as an explanation for the punishment.[9])

It seems that in many of these cases, "leprosy" and genital discharges are understood as divine punishments for misdeeds, even to the extent that when a supposedly righteous person is being struck a particular transgression has to be spelled out separately. These conditions are punishments, however, in their capacity as diseases rather than as impurities, which they are never explicitly called in these texts. There is reason to believe that skin-diseased people as well as others with unsavoury diseases or conditions were somehow kept outside or apart even before the Second Temple period, not only because of textual evidence, but also because similar attitudes to skin-diseases and genital discharges are found in other cultures and at even earlier dates.[10] Ideas of impurity are an-

---

[7] והיא מתקדשת מטמאתה. This could be regarded as a gloss. For an argument about the participles involved, claiming that they cannot refer to menstrual purification, see Chankin-Gould et al. 2008.

[8] 2 Kgs 5:10, 12, 14.

[9] According to 2 Chr 26:21, the king lived in a separate house because he was excluded from the temple. With the chronicler, however, we are well into the Second Temple period.

[10] Milgrom refers for example to a Babylonian kudurru inscription (1991, 805), a Mari letter (818, 911), and a Šurpu incantation (911); cf. a number of comparative references with regard to childbirth and genital discharges (763–768). See also Herodotus (*Herodotus* 1:138) on the isolation of "lepers" among the Persians, and Pliny the elder about menstruation (*Nat.* 7:63–66).

cient and as I suggest in chapter 2, we may consider psycho-biological reasons for their existence and development as part of our explanations.

Food taboos also belong to those phenomena that are found across cultures, and lists of unclean (*tame'*) foods are found already in Deuteronomy (14:3–21). In the narrative of Samson (Judg 13), neither the future nazirite to be born, nor his mother, are supposed to eat anything unclean. The concept of unclean food is also found in Hos 9:3–4 where it is associated with foreign lands (Assyria), but also, interestingly, with the bread of mourners. Another possibly early piece of evidence for the idea of gentile lands as unclean is found in Amos 7:17. Both of these references have, however, been attributed to later redaction, on other grounds (see below).

The pre-exilic period might also have known a basic idea of the impurity of corpses and it seems reasonable that corpses were increasingly being buried outside of Jerusalem already before the exile, although a more developed notion of corpse impurity was not yet in place; in 2 Kgs 13:20–21, Elisha's bones cause miraculous resuscitation with no hints of any corpse impurity being indicated. In the narrative of Josiah's reform, however (2 Kgs 23), human bones are used for defiling (*timme'*) the altars and the *bamot*. The evidence is ambiguous, however. While there are archaeological indications that tombs outside of the Jerusalem city wall may have been emptied when the city expanded from the time of Hezekiah, Ezekiel, or rather, the Lord's voice in Ezekiel, complains about the corpses of the kings of Judah being buried close to the temple (Ezek 43:7–9), a practice attested by the books of Kings as well as by Chronicles.[11] It seems reasonable to suggest that corpses were generally buried outside of settlements, with rulers or important people as possible exceptions, but perhaps more for practical reasons than because of notions of impurity.

Although there is no reason to doubt the existence of a number of ideas of impurity in the pre-exilic period, it is difficult to know exactly what they looked like. The texts that we have available, such as the Deuteronomistic history and pre-exilic prophets, are mostly shaped and redacted during and after the exile.[12] But even if certain statements may be suspected as glosses, there is enough evidence for basic conceptions. The "spread" witnessed during the Second Temple period was grounded in former ideas and practices, although crucial impulses for further development came from without.

---

[11] Broshi 1974; Wright 1987a, 115–128.

[12] The Book of the Twelve was redacted through several steps. Even the pre-exilic prophets Hosea, Amos, Micah and Zephaniah were first collected and given an exilic redaction, then were subject to further post-exilic redactions during the Persian period. Cf. Schart 2000; Wöhrle 2006. For the redaction of the Deuteronomistic history in general, see Römer 2005.

Purity and the Persians

Ritual purity considerations as we know them from Jewish texts seem to have developed together with the Second Temple. The priestly sacrificial laws (Lev 1–9) and the legal texts concerning the impurity of food, "leprosy" and genital discharges (Lev 11–15) presumably have their roots in pre-exilic and exilic practices and instructions, but today most scholars would date their redaction to post-exilic times,[13] although some still defend an earlier date.[14] Some consider the sacrificial laws to originate with memoranda or check lists formed during the exile, in view of hopes of a resumed cult in Jerusalem.[15] These would then have been joined with the purity laws and integrated with a priestly narrative in the early 5th century BCE, during Persian times, and added to some decades later, before P was finally included in the Pentateuch.[16]

Developed ideas of corpse impurity as well as ideas of gentile impurity most probably belong to post-exilic times. While a basic understanding of human corpses as impure could be assumed to date back in time, there is no early evidence for a conception of corpse impurity as a contact contagion. Hos 9:4, referred to above, could imply the idea of foodstuff being contaminated by corpse impurity; the mention of becoming impure (*yitamma'u*) by eating the bread of mourners (*lechem 'onim*) is conspicuous. This passage, however, is subject to suspicions of being part of late redaction.[17]

The same passage also associates unclean foods with foreign countries: "they will eat unclean food in Assyria" (Hos 9:3). However, similar considerations apply to the issue of gentile impurity. The passage from Amos 7:17, also referred to above, that talks of exile in an "unclean land" (*'adamah $t^e me'ah$*), is also probably part of at least exilic redaction.[18] Conceptions of gentile impurity or "genealogical impurity" are sometimes discussed as a fourth category, in addition to food laws, "ritual" purity and "moral" impurity.[19] It should be noted, however, that the passages mentioned so far imply at most the impurity of non-Israelite territory. Ideas of "genealogical impurity," based on the conception of lay Israelites as "holy seed," only surface in the texts from the times of Ezra and

---

[13] Nihan 2007; Römer 2008.

[14] E.g., Milgrom 1991; Knohl 1995. See Schwartz 2009 about the relationship between the relative dating of H and P, and the issue of a post-exilic dating of P.

[15] Attempts to define a specific Gattung or genre for the sacrificial laws have not met general acceptance; See Watts 2003. For Lev 1–3, see Nihan 2007, 219, 220–231.

[16] Nihan 2007, 215–231, 379–394.

[17] Yee 1987, 189, 198–207. The grounds for this have nothing to do with the issue of purity as such.

[18] Nogalski 1993, 87–88 and n. 43.

[19] Cf. Meier 2009, 343–348.

Nehemiah.[20] These ideas did not find their way into the legal texts of the Torah, however.

This is different from the case of corpse impurity. The idea is present in Lev 21:1–4 and 22:4, which is part of the so-called Holiness Code that mediates between Deuteronomy and the priestly laws, and must be dated later than the first half of Leviticus, probably to the latter half of the 5th century BCE,[21] i.e., well into the Persian period. Here it only concerns priests, however. Corpse impurity rules relating to lay people do not appear in the purity laws of Leviticus, but in the book of Numbers. I am inclined to follow an increasing number of scholars who regard Numbers as consisting of narrative non-P traditions and additional legal material, redacted at one of the latest stages in the formation of the Pentateuch. What was formerly understood as P texts in Numbers should rather be understood as post-P redaction, and the writing is probably the latest of the Pentateuchal books, being edited during the early 4th century BCE.[22] The strict commandment of expulsion (Num 5:2–4) as well as the rule concerning corpse contamination and the preparation of ashes from the red cow (Num 19:1–22) have been understood as resulting from one of the latest stages of "theocratic redaction" of the book. In spite of this, these rules are still in some respects less detailed than the purity regulations in Leviticus. The war-camp regulations (Num 31:19–24) are subject to similar considerations; they can be understood as representing an even slightly later phase of such redaction, re-flecting a proto-chronistic theology.[23] If these views are accepted, texts that re-flect a somewhat developed idea of corpse impurity all date from the Persian period, and those that relate to lay people are no earlier than the 4th century BCE.

While these considerations do not rule out an earlier background for ideas of corpse impurity, they suggest that this concept developed relatively late in comparison to other types of impurity, although as already pointed out, we can-not say much about ideas of impurity during the pre-exilic period at all. It seems that the exile triggered further development of conceptions already entertained and also added new aspects. The encounter with Babylonian and Persian relig-ion should have played a role. Similarities with the even more developed purity system in Zoroastrianism have since long been noted.[24] Achenbach refers to

---

[20] Similar ideas are also found in the book of Jubilees and 4QMMT. For a discussion of the origins of a concept of gentile impurity and its development, see Hayes 2002.

[21] Nihan 2004. Cf. Knohl 1995, 71–106, but with other dates.

[22] Nihan 2004, 120–122; 2007, 554–555, 570–572; Achenbach 2003, 499–528.

[23] Achenbach 2003, 615–628.

[24] Nyberg 1937, 378; Boyce 1996, 294–324; Choksy 1989, similarities with Judaism noted on pp. 12, 14–15, 50, 61, 79, 93–94, 103, 105.

contemporary purity rules in Persian religion, which refer to skin diseased and corpse-contaminated people as well as to menstruants, when discussing the strictures of Num 5.[25]

Although the reconstruction of Iranian religion with the help of the texts of the Younger Avesta is fraught with difficulties, much of the material is generally considered to be of ancient origin.[26] For purity laws the Avestan text called *Vidēvdāt* or *Vendidād* is the most important. Colpe has argued for an analogous structure of this text and Leviticus. Whether or not this is accepted, suggestions of contact and influence during the 5th century BCE are very reasonable.[27] The purity issues discussed in *Vendidād* cover both discharges and corpse contamination; instructions concern the separation or isolation of both categories and include details about contact contagion, distances to be kept, vessels used for serving food or for purificatory sprinkling, and a list of body parts to be treated that includes but by far exceeds those extremities that are involved in the purification rite of the "leper" in Leviticus.[28]

Drawing on *Vendidād* and other texts, both Boyce and Choksy have outlined Zoroastrian purity laws. The dualistic context places purity together with goodness and impurity with evil, within a demonic framework.[29] Impurity thus becomes the result of demonic influence and purification rites take on a clear apotropaic or exorcistic character.[30] The strongest impurities come from the human corpse and from all issues that leave the living body, whether in sickness or in health. The more righteous or holy a person has been, the more impure the corpse becomes. The most impure corpses are those of priests. Professional corpse-bearers are made very impure and have to keep separate and eat from separate vessels. A ritual is employed to diminish the contagion of a corpse. Even indirect contact with an impurity can defile. Purification rituals (*baraš-nūm*) for the strongest impurities can take up to nine days and assume degrees of impurity as well as graded purifications. Impure emissions include blood and semen, especially menstrual blood; menstruants withdraw and have to sleep alone. After childbirth the mother is isolated for 40 days. Other conspicuous details are the use of hard materials such as metal and stone for preventing the spread of impurity, the use of drawn water for purification, and the category of

---

[25] Achenbach 2003, 500–504. Achenbach refers among other things to evidence for Zorastrian practices from Herodotus and from *Vidēvdāt* (or *Vendidād*).

[26] Malandra 1983, 28–31; Boyce 1996, 17–21, 265–266.

[27] Colpe 1995 (= Colpe 2003, 649–660).

[28] See e.g. *Vendidād* 3:15–21; 5:27–62; 8:23–25, 40–71; 16:1–18. Much of chapters 5, 6, 7, and 8 deal with corpses and corpse impurity.

[29] For Iranian demonology, see also Colpe 2003, 316–326.

[30] Cf. among other texts the exorcist purification formulas in *Vendidād* 10.

khrafstra – evil animals, such as insects, reptiles and beasts of prey that are good to kill.[31]

It is difficult to avoid noting certain analogies with the development of Jewish purity law beginning with the texts that were shaped and redacted during the Persian period. Besides discharge laws and a growing concept of corpse impurity, the food and contagion laws of Lev 11 focus on animals similar to the *khrafstra*; the categories of "swarmers" together with birds of prey and certain quadruped carnivores cover most of the same ground as the "demonic" animals in Zoroastrianism,[32] although in Leviticus the focus is on not eating and not touching carrion. The idea of certain materials not being conducive to impurity comes up as a question for discussion in Second Temple Judaism a little later.[33] Rituals for diminishing initial impurities also develop in due time, as we will see in subsequent chapters.

The strict rules of isolation that we find in Num 5 thus have a correspondence in Persian religion. Although the isolation of the skin-diseased do not figure as clearly in Zoroastrian texts themselves, the practice is confirmed by Herodotus, who says that the Persians neither allow "lepers" to enter a town, nor to associate with other people.[34] Some of the other issues that are further developed and discussed during the Second Temple period also find at least partial analogies in Persian texts. Contact with Persian religion during the exile seems to have provided a crucial impetus not only for certain generally acknowledged theological ideas,[35] but also for the further development of Jewish purity paradigms in the Second Temple period, in particular the concept of corpse impurity and purification from it with regard to lay people.[36]

---

[31] Boyce 1996, 294–324; Choksy 1989.

[32] Choksy 1989, 14–15.

[33] I.e., the issue of stone vessels not being susceptible to impurity, except perhaps in Qumran. Deines 1993; Kazen 2002, 81–85; Magen 2002; for further discussion and references, see below, chapters 6 and 8. For stone vessels in Qumran, see Eshel 2000. Cf. Boyce 1992, 95–96.

[34] *Herodotus* 1:138: ὃς ἂν δὲ τῶν ἀστῶν λέπρην ἢ λεύκην ἔχῃ, ἐς πόλιν οὗτος οὐ κατέρχεται οὐδὲ συμμίσγεται τοῖσι ἄλλοισι Πέρῃσι·

[35] E.g., divine creation in seven stages, resurrection (cf. Boyce 1982, 188–195). The encounter with the Persians quite likely influenced further developments of angelology and contributed to apocalyptic dualism. Cf. Zaehner 1961, 33–61.

[36] Boyce 1982, 189–190; Achenbach 2009. Vered Noam has recently argued that the "tannaitic concretization of impurity lacks any connection with a demonic universe" (Noam 2010, 102). While this may be true regarding the *tannaim* – even though I find it a slight exaggeration – and while this shows that "realism" does not necessitate "a connection between a naturalistic perception of impurity and threatening metaphysical images of it" (103), it constitutes no argument against Second Temple concepts of impurity evolving out of a fairly demonic world-view within the context of the exilic melting pot.

Temple and life

The development of purity rules during the early Second Temple period took place within the framework of the establishment of Jerusalem as a temple-state under Persian sovereignty.[37] The holiness paradigm that grew out from a Deuteronomistic base emphasized that the divine presence required a high degree of holiness and purity; the lack of adherence to holiness laws was interpreted as the reason both for the expulsion of the former inhabitants of the land and for the recent exile. Through a commitment to holiness the people could prevent this from happening again.[38]

The holiness laws differ from those of previous law collections in certain regards. This is often expressed as an extension of the sphere of holiness; the land was considered holy and immigrants were almost fully included by the legislation, both with regard to its benefits and obligations.[39] Not only are foreigners envisaged as objects of humanitarian concern, but they are supposed to follow holiness law to an extent that is not the case earlier; many laws are expressly said to concern Israelites and foreigners alike, and on some points there are contradictions with earlier rules.[40] This can be explained by social and political circumstances in which a fairly limited Israelite community within a small temple state struggles to regain their identity and prevent previous mistakes from being repeated. Immigrants are no longer limited to a small and vulnerable minority, but are part of a mixed society and sometimes wealthy and land-owners.[41] The holiness required for God's continuous presence in the Temple cannot be upheld unless laws of holiness and purity are followed by the whole population. The holiness of the land in reality meant the holiness of a limited temple state, at least to begin with.

From such a perspective we can better understand the diverse interpretations that developed during the Second Temple period. On one hand, the so-called "extension" of holiness to all of the land and holiness laws to include all of its inhabitants, can be seen as intent on the protection of the Temple and the divine presence, within the bounds of a limited temple state. On the other hand, underlying ideas of impurity from previous times did not solely relate to temple visits, worship, or sacrifice, but were associated with repulsive foods and human conditions that were avoided for their own sake. As the renewed Israelite community grew and became consolidated during the Persian era, later to gain

---

[37] For general descriptions of Yehud during the Persian period, see Grabbe 2004; Knowles 2006.

[38] Lev 18:24–30; 20:22–26; 26:23–45.

[39] Lev 17:15–16; 18:24–30; 19:33–34; 20:2–5; 24:10–23; 25:35–55.

[40] Cf. Nihan 2004.

[41] Nihan 2009.

independence and expand further under the Hasmoneans, ideals for holiness could range from embracing all Israel to being limited to the temple. Ambitions for purity could similarly be limited to issues pertaining to the cult, or embrace everyday life in all its aspects. Both "minimalists" and "maximalists,"[42] or the expansionist and non-expansionist agendas that sometimes seem to collide as the Second Temple period unfolds, can thus be understood as originating with, or emanating from, the same early post-exilic context. To ask whether purity was originally an issue in view of the cult or in everyday life is futile. Both spheres are relevant in the developments that take place during the Second Temple period, although the emphasis varied between different groups and interests.

The holiness paradigm and its development both with regard to the cult and to everyday living also helps explaining the use of impurity language for a number of behaviours or actions that are deemed offensive, but at first sight seem difficult to subsume under one category. Most of those issues of what is often called "moral impurity" that are discussed in the Holiness Code deal either with sex and eating, i.e., issues of everyday life, or with issues of cult and worship, such as illicit mantic practices and idolatry.[43] "Home" and "Cult" also seem to be the two arenas for other types of behaviour for which impurity language is subsequently being used as the concept develops and expands throughout the Second Temple period and beyond. To set these areas against each other is not meaningful.

Issues of impurity

The expanding use of impurity language has, however, been a bone of contention through more than a century of discussion. Contradictory understandings of the relationship between impurity and sin in Judaism have been discussed by scholars at least since the time of Hoffmann and Büchler,[44] and an important contribution to the debate was offered by Klawans a few years ago.[45] This is only part of the larger discussion concerning the relationship between morality and ritual in religion, which has been going for at least as long, with roots back to people like Robertson Smith and Durkheim.[46] Sociological and anthropologi-

---

[42] Alon (1977, 232–233) spoke of a tendency towards restriction or limitation and an expansionist tendency; Milgrom uses the terms "minimalist" and "maximalist" (1990, 85). I prefer to speak of expansionists and non-expansionists.
[43] Lev 18; 20; 19:31; 20:1–3; cf. Klawans 2000, 26–31 and my discussion in Kazen 2002, 200–211, and below, chapter 2, etc.
[44] Hoffmann 1905–1906; Büchler 1928.
[45] Klawans 2000.
[46] Cf. Klawans 2006, 32–38; Stark 2001.

cal perspectives have been important in this debate and one of the most influential voices when it comes to purity and impurity in this regard has been Mary Douglas, who moved from an understanding of impurity as matter out of place to a theological symbolism,[47] none of which I have found easy to embrace. Anthropological considerations rather, in my thinking, suggest biological and cognitive approaches. Some of these issues are touched upon in chapter 2, and I have also discussed them elsewhere.[48]

Another debated area concerns the many irregularities or discrepancies that are evident both within and between various purity laws. It is a well-known fact that the rabbis homogenized some of these rules and drew conclusions from the wording of one for the interpretation of another, since many details were left unanswered by the texts and new questions emerged continuously.[49] At the same time, discrepancies could be exploited for supporting particular interpretations over against others, often with the intent of giving room for exceptions and lenient rulings.[50] It is not always evident, however, to what extent such irregularities in the texts are actually intended, the result of presuppositions behind the texts, or indications of diverse origins and complicated processes of growth and redaction. Some of these issues are dealt with in chapter 3.

Closely related to the previous question is the notion of a purity "system." Such a system can and has been built on the basis of rabbinic evidence, but even then it is a construct, by necessity negotiating a number of viewpoints, all of which are not fully reconcilable.[51] Do we have reasons to believe that notions of impurity and purification during the Second Temple period were more or less coherent than at a later stage? The question becomes acute when we deal with the texts found at Qumran; do these provide us with material for construing a Qumran purity system or are they just evidence for various unconnected ideas of impurity and contamination in the context(s) to which they might be assigned? Harrington and Werrett could be mentioned as representatives of two differing positions.[52] Although I do not attempt to answer these questions systematically, they are touched upon in several instances, and chapter 4 discusses notions of graded impurity and graded purifications in Qumran texts and how they relate to more general practice during the Second Temple period.

---

[47] Douglas 1966; 1999; 2003. Cf. the criticism by Lemos 2009.
[48] Kazen 2008; 2011b, forthcoming.
[49] Cf. *m. Zabim* 5.
[50] Cf. *m. Nid.* 8:1–3.
[51] See below, in particular chapters 3 and 5, as well as the chart in the Appendix; cf. Kazen 2002, 5–7, 78–81.
[52] Harrington 1993; 2004; Werrett 2007.

Two classical problems concerning purity practices in Early Judaism have to do with the isolation/expulsion of certain impurity bearers and the practice of eating ordinary food (*chullin*) in purity. Both are given lengthy treatments by Sanders,[53] and the latter question in particular has been subject to a long and irreconcilable conflict between Sanders and Neusner.[54] The question of isolation and/or expulsion is discussed in chapter 5, especially with a view to female dischargers. Chapter 6 takes up the issue of hand-washing before meals and the claim that Pharisees would have aspired at a priest-like behaviour. Both questions are relevant in the study of the New Testament, since they are issues in the Jesus tradition and its interpretation. Questions about Jesus' behaviour are thus dealt with in these chapters, although they are not a main concern, as they were in *Jesus and Purity*.

Chapter 7 deals with corpse impurity from the perspective of the Lukan parable of the Good Samaritan. In chapter 8, the focus is on the attitude of the historical Jesus, since this chapter reviews the chapter on purity in Meier's latest volume of *A Marginal Jew*. Here several of the issues already discussed are revisited and some further contributions to the interpretation of Mark 7 are offered.

These are not the only issues relating to impurity and purification rituals at the end of the Second Temple period that are debated by scholars today. There are other problems, too, that are not dealt with extensively, but only touched upon briefly or not discussed at all. The question of gentile impurity is one;[55] the dating of rabbinic traditions is another,[56] only to mention a few. I hope, however, that in dealing with those issues that do come up for discussion in this book I have contributed somewhat to the ongoing conversation.

---

[53] Sanders 1990.
[54] Neusner 2007c.
[55] Hayes 2002.
[56] Instone-Brewer 2004; 2010 (forthcoming); Chilton et al. 2010; Stemberger 2010.

Chapter 2

Impurity, Ritual, and Emotion:
A Psycho-Biological Approach[1]

Introduction

Although the field of Biblical studies has more often than not been prepared to integrate a number of new methods for interpreting ancient texts and their history, impulses have usually come from the humanities and the social sciences. In the present chapter I attempt to employ tools from the cognitive sciences to explore the role of three important emotions – disgust, fear and a sense of justice – for ideas of impurity, including some of the rituals employed in handling it.

In the introductory chapter of the recent book *Explaining Christian Origins and Early Judaism*, Petri Luomanen, Ilkka Pyysiäinen and Risto Uro describe the cognitive science of religion as "a new multidisciplinary field that emerged in the 1990s, drawing on cognitive science, cognitive and developmental psychology, neuroscience, evolutionary biology and anthropology."[2] While this is a fair summary of a still emerging umbrella field of studies, I believe that social-scientific perspectives still tend to dominate the playground and that cognition is mostly focused on rational mental activities.

It would be far from my intentions to question the importance or legitimacy of such approaches. I think, however, that tools from the natural sciences – evolutionary biology and neuroscience, naturally complemented by developmental psychology – are somewhat underexploited, even by biblical scholars with cognitive interests. In the following I will thus emphasize emotional aspects of cognition when interpreting texts dealing with impurity and purification. This stance is to be understood neither in opposition to, nor in tension with, what I understand as the present state of affairs, but only as an exciting and hopefully fruitful continuation.

---

[1] Presented at the Workshop on Ritual in Early Judaism and Early Christianity, Helsinki, August 26–29, 2009. For a broader discussion of the use of cognitive methods and the role of emotions for biblical interpretation, see my forthcoming book on emotions in biblical law (Kazen 2011b, forthcoming).

[2] Luomanen, Pyysiäinen and Uro 2008, 1.

As pointed out by Luomanen, Pyysiäinen and Uro, a traditional social science perspective, with its emphasis on social *distance* or a cultural *gap* between the world of an ancient text and modern interpreters, runs the risk of becoming one-sided. A cognitive perspective may counter-balance this by giving attention to the other side of the coin: cultural *similarities* in thought and categorization, providing a cross-cultural base for interpreting various recurring phenomena.[3] To this I would add that such similarities may often be understood as consisting of a common *emotional* mind-set. Cognitive patterns must be taken to include and to a large extent consist of emotional reactions, which are shared not only across human cultures, but to some extent even across intelligent species, since they are biologically based and have evolved through millions of years.

The role of emotions should also be taken into account when so-called "epidemiological" transmission models for cultural evolution are discussed and applied. Concepts and beliefs that somehow correspond with human intuitions are often understood to have had an adaptive advantage in cultural evolution. Since they "trigger intuitive mechanisms of mind [they] are naturally selected for cultural transmission."[4] We must not forget, however, that these "intuitive mechanisms of mind" to a large extent are based on emotions.

The role of emotions for human behaviour

Descartes' famous saying: *cogito, ergo sum* (I think, hence I exist) characterizes the modern Western paradigm, in which mind is seen as separate from matter and rationality is the opposite of emotion. Within such a paradigm, human behaviour is primarily regarded as the result of rational activity. Today, however, the Cartesian paradigm is questioned in favour of a concept of an embodied mind.[5] From an evolutionary perspective, beings existed before mind, and consciousness and thinking developed gradually.

In *Descartes' Error*, Antonio Damasio thus reverses the Cartesian *dictum*, claiming: "We are, and then we think."[6] Damasio's evidence from neurobiological research for the importance of bodily sensations and emotions for a functioning rationality are frequently quoted in scholarly literature.[7] His examples include patients with prefrontal damages, who display deficits in secondary emotions, while on the surface rational capacity and primary emotions seem to

---

[3] Luomanen, Pyysiäinen and Uro 2008, 16–18.
[4] Luomanen, Pyysiäinen and Uro 2008, 7.
[5] Lakoff and Johnson 1999, 16–44, 235–266.
[6] Damasio 1994, 248.
[7] Damasio 1994. Cf. Damasio 1999; 2003. Damasio is often referred to, e.g. Rottschaefer 1998, 162; Peterson 2003, 89–91; Gärdenfors 2005, 87–93.

remain intact.[8] One of Damasio's case studies, "Elliot," made choices with detrimental results for his own person, in spite of reasoning logically, foreseeing in theory various outcomes.[9] Other examples include the patient whose lack of emotional capacity made him behave rationally, without panicking, when driving on an icy road, but unable to make simple decisions.[10] Decision-making and action were seriously impaired by a reduced emotional capacity. The constant interaction between the brain and the entire organism suggests an "embodied mind" and a "minded body." "It does not seem sensible to leave emotions and feelings out of any overall concept of mind" says Damasio, and "mind derives from the entire organism."[11] Thus emotions are intimately involved in human reasoning, judgement and behaviour.[12]

The role of emotions for moral behaviour has been discussed since Antiquity. Even for Plato, they were not always on the bad side; the cognitive emotions housed in the middle, spirited part of the human soul had at least some evaluative capacities, and there is a tendency to upgrade the value of emotions in his later works.[13] Aristotle, who was less reserved than Plato, acknowledged their necessary role for a good social life.[14] The Stoics, however, regarded emotions as irrational cognitive activities, in line with their ideal of *apatheia*.[15] There were, of course, nuances; as Troels Engberg-Pedersen has pointed out, Marcus Aurelius gave room for a type of enlightened emotion that did not leave out every attachment to the particular, the here-and-now.[16]

In general, however, our cultural and philosophical heritage does not suggest a harmonious relationship between cognition and emotion. The function of reason, said Immanuel Kant, unlike other organs of the body, and unlike the instincts, is not to preserve the human organism, but to produce human morality. David Hume, however, claimed that reason was subordinate to the emotions.[17] From an evolutionary point of view, Kant was wrong; the evolution of

---

[8] Primary emotions are for example direct responses of fear or anger to sudden stimuli, while secondary emotions are conceived reactions to anticipated or imagined events. Cf. Damasio 1994, 129–139.

[9] Damasio 1994, 44–51, 191–196. "The defect appeared to set in at the late stages of reasoning, close to or at the point at which choice making or response selection must occur. ... the defect was accompanied by a reduction in emotional reactivity and feeling. ... Elliot's reasoning prevented him from assigning different values to different options, and made his decision-making landscape hopelessly flat" (50–51).

[10] Damasio 1994, 193–194.

[11] Damasio 1994, 158, 225.

[12] Damasio 1994, 245–252; cf. Kekes 1992, 444.

[13] Knuuttila and Sihvola 1998, 1–19.

[14] Knuuttila and Sihvola 1998, 16.

[15] Brennan 1998.

[16] Engberg-Pedersen 1998.

[17] Teehan 2003, 53.

uniquely human cognitive capacities can be explained by their adaptive value. Reason assists the survival of the organism by responding to the biologically grounded needs that express themselves through the emotions. Hume was closer to the truth, if we, as John Teehan suggests, can forgive his rhetorical excesses.[18] Reason and emotion are both evolutionary strategies with the same end and morality results from "our emotions, our cognitive processes, and the complex relationship between the two."[19]

The concept of an embodied mind is just as important when we discuss *ritual* behaviour. The relationship between ritual and morality is a complex one and a cause of disagreement among scholars. A functionalist approach with roots from Robertson Smith and Durkheim tends to look at rituals as sanctioning the moral norms of society. Mary Douglas saw rituals such as the purity laws as symbolic systems related to the human and the social body. It seems to be a common idea in sociological and anthropological studies that ritual considerations have moral consequences in one way or another. I am hesitant, however, to read rituals as symbols of the social body or as allegories of a moral system.[20] As Tracy Lemos has pointed out, "the type of analysis that seeks ever to schematize almost always sees ritual as secondary to belief and the body as secondary to the mind."[21] Such an approach presupposes an inherent divide between ritual and morality that I find anachronistic and culturally biased. The dichotomy between morality on the one hand and convention, whether social or ritual behaviour, on the other, is only typical of modern Western thought, as Richard Shweder has repeatedly shown – something that poses problems for developmental psychology in the tradition of Piaget and Kohlberg. When morality is understood in a broad sense, as in Shweder's "big three" domains, ethics of autonomy, community and divinity,[22] it embraces ritual concerns, such as purity, too.

Provided that the moral-ritual divide, so often taken for granted by scholars, is little more than a cultural construct, how are we to explain what might to us seem as an uneasy blend of the two, in ancient contexts? Where do we find common denominators for moral and ritual behaviour? I suggest that we should look for underlying cognitive-emotional experiences. In the following, I will

---

[18] I.e. Hume's statement that reason ought to serve and obey the emotions. Teehan 2003, 53.

[19] Teehan 2003, 58.

[20] Cf. William Gilders who emphasizes the function of rituals for hierarchical indexing. Gilders 2004.

[21] Lemos 2008. The paper has subsequently been published (Lemos 2009) but without the phrase that I have quoted above.

[22] Schweder, Much, Mahapatra and Park 1997.

exemplify with ideas of impurity and rites of purification, relating them to the emotions of disgust, fear and a sense of justice.

Impurity and disgust

In the priestly laws, purity language is used in three different contexts: for clean and unclean animals, for bodily transferable contact-contagion, and for serious immorality. Jonathan Klawans has demonstrated how three grave sins (certain sexual sins; idolatry, especially child sacrifice; murder) were regarded as defiling in the Holiness Code (Lev 17–26), conveying impurity to the sinner as well as to the land, although not in the sense of a removable contact-contagion.[23] The idea of defiling sins was then according to Klawans expanded to include a broader category of misdeeds, leading up to the merging of moral and ritual impurity found in Qumran.[24]

I have elsewhere discussed the problems involved in separating moral and ritual impurity, as well as the idea that the Pharisees had already compartmentalized the two to the extent that appears in Tannaitic literature.[25] The latter suggestion is not corroborated by evidence and neither priestly purity legislation nor Tannaitic discussion about purity is void of moral implications.[26] The three "systems" overlap: the dietary laws in Lev 11 transmute into a discussion about animal carcasses and their defilement by contact, which is a "ritual" problem, while the prohibition of sex during menstruation is found not only in Lev 15 but also in the Holiness Code (Lev 18; 20), where "moral" aspects are involved.[27] The isolation of the skin diseased person and, according to Num 5, of the *zav* as well, is certainly based on ritual considerations, but would have been stigmatizing also in a moral sense, which fits the observation that these diseases were regarded as punishments and related to moral failings.[28] The *chattat* sacrifice, translated by the LXX as *hamartia*, was effective for removing ritual impurity as well as moral offence; to this we will return shortly.

While there are moral aspects to the idea of purity in ancient Judaism,[29] purity does not cease to be a ritual category when associated with moral matters. A common denominator for various uses of purity language can be found in a

---

[23] Lev 18–20, cf. Num 35:33–34. Klawans 2000, 26–31.
[24] Klawans 2000, 43–60, 67–91. For a summary, see 158–162. See however Himmelfarb 2001, who considers the association of sin and impurity in Qumran as primarily evocative rather than halakic.
[25] Kazen 2002, 209–214, 216–218. Cf. Klawans 2000, 92–117.
[26] The lack of evidence is actually admitted by Klawans himself (2000, 150). Cf. *m. Ker.* 2:3; *m. Neg.* 12:6; *t. Neg.* 6:7; *Sifre* to Num 5:3; *b. 'Arak.* 16a; *Lev. Rab.* 17:3; 18:4; *Num. Rab.* 7:1, 10.
[27] For further discussion, see Kazen 2002, 207–211.
[28] Num 12:9–15; 2 Sam 3:29; 2 Chr 26:16–21. Cf. Kazen 2002, 217–218.
[29] Kazen 2002, 214–222.

negative emotional response to threatening stimuli, a reaction of disgust towards revolting or objectionable substances and towards states associated with
such substances, or towards behaviour evoking similar feelings. As I have laid
out the argument in more detail in a previous article, only a brief summary will
be offered here.[30]

Disgust has been understood as originally relating to taste.[31] This is the case
in two of the classical discussions of disgust, Darwin's evolutionary account[32]
and a psychological article by Andras Angyal.[33] A third classical discussion of
disgust is the phenomenological study by Aurel Kolnai,[34] which gives more
emphasis to smell than to taste, as it explains a broader range of disgust reactions. Similar considerations are voiced by William Miller in his historical and
socio-political study on disgust. Both smell and touch are understood to be just
as important.[35] In a large study on the role of disgust in arts, aesthetics and philosophy, Winfried Menninghaus relates disgust to modern aesthetic culture, to
cultural theory and psychoanalysis.[36] Susan Miller's recent monograph regards
disgust as a "gatekeeper emotion" that rejects contact in a "refusal to integrate
something into the body or being."[37] However, it readily "changes horses from
body offenses to behavioral affronts."[38] Both Kolnai and Susan Miller point out
that death as such does not seem to be a primary stimulus of disgust, but disgust
is rather directed towards death in the form of decayed life. It is not the qualities
of death but the significance of those qualities that disgust us.[39]

Paul Rozin is well-known for his empirical-psychological research. Facial
expressions, centring around the mouth and the nose, as well as nausea, suggest
an original association of taste and disgust. Disgust developed as a primary reaction to protect an organism from oral incorporation of harmful substances, but
inhaling and contacting should be subjected to similar considerations. "Core
disgust" as a primary emotion thus involves taste, smell and touch; all three
cause instant recoiling from that which is experienced as objectionable. When
sight and memory are included, a secondary aspect is added and disgust may be

---

[30] Kazen 2008.
[31] As suggested by the etymology of the English word.
[32] Darwin 1989 [1890, 1st ed. 1872].
[33] Angyal 1941.
[34] Kolnai 2004 [1929].
[35] Miller 1997, 6, 12, 60–79.
[36] Menninghaus 1999.
[37] Miller 2004, 59.
[38] Miller 2004, 67.
[39] Miller 2004, 187–188. Cf. Menninghaus's point that disgust is not directed towards the
corpse as such, but towards the *rotting* corpse (1999, 7).

triggered by the mere *thought* of a number of situations, with neither taste, nor smell or touch actually being there.[40]

Rozin defines disgust triggers as relating to nine different areas: "food, body products, animals, sexual behaviours, contact with death or corpses, violations of the exterior envelope of the body (including gore and deformity), poor hygiene, interpersonal contamination (contact with unsavory human beings), and certain moral offenses."[41] Most people agree that disgust triggers are learned through socialization, and that "the specific objects, events, and behaviors within these categories that elicit disgust vary across cultural contexts."[42] Apart from a primitive reaction to bitter taste,[43] disgust seems to be a distinctly human trait. Rozin and colleagues provide a scheme for the development of disgust from distaste and core disgust through stages of animal-nature and interpersonal disgust to a reaction to moral offences.[44]

Disgust is involved in moral evaluation, to the point that it has often become a metaphor for a sense of what is morally inappropriate, even for issues or experiences that do not elicit the feeling itself.[45] Disgust then becomes a way of phrasing a value judgement. As a socially conditioned emotion, it is at times morally mistaken.[46] Martha Nussbaum has emphasized the risks of utilizing disgust as a normative pointer; for such purposes it is quite useless.[47] At its core, however, it is a bodily reaction, similar to fear,[48] against that which is understood as dangerous for human life and threatening society with dirt, disorder, decay and death.[49] Coping strategies include rejection and avoidance, as well as removal of that which causes offence.

When we look at the three contexts in which purity language is used in the priestly legislation, we find that emotional disgust offers a coherent explanation. First, in the dietary laws (Lev 11), following the basic instruction prohibiting unclean quadrupeds for food, we find three sections on water animals, birds and

---

[40] Rozin, Haidt and McCauley 2000, 637–653. Cf. Miller 1997, 60–88.

[41] Rozin, Haidt and McCauley 2000, 637. Whether all of these areas apply globally or just to those Western societies from which most of the researchers involved come is a matter for discussion.

[42] Looy 2004, 223; cf. Rozin, Haidt and McCauley 2000, 647–648.

[43] Looy 2004, 223.

[44] Rozin, Haidt and McCauley 2000, 644–647; cf. Rozin, Haidt, McCauley and Imada 1997, 65–82.

[45] Cf. Rozin, Haidt and McCauley 2000, 643.

[46] Kekes is quite clear on the fact that disgust's involvement in moral evaluation does not mean that universal moral rules can be based on a universally felt deep disgust, or that disgust can be defended as an appropriate moral reaction (Kekes 1992, 438, 441).

[47] Nussbaum 2004, 13–15, 72–171.

[48] Cf. Miller 1997, 25–28.

[49] Kekes 1992, 435, 438–443; Rozin, Haidt and McCauley 2000, 642, 644–645; Cf. Miller 1997, 40–50.

winged insects (11:9–23) that explicitly call these animals detestable (*sheqetz*). The small land animals ("ground swarmers") such as weasels, rats and lizards, whose dead bodies are said to contaminate like the bodies of unclean quadrupeds, are subsequently also forbidden as food, with the same argument: they are *sheqetz* (11:41–42). Milgrom and others have suggested a structure of this chapter based on a distinction between the use of *tame'* and *sheqetz* (unclean and detestable), claiming that the former term denotes contact-contagion while the latter refers to food prohibitions. Such an easy distinction does not hold water, however.[50]

I read *sheqetz* as an emotional term for disgust. It is applied especially to "swarmers" (*sheretz*), whether aquatic, winged or earthbound, a term that probably refers to small, fast-moving and/or fast-breeding beings, thought to be self-generating from rotting substances, which would make humans feel uneasy. *Sheqetz* is also used to characterize larger water animals without fins and scales, such as molluscs and the slimiest of fish, as well as birds of prey. These are creatures that easily evoke feelings of revulsion, especially at the thought of eating them, but often at the mere idea of contact. Possibly, their association with deterioration reminds humans about their mortality and animal nature. This would represent what Rozin calls animal-nature disgust.[51] Aversion to their dead bodies is likewise easy to understand and is expressed through the command to wash everything and even destroy clay vessels or ovens that had come in contact with them (Lev 11:32–38). These prohibitions would then have been extended to corpses of clean animals rather due to systemic reasoning than because of emotional disgust. The basic instruction, however, prohibiting pigs and camels for food, can hardly be explained the same way. Only in the parallel in Deut 14 are they called disgusting, but now with the term *to'evah*, "abominable."[52]

Secondly, looking at impurity as contact-contagion, we find that the emotion of disgust can be traced with regard to the three basic types, skin disease, genital

---

[50] First, the basic instruction (11:2–8) does not refer to the forbidden quadrupeds as "detestable" but uses "unclean" for both eating and contamination, and the focus is on eating. Secondly, water animals (11:9–12) are not only "detestable" as food, but their dead bodies should be "detested" (11:11 uses both the noun and the verb שקץ). Thirdly, the call to holiness (11:43–45) warns against "uncleanness" from "ground swarmers" but connects directly to the preceding verses (11:41–42), which prohibits eating them because they are "detestable." Fourthly, the subscript (11:46–47) summarizes the law by presenting the opposites "unclean – clean" and "allowed for food – not allowed for food" in a typical parallelism. For a more detailed discussion and suggestions about the structure of this chapter, see Kazen 2008, 54–57 and 2011b, forthcoming.

[51] Rozin, Haidt and McCauley 2000, 641–642.

[52] The term is not found in P but also found in H, where it expresses a strong sense of revulsion, especially against objectionable behaviour. See further below.

discharges and corpse impurity (Lev 12–15; Num 19), too. These impurities are often associated with decomposition, rotting and decay, and purification rites especially focus on washing, as if the impure "substance" might be removed by water, washed off like literal dirt. The disgust felt towards skin disease (*tzara'at*) probably had to do with scaliness,[53] damage and decay of the "body envelope," one of Rozin's basic disgust triggers. This is clear from Miriam's punishment (Num 12), where she is likened to a half-decayed, stillborn foetus. A similar repulsive experience also applied to the various kinds of moulds on cloths and buildings, described in Lev 13 and 14. When rejection or avoidance becomes difficult, a strategy of removal is found instead: the scraping or exchange of stones in "leprous" houses as well as the burning of "leprous" clothes.

In the case of a corpse or a grave, the association with decaying matter is obvious. The biblical rules describing how corpse impurity is transmitted (Num 19:14–16) suggest that corpses were originally thought to ooze out some sort of quasi-physical substance, particularly threatening the sphere of the holy. Priests were only allowed to contract corpse impurity at the death of close relatives, and for high priests there were no such exceptions.[54] Corpse impurity rules are related to war-camp regulations (Num 31:19–24), requiring washing of body, clothes and wooden vessels, as well as the cleansing of metals with fire, after warriors and their attire had become filthied with blood and gore, suggesting disgust as a trigger in this case, too.

The evidence in cases of people with genital discharges is clear, too. I have elsewhere discussed discrepancies in Lev 12 and 15, arguing for an early view of the discharges themselves as the primary source of their impurity.[55] Remnants of such thinking can be found in Samaritan *halakah*[56] and in texts found at Qumran.[57] This implies that blood associated with decay, as well as gory or un-

---

[53] Cf. Hulse 1975, 96–100; Milgrom 1991, 774–776, 816–817.

[54] Lev 21:1–4, 11. In the Second Temple period, an extra-biblical first-day ablution had developed in order to mitigate the strength of corpse impurity, to make it possible for corpse-impure people to stay within cities. Cf. Num 5:1–3; 31:19–24 with actual practice, at least during the Second Temple period, which allowed corpse-impure within towns. See Milgrom 1978; Kazen 2002, 185–189; Kazen 2011a, forthcoming.

[55] See chapter 3 below, or Kazen 2007; Kazen 2002, 144–146.

[56] In Samaritan *halakah*, direct contact with menstrual blood causes a 7-day impurity. Other examples include detailed regulations implying that the flux or blood transmits a stronger impurity than the impurity bearer. In biblical legislation, the impurity of the discharges themselves is implied by detailed regulations concerning items underneath the discharger. Fear of contact with menstrual blood could explain why touching the bed or anything the menstruant has sat upon requires laundering (Lev 15: 21–22) while touching the menstruant herself does not (v. 19). The invisibility of male discharges on the other hand might explain why touching the *zav* necessitates laundering (v. 7). For further discussion, see chapter 3 (= Kazen 2007).

[57] See chapter 4 (= Kazen 2010a).

natural discharges, were experienced as disgusting and form the basis for the purity laws about discharges. The contempt with which dischargers are spoken of together with skin diseased people and the disabled in 2 Sam 3:29, suggests that the aversion felt against such categories of people was based on primary feelings of disgust towards their bodily conditions. Ezekiel utilizes the primary disgust of his readers for menstrual blood in order to transfer their emotional indignation to the issue of gentile idolatry (Ezek 36:17).[58]

This leads us to the third category: impure behaviour. Certain rules of the Holiness Code, particularly in Lev 18 and 20, give us some clues.[59] Here, a number of terms are used for repulsive behaviour, particularly in sexual matters, for example *zimmah* and *tevel*, both of which carry notions of offensiveness. The most conspicuous term is *to'evah* (abomination), absent in the preceding priestly laws, but frequently used in Deuteronomy and some of the prophets, mostly in relation to idolatry, and in Proverbs referring to serious sins in general.[60] The term clearly expresses a feeling of disgust at offensive behaviour and is used in the Holiness Code for same-sex relations between males (Lev 18:22; 20:13), and as a blanket term for summarizing all the incest and sexual rules of Lev 18, including bans on sex with animals and with women during menstruation (Lev 18:26, 27, 29, 30).[61] In Deuteronomy it is also used about defective sacrifice, invalid offerers, false weights and remarriage with a remarried divorcee, and in Deut 14:3, as we have seen above, to characterize all categories of unclean food, as an equivalent to *sheqetz* in P. Rather than being a metaphor, *to'evah* in the Holiness Code expresses physical and emotional disgust at repulsive behaviour.[62] In the context of Lev 18, the listed abominations are said to

---

[58] Reactions against menstrual blood are found almost worldwide, and Pliny's superstitious comments regarding its effects breathe feelings of revulsion. Pliny, *Nat* 7:64. See Milgrom 1991, 763–765.

[59] I consider H (and much of Numbers) as later than P and belonging to a redactional stage of the Pentateuch, following the lead of Knohl, Milgrom (although not accepting their early dating), Otto, Achenbach, Römer and Nihan. For an overview with references, see Nihan 2004; Römer 2008. I do not believe that P's legislation is devoid of ethical elements, so that sins against the Lord's commandments (Lev 4:2; 5:17) only refer to *cultic* matters, and that "the interpenetration of ethical and cultic considerations" comes only later, with the Holiness School (Knohl 1995, 225–230; see Milgrom's objections, 1991, 44; 2000, 1335–1336, 1397–1400).

[60] The term is also used twice in Genesis (43:32; 46:34) to convey the Egyptian view of the Hebrews and shepherds as unclean. In Exod 8:26 the Egyptians are assumed to regard the sacrifice of the Hebrews as abominable.

[61] Milgrom 2000, 1345, argues that since *to'evah* in Lev 18 is used separately only to characterize one prohibition (18:22), while several times summarizing all the prohibitions in the closing exhortation, this points to the incorporation of an older list of sexual prohibitions (18:6–23) into two reworded exhortations (18:1–5, 24–30).

[62] Cf. Milgrom 2000, 1569, suggesting a root meaning of darken, contaminate or stain. The variability of the term is emphasized by Humbert 1960, who argues that it cannot be restricted to a particularly type of sacred language.

make the land unclean (v. 27) and cause it to spit or vomit the people out (v. 28). Uncleanness and abominations are expressly paralleled (v. 30). The imagery is repeated in Lev 20:22 at the end of the corresponding list of sexual laws, where not only the land, but also God, is said to have felt disgust[63] at the repulsive behaviour of the former inhabitants (v. 23). While this refers to the preceding list of sexual sins, the conclusion (vv. 24–26) is that the Israelites whom God has separated from other people and to whom he has given the land, must themselves separate between clean and unclean animals. Repulsive sexual acts and ingestion of disgusting foods are thus combined and jointly seen as repulsive behaviour causing divine disgust to such an extent that the people would be threatened.

Impurity and fear

The divine threat associated with impure behaviour and unclean states suggests fear as another emotion involved in ideas of purity and impurity. The warnings in the dietary laws (Lev 11:43–45) implicitly threaten the people, as does the prohibition for the parturient against touching anything holy (12:4), since general knowledge of the dangers involved in contacting the cultic sphere without necessary preparations must be assumed. The threat becomes explicit in the conclusion to the laws on discharges (15:31); the consequence of impurity is death, because impurities cause the Israelites to defile the sanctuary. This is reinforced by the regulations for the high priest entering the sanctuary on the Day of Atonement, preceded by express warnings of death (16:1–2). In the Holiness Code, a number of impure or abominable behaviours, including those just mentioned above, are explicitly said to result in death, *karet*, or exile.[64] The *karet* punishment is also prescribed for the corpse-impure person who does not purify, but defiles the sanctuary (Num 19:13, 20).

Presupposing a fully monotheistic framework, these examples would only point to fear of divine punishment after defilement has occurred. As soon as we ask for underlying historical explanations, however, the picture changes. A number of purification rites contain what plausibly seem to be vestiges of more ancient beliefs in impurity resulting from life-threatening demonic powers, which need to be exorcised.

Fear manifests itself as a sudden response to direct stimuli and is often discussed together with anxiety in psychological research. Fear is usually understood to differ from anxiety by being "poststimulus" rather than anticipatory, but humans often "fear" anticipated events and the distinction is not always

---

[63] *qutz*, cf. *sheqetz* in ch. 11.
[64] Lev 17:4, 9, 10, 14: 18:28, 29; 19:8; 20:3, 5, 6, 17, 18, 22; 26:33.

easy to uphold, and not necessary for our purpose. Hence some of the discussion below might strictly speaking relate to anxiety. Fear is a subjective experience, associated with somatic and autonomic responses and it relates to coping behaviour, especially avoidance and escape.[65] Like anger, pain and feelings of hunger, fear has evolved to protect the physical organism from damage and death. Most situations in which fear is experienced can be classified into four broad categories: interpersonal situations, death/ injury/ illness, animals, and "agoraphobic fears."[66] All represent situations during the history of evolution in which fear as a protective reaction kept living organisms away from potentially dangerous contexts: hostile strangers or enemies, damaging or lethal actions, dangerous animals, and open places, lacking security, with nowhere to seek refuge quickly. Human fear is biologically based and shaped in such a way that we fear "situations that threatened the survival of our ancestors."[67] Although it evolved because it was functional, it may not always represent the most efficient response to a threatening situation.[68]

From the perspective of evolutionary biology, fear of outsiders is reasonable. Xenophobia is found with a number of social species and human children experience fear of strangers from the age of three months.[69] Ethnocentrism has some adaptive value and ethnocentric tendencies are context sensitive.[70] Ethnocentrism and xenophobia may serve to protect the integrity of the group, by reserving resources for the in-group, guarding against foreigners taking advantage of the reciprocal altruism practised within the group without contributing themselves.[71] Another partial explanation for the development of xenophobia is dis-

---

[65] Öhman 2000, 574.

[66] Öhman 2000, 575, referring to a study by Arrindell et. al., 1991.

[67] Öhman 2000, 576.

[68] As several scholars have pointed out, it is not the response itself that is the problem, but the fact that it is triggered in the wrong context or has too low a threshold. Öhman 2000, 577. Since during the course of evolution, fast discovery of threat has had high survival value, fear has evolved as a more or less automatic response to stimuli bypassing traditional pathways in the brain, to the effect that "affect precedes inference" (Öhman 2000, 578). Much research has been performed on how fear is elicited by stimuli outside the subject's awareness.

[69] McEvoy 2002, 45–46.

[70] Ethnocentrism can be understood as a "sentimental structure," the result of cultural elaboration and individual rationalization of basic evolutionary emotions (McEvoy 2002, 40). For an understanding of sentimental structures, see van der Dennen 1987, 42. The experienced availability of resources as well as cognitive recognition of the limits of group belonging, govern to a significant degree the balance between selfish and altruistic behaviours in a population (cf. Dunbar 1987). It goes without saying that, while ethnocentrism and xenophobia may have evolved due to adaptive values at some stages and in certain contexts, other circumstances make such behaviour maladaptive (McEvoy 2002, 42–45).

[71] Another effect is to block the likewise innate human propensity for empathy, which otherwise would inhibit aggression, thus making it easier to exercise violence against out-groups. Cf. Bandura 1999.

ease-avoidance; hostility towards out-group would have been adaptive since pathogens were avoided. Furthermore, out-group members would not act according to in-group practices that might have evolved to protect members from local pathogens.[72] Navarrete and Fessler suggest that "disease-avoidance mechanisms may have given rise to the association between norm violations and feelings of disgust."[73] This could provide a partial explanation to certain ideas of impurity, although it is not to be confused with popular hygienic explanations for the purity laws in general. While singular food avoidances and negative attitudes to certain irregular conditions of the body could have developed from collective experience, all attempts to explain dietary laws or purity rules at large from considerations of preventive hygiene have failed.[74]

Fear of the supernatural, divine beings or demons, was a natural part of life in the ancient world. Such fear carries traits of all four analytical categories mentioned above. Death, injury or illness was often ascribed to invisible causes, such as the influence of personal spirits or demons, regardless of whether visible causes were available in addition. Fear of death and disease is thus blended with interpersonal fear. Fear of demons is also akin to animal fear, since demons are envisaged as non-human, or post-human beings, and often take on animal traits. Like some of the real or imagined animals threatening human beings, demons are often associated with open places, deserts, waters and foreign areas, which are unsafe and in which it is difficult to seek refuge quickly or to protect oneself.

Vestiges of demon belief and demonic fear can be seen in a number of purification rites, in spite of more or less successful attempts to integrate them within a priestly sacrificial system. Following the lead of Yehezkel Kaufmann, many of these rites can be read as originally intent on exorcising demonic powers, and "retained magical features, so deeply rooted as to defy extirpation."[75] This general view has been followed by others, such as Baruch Levine and Jacob Milgrom, although they all differ on the extent as to which priestly theology managed to refashion or abolish earlier magical and demonic ideas. We will not enter that discussion here or the one about evolutionary interpretations of religion in general. Suffice it to point to those purification rites that are particularly suggestive of an underlying fear of demonic activity.

The most conspicuous of these may be the rites after the healing of skin disease, or the repair of a "leprous" house (Lev 14:1–7, 14–18, 25–29, 49–53). After inspection, purification begins with a bird rite. At the end of the purifica-

---

[72] Faulkner, Schaller, Park and Duncan 2004; Navarrete and Fessler 2006.
[73] Navarrete and Fessler 2006, 280.
[74] Cf. Houston 1993, 69–70.
[75] Kaufmann 1960 [1937–1948], 102.

tion period subsequent to the healing of skin disease, blood and oil from the *asham* offering are smeared on the right ear, thumb and big toe of the healed person. This smearing has obvious similarities with Zoroastrian practices for chasing away the corpse demoness as described in *Vendidād*, although the latter rites include the treatment of many more parts of the body.[76]

In the bird rite at the beginning of purification from skin disease, or after the repair of a "leprous" house, two "live," probably wild birds are used,[77] together with cedar wood, red wool and hyssop. One bird is slaughtered over a bowl with water, after which the other is dipped in it, together with the wood, wool and hyssop. The healed person is sprinkled and the live bird is released in the open fields. The rite is generally interpreted as transferring the disease or demonic influence to the live bird, who takes it away, never to return again.[78] In Mesopotamian religion, impurity is often seen as the result of demonic activity and a number of rituals aim at exorcising the demons, sending them back to their origin. These may be the river, the open uninhabited country, or the underworld.[79] Similarly, the Hittites thought of open areas and the underworld, together with mountain areas and foreign lands, as disposing places for impurities, although evils were generally thought of in more impersonal terms.[80]

The use of red wool in purification or disposal rites is also found in Mesopotamian transfer rituals, for example in a Shurpu ritual, in which the patient is sprinkled, although the wool itself is burnt,[81] in a Malli thread manipulation ritual,[82] or in a number of transfer rites. In a Mesopotamian healing ritual, red wool is tied to the foot of a frog that explicitly is said to return the evil to its steppe. Red wool is also used in an amulet from ancient Uruk[83] and in a Neo-Assyrian goat ritual.[84] The release of birds is mentioned in Mesopotamian and Hittite texts as carriers of evil in various rites and in prayers and incantations.[85] Numerous examples are provided by Wright and Milgrom.[86] Birds occur frequently in Hittite and Hurrian sacrificial rites in association with chtonic deities.[87] Milgrom suggests that birds are not chosen in the priestly ritual because

---

[76] *Vendidād* 8:40–71.

[77] Milgrom 1991, 833–834.

[78] Wright 1987a, 77–78. For Namburbi rituals to purify houses, see Maul 1994, 97–100.

[79] Maul 1994, 248–261.

[80] Maul 1994, 261–271.

[81] Shurpu i 9–23 (the red wool is mentioned in lines 14 and 21), in Reiner 1958.

[82] Malli i 37–40, in Wright 1987a, 41–42.

[83] Text no. 248, Vs. 4, in von Weiher 1998, 58, 60; cf. Scurlock 2002, 215.

[84] Scurlock 2002, 211–212.

[85] Maul 1994, 90–91, 93; cf. all the "bird-*namburbis*" (229–269).

[86] Wright 1987a, 80–83; Milgrom 1991, 834.

[87] For the sacrifice of three birds, see Collins 2002, 227, 228, 230. See also Milgrom 1991, 834, with a reference to Otten 1961, 130.

they are favoured by chtonic deities, but only because they transport the evil away.[88] However, the use of two birds in Ugaritic texts, as a typical sacrifice for the *'Inasu-'Ilima*, the "mankind of the gods" or divinized dead, is conspicuous, although in these texts both birds are sacrificed.[89]

The bird rite in Lev 14 is probably the surviving apotropaic rite that retains most original traits, since it is not incorporated into the sacrificial system and is not forced in under the *chattat* umbrella – perhaps because the wild birds crucial to the rite were no sacrificial animals.[90] While the priest has been made to effect the sprinkling and release, he only seems to supervise the ritual arrangements and the slaughtering. Milgrom suggests that the rite "was retained not because Israel's priests wanted it but probably because the people at large demanded it, practiced it, and would not have tolerated its deletion."[91]

A similar function to ward off demonic evil is likely for the origin of the scapegoat ritual (Lev 16). Space allows only a most cursory discussion. The ritual is barely integrated into the sacrificial system; while goats as distinct from wild birds are at least sacrificial animals, the goat for Azazel is nevertheless no sacrifice, but rather a vehicle. The identification of Azazel with a desert demon[92] has been questioned; express identification is said to be late and the sending away has even been interpreted as a liberation.[93] However, in view of the use of animals as vehicles for sending away evil elsewhere in Ancient Near Eastern texts, this must be deemed very unlikely.[94] The Day of Atonement ritual looks very much like the conflation of two rites, and Milgrom's suggestion that the cleansing of the sanctuary at one stage was accomplished by a pair of goats through a rite closely resembling the bird rite is plausible.[95] Milgrom also suggests that originally this was no calendrical rite but an emergency rite, as most similar Ancient Near Eastern rituals.[96]

Exorcistic purgation of temples by animal carcasses is known from the Ancient Near East; the most well-known example comes from the Babylonian *Akitu* or New Year's festival. Wright has collected numerous Hittite and Meso-

---

[88] Milgrom 1991, 834.

[89] RS 1.009, line 8; 24.256, line 5–6; 24.249, line 26; 24.250+, line 2, 7–8; 1.003/18.056, line 5–6, 27, 36 (?), 40; 1.001, line 21–22; 19.013, line 7–8. Pardee 2002.

[90] Cf. Milgrom 1991, 833.

[91] Milgrom 1991, 838.

[92] E. g. de Vaux 1964, 86–87; Levine 1974, 79–82; Kaufmann 1960 [1937–1948], 114–115; Milgrom 1991, 1020–1021.

[93] *1 En.* 10:4–5; cf. 11QT^a XXVI, 13. Douglas 2003.

[94] Maul 1994, 90–91.

[95] Milgrom 1991, 1044.

[96] Also, v. 34 fixes it to once a year, which might suggest that the rite had not previously been fixed to a certain time. Milgrom 1991, 1061. Cf. Wright 1987a, 17–21.

potamian parallel rituals with purification motives.[97] Often an animal or a person is sent away, adorned or accompanied by gifts of appeasement. Evil is thus returned to its origin: the open country or steppe, foreign lands, or the underworld. In a ritual from the *Shurpu* series, impure material is disposed of in the wilderness where desert deities are active.[98] The association of wilderness or open, uninhabited country with the underworld is common in Mesopotamian texts.[99] Nevertheless, Wright stresses the differences between the biblical rite and Hittite or Mesopotamian parallels: the scapegoat is just a transporter, no substitute, and Azazel is not an angry deity in need of appeasement.[100] This is true, of course, for the priestly adaptation of the rite that is described in Leviticus. As for its origin, however, Wright admits that it may have carried just those traits in which the biblical rite now differs from Ancient Near Eastern parallels due to priestly alterations.[101]

The red heifer, burned to obtain ashes for the purification water (Num 19) is another apotropaic rite, most probably originating as exorcist magic to ward off demonic threat. The rabbinic awareness of, and uneasiness with, the rite's apparent exorcist character is displayed by the oft-quoted saying of Yohanan ben Zakkai in response to a gentile question, in which he explains the red heifer rite by comparing it to exorcism.[102] While Yohanan subsequently gives a theological explanation to his disciples, the tradition is evidence for the fact that the exorcist nature of the rite was generally acknowledged, although not necessarily accepted.

The slaughtering, burning and collecting of ashes are all done by laymen. As in the bird rite, the priest's role is mainly to supervise the event, except for an initial gesture, sprinkling some blood towards the sanctuary, and throwing the cedar wood, red wool and hyssop into the fire. The same ingredients are used as in the bird rite. The rite is incorporated into the sacrificial system to the extent that is possible without loss of its crucial characteristics; it is explicitly identified as a *chattat* sacrifice (Num 19:9, 17), but almost as an afterthought, justifying its purificatory effect. Like a *chattat*, it defiles those who perform it but purifies the recipients. Unlike a *chattat*, however, the sprinkling is mainly on people, as in the bird rite. The initial gesture towards the sanctuary seems more like a forced adaptation.[103] The sprinkling of ashes seems to have been carried

---

[97] Wright 1987a, 31–74.
[98] Shurpu vii 53–70, in Reiner 1958. Cf. the role of the steppe in the Namburbi texts (Maul 1994, 48, 93, 124, 387).
[99] Milgrom 1991, 1072.
[100] Wright 1987a, 49–50, 53–54, 72–74.
[101] Wright 1987a, 73–74.
[102] *Pesiq. Rab Kah.* 4:7.
[103] Cf. Milgrom 1981.

out by minors, at least towards the end of the Second Temple period, which further attests to its origin outside of the priestly system.[104]

Yet another rite with apotropaic traits is the breaking of a heifer's neck in the case of an unsolved murder (Deut 21:1–9). The explicit purpose of this rite is to erase the collective blood guilt that otherwise would apply, in view of the fact that no murderer can be found and the blood of the victim thus cannot be avenged.[105] The rite has been subject to numerous interpretations, many of which are speculative, with little grounding in the text.[106] Its basic character as an elimination ritual, focused on the blood guilt that adheres to the land, seems nevertheless obvious to me.[107] Interestingly, the rite is said to effect *kipper*, atonement, which may cause associations to the *chattat* sacrifice, although the present rite is wholly outside of the priestly sacrificial sphere. The agents of every specified action are the elders (and judges) of the nearest town. The priests pop up in v. 5, like puppets with no active function whatsoever, although in theory they are ascribed the authority to decide in disputes and assaults. In actual fact they seem to do nothing; their purported role is fulfilled by the elders and judges. It is very difficult to avoid the conclusion that their sudden appearance is due to a redactional insertion out of priestly interests at a late stage in the textual formation, turning focus from the ancient rite to the similarly appended prayer for forgiveness (vv. 8 [or 8a], 9).[108]

The focus on blood guilt and revenge fits with the Deuteronomic law about cities of refuge (Deut 19:1–13). In cases of inadvertent murder, no danger seems to threaten the perpetrator as long as he stays within a city of refuge. In some unexplained manner, the existence of cities of refuge seems to eliminate blood guilt (19:10). According to the parallel passage in Num 35:9–34, the murderer may even return without danger after the death of the high priest. A danger does, however, threaten the people, if the murderer is not avenged in the case of advertent murder, or, when the murderer is unknown, unless the heifer rite is

---

[104] *m. Parah* 3:2–4; *Barn.* 8:1; Some of the texts found at Qumran seem to oppose this. The statement that no youth may sprinkle is heavily reconstructed (4Q269 8 ii, 6 and 4Q271 ii, 13); the crucial *na'ar* is missing in both but conjectured! The translation of 4Q277 1 ii, 7 is furthermore debated. It is, however, reasonable to accept Baumgarten's suggestion that *'lwl* is a variant for *'wll*, i.e., child (Baumgarten 1999, 118). In any case it is clear that other Qumran texts consider only priests competent for the task, see 4Q276; 4Q277.

[105] For a recent study on this rite, see Dietrich 2009. Cf the brief but comprehensive discussion in Tigay 1996, 472–476.

[106] This is one of Dietrich's points in his review of previous research (2009, 29–64). (e.g. Tigay 1996; Wright 1987b).

[107] There are good arguments for interpretating the rite as a reenactment of the murder, an elimination rite, transferring the impurity of bloodguilt from arable land to a desert place. Cf. Milgrom 1972; Wright 1987b; Tigay 1996.

[108] Cf. Milgrom 1972, 478; Tigay 1996, 475; Otto 1999, 265–268. For a different view, see Willis 2001, 149–158.

carried out. While it is not *explicitly* stated in Deut 21, collective blood-guilt seems to be associated with some kind of impurity of the land, the *'adamah* on which the corpse has been found. According to Deut 19:13, some misfortune implicitly results from the negligence of blood revenge. And according to Num 35:33–34, the land (*'eretz*) must be neither profaned, nor made impure by the shedding of blood, and the land can only have atonement (*kuppar*) for shed blood by the blood of the murderer.

This is clearly purity language related to the concept of the holiness of the land that is prominent in the Holiness Code, and associates unavenged blood guilt and thus the heifer rite with corpse impurity.[109] The contamination of the ground by corpses is, however, conspiciuous in Zoroastrian religion, where the corpse is thought of as being entered by the corpse demoness at death, and during certain circumstances subsequent purification of the ground was deemed necessary.[110] Although this applies to corpses in general and not particularly to unavenged murder, Persian burial practices seem to have been intent on protecting the earth from impurity, by the use of either burial towers or stone tombs.[111] Victims of murder that were left on the ground would, however, contaminate the earth with demonic influence.

Jacob Milgrom suggests that "corpse contamination evoked an obsessive, irrational fear in individuals."[112] This is corroborated by the fact that Herod had problems in settling Tiberias because it was built over a burial ground. In view of corpse impurity originally being associated with demonic activity this is perhaps not so surprising. The isolation and the cry of the skin diseased person ("impure, impure") to protect others from unintended contact also suggests an underlying fear (Lev 13:45–46). The obviously apotropaic vestiges of the above-mentioned rites suggest a fear of demonic influence or activity unless this is warded off by appropriate means; the bird rite and the burning of the red heifer have exorcist traits, and the scapegoat is clearly a transfer rite, too. Rites in cases of corpse impurity or murder are necessary in order to avoid misfortune or death. While in the Holiness Code the punishment for defiling the sanctuary or the land – death, *karet*, or expulsion – always comes from God, these rites suggest a wide-spread fear of other lesser powers, inhabiting the underworld,

---

[109] The relationship between the asylum laws in Exod 21:12–14, Deut 19:1–13 and Num 35:9–34 cannot be discussed here; see Stackert 2007, 31–112. Many scholars agree with Stackert that the passage in Numbers is H composition or redaction, e.g. Knohl 1995, 179–180; Milgrom 2000a, 1344 (probably); Nihan 2004, 118, n.167. According to Achenbach, however, Num 35 belongs to a late stage of theocratic redaction with a focus on holiness and presupposes the asylum law in Deuteronomy (2003, 598–600, 638).

[110] Choksy 1989, 11, 16–19. See *Vendidād* 3:14; 5:27–38; 7:1–9; 8:14–19.

[111] Choksy 1989, 17. See for example *Vendidād* 3:8–9, 12–15, 36–39; 6:44–51; 8:4–13.

[112] Milgrom 1991, 275.

wastelands or open places to which various impurities and evils are returned. The basic emotion of fear in all its aspect can thus be understood as one underlying component of ideas of impurity and rites of purification.

Impurity and a sense of justice

At first sight the connection between impurity and injustice may seem far-fetched. However, this depends on the perspective we take on justice/injustice. If we extend this concept beyond the fair distribution of goods, to personal integrity, mutual behaviour and the maintaining of an interpersonal equilibrium, including the relationship between human beings and the divine, we will find that many of the examples involving divine threat that introduced the previous section can be understood in a justice perspective, too. This applies most readily to some of the serious sins in the Holiness Code, as well as to murder in Numbers, which are interestingly said to render the land unclean (Lev 18:24–30; 19:30; Num 35:33–34),[113] but also to the eating of unclean food, which is appended to the list of abominable practices (Lev 20:25–26). Even examples of impurity through contact that are associated with divine threat, may be understood from a justice perspective as infringements on the divine sphere or trespasses against divine rights, and thus as offences committed by one party against the property or prerogatives of another, although no equal status is envisaged to begin with.

From a cognitive science perspective, the sense of justice is a more complex phenomenon than the two emotions previously discussed, involving interaction between a number of emotions. One is anger, which is often a response to unjustified behaviour or unfair treatment, not only directed towards oneself but also to unrelated others.[114] Others include envy and jealousy.[115] However, these are not the only components in indignation against unfair experiences; pride, contempt, shame, embarrassment and guilt are also involved. Since taxonomies of emotions are not only or necessarily biologically motivated, but also cultur-

---

[113] Cf. Klawans 2000, 26–36, 43–46.

[114] Cf. Krebs 2008, 235. In the latter case empathy is naturally part of the game, too. It is interesting to see how anger is discussed by various theorists and different handbooks; while some emphasize its role for a sense of justice others ignore this and limit their focus to frustration and goal blockage. Compare Lemerise and Dodge 2004 on anger in *Handbook of Emotions*, who focus on hostility, with the chapters on anger and on jealousy and envy respectively (Berkowitz 1999; East and Watts 1999) in *Handbook of Cognition and Emotion*, as well as with Haidt's short discussion of anger (Haidt 2003, 856–857) in *Handbook of Affective Sciences*. Cf. Power and Dalgleish 1997, 304–305.

[115] These two are not exactly the same. East and Watts 1999.

ally defined,[116] I find it legitimate to discuss a sense of justice as a distinct emotional complex in the present context.[117]

Building on Aristotle, we may distinguish three types of justice: distributive, commutative and corrective.[118] These labels are convenient for categorizing, but in reality the different types of justice interact. A basic sense of fairness can be traced in non-human species.[119] Anger due to goal blockages often results in negotiation and/or a restoration of balance.[120] Other reactions are displayed when unfairness is experienced as unjust distribution or partiality. Experiments with capuchin monkeys and chimpanzees suggest a sense of justice with regard to equal distribution.[121] A recent study from 2009 confirms similar reactions in dogs.[122] For our purpose, however, commutative and corrective aspects of justice are more important, relating to agreements, social contracts, reparation and revenge. A sense of fairness in canids is often connected to their highly ritualized social play, which trains them for functional social interaction.[123] Reconciliatory behaviours include lip-smacking and intense grooming among primates, soft grunting among baboons, hold-bottom postures among stump-tailed macaques, scrotum fingering among chimpanzees[124] and sexual stimulation among bonobos.[125] Ritual mock bites are used among stump-tails and canids.[126] Third party mediators are found among chimpanzees,[127] and third party enforcement of social norms among certain birds.[128] Reconciliatory behaviours relate to the need for social cooperation within a kin or a larger social group and reconciliatory strategies are used for relationship repair and to limit

---

[116] Haidt 2003, 865.

[117] Cf. Wilson 1993, 55–117, who discusses fairness together with sympathy, self-control and duty as four "sentiments."

[118] Krebs 2008, 229. Procedural justice is then understood to override all of these.

[119] Brosnan 2006. It has long been observed that primates like chimpanzees can have temper tantrums when frustrated or offended (Brosnan 2006, 155; de Waal 2007 [1982], 98–105), similar to human children, at times leading to revenge (de Waal 1989, 37–69).

[120] De Waal 1996, 173–186; de Waal 2000.

[121] When these primates were asked to do tasks in pairs, one being rewarded with cucumber and the other with grapes, those receiving the low value reward often refused to accept it after a while, something they would never do under other circumstances. Brosnan 2006, 170–179; Brosnan and de Waal 2003; 2004; van Wolkenten, Brosnan and de Waal 2007.

[122] Dogs, however, seem to lack the capacity of primates to distinguish between high and low value rewards. Not receiving a reward while its companion continues to receive it, simply puts the dog off; it stops performing tasks much sooner than when on its own with the experiment leader. Range, Horn, Viranyi and Huber, 2009.

[123] Bekoff 2004.

[124] De Waal 1989, 79.

[125] De Waal 1989, 198–222. Reconciliation was first used to describe post-conflict behaviour of chimpanzees by de Waal and van Roosmalen 1979.

[126] De Waal, 1989, 157, 165; Bekoff 2004, 501–504.

[127] De Waal 1989, 39–42.

[128] References in Brosnan 2006, 168.

the escalation of aggression.[129] Some of these gestures also have a communicatory value; they signal non-aggressive future behaviour, thus facilitating mutually advantageous post-conflict interactions.[130]

When human reconciliation rituals are studied cross-culturally, a number of behaviours can be observed, from fixed phrases of apology and physical contact, such as hand shaking or kissing, to appeasement postures, food sharing, payments of restitution and symbolic gifts. The aim is often to restore an equilibrium, which has been disturbed by the offences committed.[131] Reconciliation is related to, but not identical with forgiveness. The latter is often understood as an emotional prerequisite, while reconciliation "is a behavioral coming together that a forgiver and the forgiven may establish with trust. The offended presupposes that the offender has changed and that a more just relation will ensue."[132] From an evolutionary perspective, our sense of justice and associated reparative mechanisms have developed because of their adaptive value. While not always functional at a given time and in a given context, they can be viewed as resulting from processes of *homeostasis*, aiming at "an equilibrium unique for each society and probably each social relationship."[133]

The *kipper* rites that "effect removal" can be interpreted from this perspective, although they often carry an element of fear as well. While rites of washing or fire can be thought of as removing the "substance" of impurity, thus mainly relating to emotional disgust, and various apotropaic rites can be understood to remove threats from demons or the divine realm, thus relating primarily to fear, ransoming practices and sacrifices of restoration and purification that effect *kipper* can be taken as particularly intent on removing injustices and restoring an equilibrium.[134]

Laws on restitution and ransom have no *direct* bearing on issues of purity, but they give clues as to the role of a sense of fairness for re-establishing a balance when it has been disturbed. In the Covenant Code (Exod 20:22–23:33), most of the casuistic laws (Exod 21:1–22:16 [ET 22:17]) deal with revenge and restitution. Murder is punished with execution unless it is unintentional, in which case the murderer can seek asylum.[135] Violence against or cursing of par-

---

[129] Aureli and Schaffner 2006; Hofer and East 2000.

[130] Aureli and Schaffner 2006, 134–135; Silk 1996; 2000, 179–181.

[131] Fry 2000, 334–351.

[132] Park and Enright 2000, 360.

[133] de Waal and Aureli 2000, 376.

[134] This does not exclude that *kipper* rites also to some extent seem to remove causes of disgust and fear as well.

[135] The phrase: "to a place which I will show you" (Exod 21:13) is probably a redactionary supplement that betrays Deuteronomistic influence. Cf. Deuteronomy's version of the law of refuge cities (Deut 4:41–43; 19:1–13). The status of Exod 21:13–14 has been much discussed and while some regard these verses as secondary on linguistic and literary grounds (e.g. Schwien-

ents also render capital punishment, as does man-theft. In cases of violence between men resulting in injury, the perpetrator must pay for the victim's restoration and expenses until he is healed. Lethal violence against a slave requires
vengeance, but not if the slave survives. If someone hurts a pregnant woman
and "her children come out" he shall pay unless harm follows; then he shall
give life for life, eye for eye, tooth for tooth, et cetera. If someone destroys an
eye or a tooth of a slave, the slave shall go free. If an ox gores a man, woman,
boy or girl, it shall be stoned but the owner goes free unless the ox's behaviour
was well-known and the owner had not taken proper precautions, then capital
punishment follows, *unless* he is required to pay a *kofer* as a ransom for his life.
If the victim is a slave there is a restitution payment in silver. Restitution in
money or kind is also paid if someone neglects covering a well and an animal
falls into it, or if a goring ox kills another one. In cases of animal theft, restitution shall be two- or manifold, depending on the circumstances. A burglar may
be killed during night but not in daylight. Restitution also applies in cases of
fire out of control and safekeeping or rental of others' property or animals. Se-
duction of a non-engaged girl renders payment of the bride-price, whether the
father allows marriage or not.

Differences and similarities with other Ancient Near Eastern law collections
are well known and there is no room here for discussing them or even outlining
them in any detail; I am doing that elsewhere.[136] I am not convinced by Anthony
Phillips' theological idea of a clear division between criminal and civil law,
according to which monetary compensation can only be made for property but
never for criminal offences since they require capital punishment.[137] I rather
follow Bernard Jackson who thinks that it was always possible to settle issues
with monetary compensation instead of physical retaliation.[138] While Jackson
may perhaps be overstating his case, it is reasonable that compensation presented a favourable alternative, since it increased the strength and status of the

---

horst-Schönberger 1990, 39–42; Jackson 2006, 120–121), others defend their place (Wright
2009, 163–165). A dependence on the altar law (Exod 20:22–26) seems reasonable for many
reasons (Wright 2009, 165; Stackert 2007, 34–38). The phrase about appointing a place seems,
however, to be a secondary qualification, implying that in view of cult centralization the altar in
v. 14 cannot be *any* altar, but then leaving the mention of that altar somehow unexplained. One
may thus conjecture an original mention of the altar as a place of refuge in Exod 21:13, rather
than a reference to the establishment of a place for asylum in the future. The alternative would
be to claim a cultic meaning of *maqom* (place) in Exod 21:13, which Deuteronomy then re-
interprets as "city" (See Stackert 2007, 31–112).
[136] See Kazen 2011b, forthcoming.
[137] Phillips 2004, 2–24, 43. Wright 2007, arguing for the dependence of the Covenant Code on
Hammurabi's law (cf. Wright 2003), sees no theological rationale for the former's modifica-
tions of the latter (76).
[138] Jackson 2002, 21.

family or clan of the victim, while saving the perpetrator from loss of bodily functions or life. Jackson and others are thus to be believed when they point out, against Phillips, that laws prohibiting *kofer* in case of outright murder (Num 35:31–32), or the proverb stating that a *kofer* is useless in the case of raging jealousy (Prov 6:32–35), suggest that monetary compensation was a live alternative even in cases of murder and adultery.[139] I favour the view that the practice of *kofer* was known and practised at an early stage, not least in view of the provisions of other Ancient Near Eastern law codes, and that it reflects pre-institutionary and self-regulating customary law.[140] The priestly redactors seem to have looked at it with suspicion and denied it in favour of the more recent innovation of cities of asylum, partly due to increasing institutional control.[141]

In the past, an evolutionary approach has been common, suggesting a linear development from personal revenge, through formalized retaliatory norms, to monetary compensation.[142] This appears too simplistic, however, as other Ancient Near Eastern law codes from Sumer to the Hittites, dated to the second millennium BCE or even earlier, frequently give options of monetary compensation rather than talion, and payment rather than death.[143] Possibly, an increasing recourse to monetary fines may be a corollary to an increase in state power and the growth of state intervention, and could thus depend on the level of centralization.[144] In early Judaism, Josephus as well as the Pharisees, followed by the rabbis, seem to have interpreted talion law as allowing for, or even demanding the alternative of compensatory payment.[145] If this "development" came

---

[139] Jackson 2006, 133–138, 157–166.

[140] Jackson 2002, 12–17; 2006, 387–430.

[141] Cities of asylum possibly come from the time of Josiah's reform as a result of pre-exilic cult centralization. Before that, local shrines functioned as asylums. For further discussion, see Stackert 2007, 31–112; cf. note 130 above. The main passage for cities of asylum is Deut 19:1–13 (cf. 4:41–43), which spells out the conditions for asylum (unintentional killing). Here, nothing is said either positively or negatively about redeeming the perpetrator by a *kofer*, like in Num 35:31–32. I understand both the Holiness Code and Numbers as belonging to the latest strata of the Pentateuch.

[142] Cf. Blau 1916; Sulzberger 1914; 1915a; 1915b. For a late example, see Parisi 2001.

[143] The Sumerian laws of Ur-Namma (ca. 2100 BCE) have an elaborated price list for various bodily damages. This is the case with the Akkadian laws of Eshnunna, too (ca. 1770 BCE).

[144] Cf. Phillips 2004, 68–69.

[145] Parisi 2001; Jackson 2002; This is first argued by Blau 1916, 345. Josephus suggests that talion law applies "unless indeed the maimed man be willing to accept money; for the law empowers the victim himself to assess the damage that has befallen him and makes this concession, unless he would show himself too severe." *Ant.* 4:280. Philo, on the other hand, mentions no such exceptions, but finds monetary penalties for bodily damage insufficient (*Spec. Laws* 3:181–182). Josephus also suggests that the Pharisees were less severe than the Sadducees with regard to punishment (*Ant.* 13:294; 20:199); according to *m. Mak.* 1:6 the latter at least interpreted talion law literally. According to the medieval scholiast's commentary to the *Megillath Ta'anith*, Boethusians believed in a literal interpretation of talion law, but the historical value of this tradition may be doubted. The rabbinic arguments for and against interpreting talion law

comparatively late in Israelite society, it may result from differences in state organization and function.[146]

Laws on restitution and ransom express a popular sense of justice, aiming to limit aggression and restore a disturbed equilibrium, and we may argue that they evolved culturally and were continuously re-interpreted because of their adaptive value. While monetary compensation came to be applied to all sorts of cases, there are basic distinctions between simple compensatory payment and *kofer* or ransom. In most cases when property can be restored or exchanged for money, a payment of silver (*kesef*) or "full restitution" or "appeasement" (*shallem y^eshallem*) is prescribed. In cases of theft, there is an over-compensation that may be explained either as an appeasement in view of the wrongs committed against the owner, or as a deterrent towards potential thieves, or as both. When damages cannot be restored by monetary payment, however, the talion principle may be understood as an alternative way of achieving an equilibrium and thus satisfying a sense of justice. While the damage cannot be undone, the offending party is made subject to a similar loss. I suggest that when a *kofer* is involved, however, the value of what is at stake *cannot* really be compensated for. In the Pentateuch this applies to the owner of the goring ox (Exod 21:29–30), census-taking (Exod 30:12–16); unintentional murder and cities of refuge (Num 35:30–34), i.e., what is at stake is somehow the value of human life. Outside of the Pentateuch a *kofer* is involved with regard to payments in a variety of extraordinary circumstances that do *not* correspond to simple compensation for lost or damaged property.[147] In many of these cases there is also a notion of offence involved. *Kofer* is not simply a compensatory payment; it does not effect full restitution (*shallem y^eshallem*), but rather acts as a symbolic token towards the victim or the victim's relatives. A *kofer* depends on the offended party and cannot restore the balance, only act as a reconciliatory action, a mitigating gesture, signalling a change in future behaviour. While the monetary value should not be down-played, it is also a sign of reconciliation, even an implicit assurance of a change in attitude, which can be accepted at will by the offended

---

literally are found in *b. B. Qam.* 83b–86a; cf. *b. Sanh.* 79. The principle of evaluating bodily injuries is already underlying the *Mishnah* (*m. B. Qam.* 8:1). For other references, see Crossley 2004, 103.

[146] Rather than from theological convictions, as Phillips (2004, 43–44, 49–73) thinks. As Jackson (2006, 389–406) has pointed out, the *mishpatim* of the Covenant Code can function as self-administered laws that do not require a developed judicial system, but may be practised on family and village level, legitimated by general consent. This suggests a relatively limited role of the state in judicial matters.

[147] 1 Sam 12:3; Amos 5:12; Isa 43:3; Ps 49:8 (7); Prov 6:35; 13:8; 21:18; Job 33:24; 36:18. Cf. Finkelstein 1973, 183 n. 46, who argues that ransom is not to be understood as "wergild," corresponding to the value of the victim.

party. When accepted, it removes the offence, and thus restores a *fictional* balance, a mitigated equilibrium.

The meaning of the *kipper* rites is a constant bone of contention among biblical scholars. Today, most scholars derive the pi'el verb either from the cognate Akkadian *kuppuru* ("to wipe off, cleanse") or from the noun *kofer*, or from both.[148] The ambiguity relates to the use of *kipper* in contexts of both sin and impurity. In the descriptions of the holocaust bull in Lev 1:4 and of the *chattat* offerings in Lev 4–5, the priest is explicitly said to "effect atonement" (*w^{e}kipper*), usually resulting in forgiveness (*w^{e}nislach*).[149] This is the case with the *asham* offering in Lev 5 too and the formula *y^{e}kapper/w^{e}kipper ... w^{e}nislach* keeps recurring (Lev 5:16, 18, 26 [ET 6:7]). In the purity laws, however, holocausts as well as *chattat* and *asham* offerings, and in some cases even *minchag* offerings, are employed by the priest in order to effect purification; the formula runs: *w^{e}kipper ... w^{e}taher* (Lev 12:7, 8; 14:20, 53).[150] In the Day of Atonement rituals (Lev 16), *kipper* is frequently employed to describe the effect of the priest's activity and once, towards the end (Lev 16:30) the purpose is explicitly stated as *l^{e}taher*.[151] For this reason, Milgrom has argued that *kipper* never means "atone" but always "purge" or "purify," with the strained result that the offences forgiven in Lev 4–5 cannot be the original ones, but the additional sin of indirectly causing defilement to the sanctuary.[152] However, the use of the verb elsewhere suggests that such a narrow understanding is hardly viable.[153]

---

[148] Earlier attempts to derive *kipper* from the Arabic *kafara*, meaning "to cover" are generally rejected. Cf. Sklar 2005, 44–45, especially n.2; Gilders 2004, 28–29. It is rather associated with *kuppuru*; see Milgrom 1991, 1079–1084; Levine 1974, 56–63. For further discussion of the Akkadian stem *kuppuru*, see Wright 1987a, 291–299. Maul (1994, 80) suggests that the "'Sitz im Leben' von *kuppuru*... ist im Bereich der Kosmetik zu suchen. *kuppuru* ist nichts anderes als ein *peeling*." Levine claims two forms of *kipper*, deriving from *kuppuru* and *kofer* respectively (1974, 67–77). He is followed in this by Gilders (2004, 29) and some other scholars. Others, like Sklar (2005, 4–5), point out the difficulty in trying to keep two distinct meanings of the verb apart.

[149] Lev 4:20, 26, 31, 35; 5:10, 13. The exception is Lev 5:6, but here we must assume forgiveness as implied from the context.

[150] The abbreviated statement, without *w^{e}taher*, also occurs in Lev 14:18, 19, 21, 29, 31; 15:15, 30.

[151] Verses 29–34 are often considered as H redaction. For references and a discussion, see Nihan 2007, 345–350.

[152] The original offences are taken care of by the feeling of remorse (Milgrom 1991, 254–256). Milgrom's explanation depends on his theory of defilement of the sanctuary from afar as well as on the use of prepositions (1991, 255–256, 316–318, 991–1000). Both arguments have been challenged (Maccoby 1999, 165–192; cf. Kazen 2002, 211–214).

[153] In the Holiness Code, an *asham* offering is prescribed for a "minor" sexual offence, with which the priest brings "atonement" and the man is forgiven (*w^{e}kipper ... w^{e}nislach*) (Lev 19:22). In Numbers, the ambiguous use of *kipper* is continued. In Num 5:6–10, an undefined case of compensation or restitution is described, in which the offending party also gives a "ram of atonement" to the priest with which he brings "atonement" (*y^{e}kapper*). The exact nature of

It seems that *kipper* rites often function as a *kofer*, removing injustice, imbalance and offence, restoring a fictional balance, a mitigated equilibrium,[154] between human beings and the divine power. In cases of impurity, holocaust and *chattat* sacrifices for the post-natal bleeding of the *yoledet* (Lev 12:6–8), for pathological discharges (15:13–15, 28–30), and on the day of atonement (16:3–19, 30), holocaust, *minchag*, *asham* and *chattat* sacrifices for the healed skin diseased (14:10–31), and the bird rite for a "leprous" house (14:49–53), are all carried out by the priest to effect *kipper*. Effecting *kipper* through the bird rite for a "leprous" house is somehow anomalous and may result from this section being a fairly late extension of *tzara'at* laws; the idea of *kipper* is not present in the application of the bird rite for skin diseased persons. In the other cases, however, the aim seems to be not only a removal of the impurity itself, but also a restoration of balance. The presence of impurities such as genital discharges and skin disease somehow encroaches upon the divine sphere and compromises divine holiness and presence. It is not an issue of upholding fair conditions between equals; the divine power can have absolute claims with regard to human beings. But human impurities – like any human offences, that is, sin – seem to cause divine offence and indignation comparable to that of injustice, theft, violent assault or unfair distribution among human beings. Consequently, the Nazirite who has become accidentally corpse-impure must also sacrifice a holocaust and a *chattat* to effect *kipper* (Num 6:9–11), although this is not normally required after corpse impurity, since he has compromised the divine sphere of holiness in which he had been partaking.[155] Similarly, the consecration of the Levites requires a holocaust and a *chattat* sacrifice for their permanent sanctification. In both cases we could speak of a fictive balance being

---

the offering is not stated. In the Nazirite law, unintentional defilement by a corpse requires "atonement" (Num 6:11). The consecration of the Levites is accompanied by sacrifices that effect "atonement" with the purpose of their purification (*l*ᵉ*taharam*) (Num 8:12, 21). Inadvertent sins require sacrifices, and like in Lev 4–5 the priest effects "atonement" and the sinner is forgiven (*w*ᵉ*kipper ... w*ᵉ*nislach*) (Num 15:25, 28). The festal calendar also mentions "atonement" as the purpose of sacrifices at various festal days (Num 28:22, 30; 29:5).

[154] This is also how the verb *kipper* is employed in non-sacrificial settings outside of the Pentateuch (1 Sam 3:14 [hitpael]; 2 Sam 21:1–9; Isa 47:11; Jer 18:23; Prov 16:14). The exception may be the Psalms, where *kipper* can be translated more generally as "forgive." However, a sense of *kofer* is possible here, too. Cf. Dan 9:24. In 2 Chr 30:18 Hezekiah prays for the people that *God* shall effect removal (*kipper*) for them, and in the context this would mean to overbear the offence that is caused by people not being properly purified. It is thus less of a "removal" of impurity than a waiving of the conditions. In Ezekiel as well as in 1 Chr 6:34 (49), *kipper* is used as in the sacrificial laws of Leviticus.

[155] The subsequent *asham* for re-entry into the Nazirite state (vv. 11–12) and the series of sacrifices for exiting this state (vv. 13–20) cannot be discussed here. However, neither of these sacrifices is said to effect *kipper*.

established, by the divine power accepting the "unequal" participation of human beings in his holy sphere through the mitigating tokens of the *kipper* rites.

In several cases the concept of *kipper* is also associated with fear of divine punishment, and an underlying fear of demonic powers can be detected. In the wake of Korah's rebellion, Aaron effects "atonement" by burning incense (Num 17:11–12 [ET 16:46–47]).[156] In Num 31:48–54, the soldiers give a *qorban* to Yahweh, to effect "atonement" for their lives; the verb is used synonymously with *kofer*, as in the passage on census in the Covenant Code (Exod 30:12–16), where both verb and noun occur.[157] *Kipper* is also used in the already mentioned rite of breaking a heifer's neck (Deut 21:8). The apotropaic function is evident in these examples and they involve emotional fear. While not expressly relating to impurity, they display the double function to avert danger and restore balance.

In cases where sacrificial rites are used to effect *kipper* for impurities, similar conditions seem to apply. These rites aim at removing offences and restoring the balance required by a fundamental sense of justice. Without such a balance, divine revenge is to be expected. Offences causing such instability to the "system" must be dealt with; threats due to the imbalance need to be averted by a *kipper* act or rite, usually involving an *asham* or a *chattat* sacrifice. These sacrifices are offered to the deity, who is very much envisaged in human and emotional terms. God reacts emotionally against "unfair" disturbances of a hierarchically defined equilibrium envisaged in the human-divine relationship, a relationship in which the human part is always found wanting. In cases of sins of ignorance or negligence as well as in cases of impurity there is a perceived offence; humans have transgressed the divine order in ways that cannot be solved by compensation or restitution. Divine authority and sanctity have been somehow compromised. The offerings effecting *kipper* are not understood as full restitution or payment for wrongs against the deity, but as ritualized appeasement behaviours, mitigating tokens of reconciliation, appealing to the offended party for emotional acceptance and acknowledgment, thus restoring a fictive balance. Although effecting *kipper* does not by definition require sacrifices, it seems that the priestly authors and redactors of the Pentateuch restricted mitigating rites, intent on removing serious offence, to the newly centralized sacrificial cult, while suppressing popular *kofer* practices.[158] They did not, however, necessarily reserve *kipper* rites to blood sacrifices. Both fear and a sense

---

[156] Phinehas does the same by killing Simri and the Midianite Kosbi (Num 25:11–13).

[157] Gilders argues for this passage being an interpolation by a late redactor (2004, 172–173). Cf. Nihan (2007, 31–33, 609, 614, 619), who regards Exod 30–31 as part of a late redaction.

[158] This does not exclude the possibility that a cultic use of *kipper* rites could also have had a social function, as suggested by Albertz 2001.

of justice seem to constitute the emotional bedrock on which a number of purificatory rites are built.

Conclusions

Biologically based emotions play a crucial role in human activities, including ritual concepts and behaviour. The emotions discussed in this chapter, disgust, fear and a sense of justice, have all evolved because of their adaptive value and their development in the human being has been further shaped by cultural factors. They all have a bearing on ideas of impurity and the formation of various rituals for purification. A better understanding of these emotions contributes to our interpretation not only of the purity texts, but also of underlying concepts and practices.

We have seen that disgust can be understood as a common denominator underlying all three categories of impurity, and many of the generally accepted disgust triggers can plausibly be associated with various impurities. Coping strategies involve rejection, avoidance and removal. Water purification rites enact the removal of offensive "substances." Emotional disgust is expressed at certain foods, bodily conditions and offensive acts, especially serious crimes and sexual and cultic behaviour associated with non-Israelites.

We have also found emotional fear behind a number of apotropaic purification rituals that seem to lie at the intersection of the priestly cult with popular religion. Fear of becoming, and especially remaining impure is bolstered by divine threats, but under the surface demonic influence is detectable. Fear of divine beings or demons can be understood to involve all four components that are generally acknowledged. The rites discussed contain a number of traits that are plausibly associated with demons and their habitats, with parallels available in other Ancient Near Eastern texts.

Finally, we have explored the role of a sense of justice, not only for ancient ideas of restitution and ransom, but also for the concept of *kipper*, especially for those sacrificial rites that are employed for effecting "removal." Although associations are less straight-forward, *kipper* rites can be understood as ritual reconciliatory gestures aimed at a fictive or symbolic restoration of an equilibrium that has been disturbed by "unfair" trespasses of a hierarchically defined divine-human relationship. In this case we may in fact suggest a close interaction between a sense of justice, fear and emotional disgust; removal rites deal with the causes of all three.

Chapter 3

Explaining Discrepancies in the Laws on Genital Discharges[1]

Introduction

At the end of the Second Temple period the purity laws of Lev 12 and 15 were read "systemically" with regard to the mechanisms of contamination and the purificatory measures to be taken by various impurity bearers. The contamination potential and purification rituals of different genital dischargers were to a large extent harmonized. However, when these laws are read without harmonizing, a number of discrepancies become obvious.

In this chapter, discrepancies at the surface of biblical texts are examined and discussed from a variety of perspectives: as presupposing a systemic shaping of legal material; as revealing a gender issue, especially with regard to female involvement in the cult; as signs of an underlying view of genital fluids as ultimate sources of contamination; and finally, as vestiges of fears and beliefs in demonic influence through various types of impurity.

The discrepancies that are dealt with are basically as follows: The person who touches a *zav* (זָב) has to launder, wash, and is unclean until the evening (Lev 15:7). The person touching a menstruant, however, is only said to become unclean until the evening (v. 19), and nothing whatsoever is said about touching a *zavah* (זָבָה). Similarly, the *zav* is said to contaminate people and vessels by touch, unless he has washed his hands (vv. 11–12). Nothing, however, is said about female dischargers contaminating by touch. The *zav* is given a more elaborate treatment on some points: he contaminates by spitting (v. 8), and everything upon which he sits when riding is contaminated (v. 9).

When we look at purification rituals, we find that the *zav* is required to launder his clothes and wash on the seventh day, as well as to bring a sacrifice on the eighth (vv. 13–15). Nothing is said about the menstruant, and while the

---

[1] An earlier version of this chapter was published as "Explaining Discrepancies in the Purity Laws on Discharges" in *Revue Biblique* 114 (2007): 348–371. The article develops and elaborates on a section in my dissertation (Kazen 2002, 139–154). The *RB* article has been only slightly revised here.

zavah is to wait for seven days and then bring a sacrifice (vv. 28–30), there is
no mention of washing or laundering.

Turning to the *yoledet* (יוֹלֶדֶת) of Lev 12, her impurity during the first stage
(one or two weeks) is likened to that of a menstruant (vv. 2, 5). Nevertheless,
during her second stage impurity (another 33 or 66 days) she is not allowed to
touch anything holy or enter the sanctuary (v. 4), and the period should be ter-
minated by a sacrifice (vv. 6–8). Nothing is said, however, about any washing
or laundering.

Systemic reading in Second Temple Judaism

An "equalizing" tendency is obvious in rabbinic texts, as a result of systemic
reading. This is clear from the discussion in *m. Nid.* 4:3:

> The blood of a woman who has not immersed after childbirth -
> The House of Shammai say, "It is like her spit and her urine."
> And the House of Hillel say, "It imparts uncleanness wet and dry."[2]

Without defining the exact disagreement between the Houses, we notice that
bathing is taken for granted in the case of the *yoledet*, although it is not explicitly prescribed in Lev 12. The menstruant's immersion in a *miqveh* at the end of
her period is so self-evident that the fact itself is seldom mentioned in the *Mishnah*. When it is, it is taken for granted.[3] As for the *zavah*, her immersion was
taken for granted too. She is regarded slightly more unclean than the *zav*, because she could render a man unclean for seven days by intercourse. For all
other practical purposes, she is included in some of the legislation concerning
the *zav*, separately identified only at times.[4] Immersion was widely practised
during the first century CE, as is evidenced by frequent findings of *miqvaot*.[5]
There are no reasons to doubt that this practice included all severe impurity
bearers, men and women, already at the end of the Second Temple period.

Similarly, the contamination potential of various genital dischargers is
clearly regarded as equal, according to *m. Zabim* 5:6:

> He who touches the *Zab* and the *Zabah* and the menstruating woman and the woman af-
> ter childbirth and the *mesora*, a bed or a chair [that any of these have lain or sat upon]
> imparts uncleanness at two removes and renders [heave offering] unfit at one further
> remove. [If] he separated, he imparts uncleanness at one remove and renders unfit at

---

[2] Quotations from the Mishnah in this chapter are taken from Neusner 1988.
[3] *m. Miqw.* 8:1; *m. Miqw.* 8:5. That the menstruant is required to immerse is self-evident in
rabbinic Judaism, and the *miqveh* survived in post-temple times only for the sake of menstruants. Maccoby 1999, 43. Cf. Sanders 1990, 143.
[4] *m. Kelim* 1:4; *m. Zabim* 5:6.
[5] Cf. Sanders 1990, 214–227, 355 n.28 and 1992, 222–230. For further discussion and more
references, see Kazen 2002, 74–76.

one further remove. All the same are the one who touches and the one who shifts, and all the same are the one who carries and the one who is carried.[6]

The discrepancies in biblical legislation between touching and being touched by different impurity bearers were not relevant for the Rabbis. The anonymous saying in *m. Zabim* 5:1 is clear:

> He who touches the *Zab*, or whom the *Zab* touches,
> he who moves the *Zab*, or whom the *Zab* moves
> imparts uncleanness to food and drink and utensils
> which may be cleaned through rinsing when [he is in] contact but not when he carries.

A similar equalizing tendency is found in texts from Qumran, providing strong evidence for a systemic reading being presupposed already in Second Temple Judaism. A case for this has been argued from 4QD (4Q266–273) by Martha Himmelfarb. She defines this text as a commentary on Leviticus, pointing out that the subjects treated were those that the Torah did not organize clearly enough, and that there is nothing sectarian about this systemic interpretation of 4QD.[7] "Thus they [the laws of 4QD] organize the purity laws of Leviticus more clearly than Leviticus does and make explicit connections that the Torah fails to make."[8]

Other fragments from the same cave, 4QTohorot (4Q274, 276–278), provide further arguments for the case in question. While it is not clear whether the rinsing of hands to prevent contamination applied to the *zav* only or to other dischargers as well,[9] we find that all dischargers are basically considered to contaminate in the same way. In 4Q274, fragment 1, different impurity bearers, at their purifying stage of seven days, are instructed not to touch other impure people, thus incurring an added impurity.

> 4b And the woman discharging blood (*zavah dam*) for seven days shall not touch the man discharging (*zav*) or any utensil [t]hat the man discharging (*zav*) has touched or lain
> 5 on or that he has sat on. And if she touched, she shall launder her clothes and bathe, and afterwards she may eat. And with all her strength she shall not mix during her seven
> 6 days in order n[o]t to defile the camps of the ho[ly] (ones) of Israel, and also, she shall not touch any woman [discharg]ing blood (*zavah dam*) for man[y] days.
> 7 And the one who counts, whether male or female, shall not tou[ch the man discharging (*zav*) in] his [dischar]ge (or) the menstruant in her (initial) *niddah* (bleeding), unless she is pure from her [*nidd*]*ah* (bleeding), for behold,

---

[6] Cf. Harrington 1993, 230–231. Sanders 1990, 208–209, doubts that "the Pharisees operated by this principle," but misunderstands the passage. For a discussion, see Kazen 2002, 152, n. 343.

[7] Himmelfarb 2004, 155–169.

[8] Himmelfarb 2004, 168.

[9] Cf. 4Q277 1 ii, 10–11: "And anyone touched by [a man who has] a flux [   ] [and whose] hand[s were not] r[in]sed in water becomes [unclean]" (Baumgarten 1999, 116).

8 *niddah* blood is considered like a discharge [to] the one touching it. And if a semen emission com[es forth from a man] – his touch i[s] unclean. And [anyo]ne who touches a person from all
9 these unclean ones during the seven days of [his] puri[fication] shall [no]t eat, as if he were defiled by [a human cor]pse, [and he shall b]athe and wash (his clothes) and afterwar[ds] [Col ii, 1] he shall e[at …[10]

The underlying premise is that impure persons contaminate not only pure, but also purifying people. Those purifying thus had to be instructed to avoid other impurity bearers, especially those with the same type of impurity as themselves, whom they, probably, had been associating with, during expulsion or quarantine. These restrictions self-evidently applied to clean persons as well; otherwise they could not be applied to purifying or impure people. A menstruant is not to touch a *zav* or a *zavah* alike.[11] No (purifying) person should touch any *zav* or any menstruant. It is implied that different impurity bearers are equalized as to their contamination by the fact that different types of discharges are put on the same level. Finally, touching a genital discharger is compared to corpse-defilement. Following Baumgarten's reconstruction,[12] the last lines (8b–9) can be taken to summarize the preceding rulings, thus referring to any of the previously mentioned purifying persons, male or female (line 7: אם זכר ואם נקבה). Bathing and laundering (clothes) is a common requirement for all, and this applies regardless of which type of impurity bearer that has been contacted. The equalizing tendency is further underscored in lines 7b–8a:

for behold, *niddah* blood is considered like a discharge [to] the one touching it. And if a semen emission com[es forth from a man] – his touch i[s] unclean.[13]

The point seems to be that since discharges and menstrual blood are equally impure, contact with a menstruant should be avoided to the same extent as contact with a *zav*. And, adds the text, this applies to the semen-emitter as well. If the whole passage is not to be taken as a jumbled hotchpotch of unconnected

[10] 4Q274 1 i, 4–9; ii, 1. My translation. For a reconstruction, translation, and discussion of this text, see chapter 4 below (= Kazen 2010a).
[11] Since Lev 15 is not explicit about touching or being touched by a *zavah*, the comment that she should not mingle (תתערב) is difficult to interpret. Qimron suggests that it refers to intercourse (cf. Baumgarten in DJD 35, 102, n.2), but the term belongs to a ritual context in most texts found at Qumran (cf. Milgrom 1995, 63).
[12] I follow Baumgarten's [רתו]טה (1999, 100–101), which is preferable to Milgrom's [רתם]טה (1995, 59–60), i.e. "*his*" rather than "*their*" purification; this does not exclude ambiguity, but for reasons explained in the following chapter I take this to refer to the purifying person who during his period of purification must not touch the fully impure. Hence the end of line 7 should not be misinterpreted as a concession as Milgrom's restoration and translation of lines 8 and 9 has led Harrington to do (1993, 85–86). See chapter 4 for further discussion.
[13] Here I follow Eisenman and Wise in reconstructing יחשב לנוגע בו; the resulting translation is close to that of García Martínez and Tigchelaar 2000, 628–629. For a discussion, see chapter 4.

instruction, the underlying premise must be understood: no distinction is being made between touching or being touched; all types of purifying persons are to avoid physical contact with any kind of impurity bearer, since they contaminate in basically the same way.

We thus find evidence both in rabbinic texts and Qumran fragments for a systemic reading and an equalizing interpretation being presupposed in halakic discussions at the end of the Second Temple period.[14]

Systemic shaping in the text of Leviticus

Although most of the discrepancies were harmonized during the Second Temple period, this does not prove that the purity laws were always read systemically. One obvious possibility, however, is to regard a *basic* systemic reading as presupposed in a redactional process that is supposed to have shaped the laws about discharges into their present form. Such presuppositions are admittedly speculative when no sources are present or not even possible to reconstruct with certainty.[15] Rather than imagining a particular instance for the redaction of literary source documents, we should perhaps think more in terms of a continuous development of legal texts. Also, since the priestly writers, at least in part, framed their laws as though they were given at a period in the distant past, we should not expect an exact correspondence between their formulations and contemporary practices.[16] Nevertheless, there are enough of discrepancies that cannot be explained from imagined wilderness conditions, which need to be explained, suggesting diverse origins in time and/or place for the legal material included and shaped by the priestly writers.

Several interpreters point out that the discussions about female dischargers (Lev 15:19–30) are made dependent on the previous basic regulations concerning the *zav* (15:2–15). The whole chapter would thus have been formed from a systemic point of view.[17] As the *zav* is first treated, the menstruant and the *zavah* incorporate certain traits of the former. This is clear from the attempts of

---

[14] The antiquity of the *presuppositions* of the discussions in *m. Zabim* and *m. Niddah* is thus corroborated by material from Qumran. Cf. Neusner's argument from form-critical considerations (1977, 3).

[15] Cf. the relative difficulty of discussing redaction in the Gospel of Mark as compared with Matthew and Luke.

[16] I am grateful to Baruch Schwartz for pertinent comments on these issues (personal correspondence).

[17] Ellens (2003, 29–43) has argued for a conscious ABBA structure that organizes the text in order to achieve gender symmetry, contrasting the viewpoints, grammar, vocabulary and structure of the material, transforming the common understanding of menstruation as "unhealthy" or anomalous. (The arguments are further developed in 2008, 47–72.) This organization is far from complete, however, and discrepancies still abound.

the author to parallel the symptoms of the menstruant with those of the *zav*, which has lead to a somewhat clumsy construction in Lev 15:19 (וְאִשָּׁה כִּי־תִהְיֶה, in אִישׁ אִישׁ כִּי יִהְיֶה זָב מִבְּשָׂרוֹ זוֹבוֹ) that parallels 15:2 (זָבָה דָּם יִהְיֶה זֹבָהּ בִּבְשָׂרָהּ), in spite of specific terminology being available (v. 33:הַדָּוָה בְּנִדָּתָהּ).[18] A systemic reading is encouraged by the fact that זָב is being used inclusively about both men and women in the concluding v. 33 (הַזָּב אֶת־זוֹבוֹ לַזָּכָר וְלַנְּקֵבָה).[19]

Granted that this chapter is systemically shaped, Milgrom's suggestion that not only the *zav*, but all dischargers, are supposed to purify in spring water (Lev 15:13), like other seven-day impurity bearers (Lev 14:5–6, 50–52; Num 19:17), is probably true. While this is not mentioned in the case of female dischargers, it is implied, since the regulations concerning the latter abbreviate those preceding, concerning the *zav*.[20]

An important argument, developed by Wright and Milgrom, is that the expression יִטְמָא עַד־הָעֶרֶב ("unclean until evening," e.g. in 15:19) always implies ablutions, i.e. washing the body. This can be deduced from several instances of parallel instructions, where the expression is used in one place with, and in another place without bathing being mentioned.[21] Assuming this to be the case, Harrington argues that since those who touch a menstruant are unclean until evening (15:19) and thus must bathe, this must *a fortiori* apply to the menstruant herself.[22] Based on a similar logic, Wright suggests that the menstruant must launder her clothes too, as must those who touch her bed.[23]

The purification requirements of the *zavah* (15:28–30) mention only a sacrifice. If these requirements are seen as abbreviating the requirements of the *zav*, laundering and bathing must be implicitly understood from v. 13.[24] Sacrifices are, however, explicitly required only from the *yoledet*, the *zav* and the *zavah*, but not from the menstruant (12:6–8; 15:14–15, 29–30). Are we to harmonize from a systemic reading in this case too, or is the discrepancy intended? Explaining the difference by the non-pathological character of menstruation is hardly credible; that should have applied to the *yoledet* as well.[25] Practical considerations have been suggested: menstruants cannot be expected to afford sac-

---

[18] Gerstenberger 1993, 186. It should be noted that זָבָה is the technical term in Rabbinic Hebrew for a woman with long-term discharges of blood. In Lev 15, both זָבָה and דָּוָה are used for the menstruant, and the "rabbinic" זָבָה is referred to in v. 25 by the even more roundabout phrase אִשָּׁה כִּי־יָזוּב זוֹב דָּמָהּ יָמִים רַבִּים בְּלֹא עֶת־נִדָּתָהּ.

[19] Cf. Milgrom 1991, 948.

[20] Milgrom 1991, 923–924, 934–935.

[21] Milgrom 1991, 919. Cf. Wright 1987a, 185, n.38; Harrington 1993, 117–120.

[22] Harrington 1993, 228–229.

[23] Wright 1987a, 191, n.44.

[24] Wright 1987a, 193, especially n.47. It seems as if Wright assumes the same purification rites to apply also to the *yoledet* (195).

[25] For a linguistic argument for associating menstruation with illness, see Ellens 2003, 29–32.

rifices monthly.[26] This is a questionable argument, however, since regular menstruation through the fertile period is a fairly recent phenomenon, dependent on modern family structures and birth control. Most women were pregnant or breast-feeding during the major part of their fertile period. Possibly menstruation is considered a slighter impurity than the others, since it is of shorter duration, and is not followed by a seven-day purification period. Menstruation impurity is actually more equivalent to the seven-day *purification* period of the other impurity bearers. The impurity of the menstruant could thus be regarded as milder than that of other dischargers.[27]

So far we have seen that a systemic reading of the biblical legislation seems natural in many cases, but is not always self-evident. The question of contamination through physical contact is particularly tricky. Taking the differences at face value, Fonrobert concludes that not only did the menstruant and the *zavah* fail to transmit impurity by touching, but also the *zavah* could even be touched.[28] The opposite view is held by Trummer, who suggests that rules about discharging women touching clean people are absent because this was simply unthinkable.[29] I would regard both standpoints as oversimplifications.

In the case of a clean person touching a discharger, a systemic reading would mean that one is contaminated and has to purify in the same way after having touched a menstruant (15:19) as after having touched a *zav* (15:7), i.e., including laundering. Wright argues that since laundering is required from a person having touched something upon which a menstruant lies or sits (vv. 21–22), it must logically be required from someone directly touching her.[30] Against this, Milgrom argues that, although the phrase יִטְמָא עַד־הָעָרֶב implies bathing, it never includes the laundering of clothes.[31]

There is thus an apparent tension between v. 19 and vv. 21–22 that demand laundering from those touching the menstruant's bed and seat. The problem is made even worse when the *zavah* is considered. While both washing and laundering are demanded from the person touching her bed or seat (v. 27), nothing is said about touching the *zavah* herself. This can be explained in different ways. Since the *zavah* is explicitly compared to the menstruant (vv. 25–26) and since the menstruant is actually referred to as a *zavah* too, it could be argued that the

---

[26] This is the argument of Milgrom 1991, 935. It could be argued that while childbirth is natural too, it does not occur so often; hence a sacrifice could be afforded.

[27] This fits with Milgrom's theory of sacrifice as a consequence of having polluted the sanctuary from afar (cf. Milgrom 1991, 999). His idea of airborne impurity has been seriously criticized, however (Maccoby 1999, 165–192; cf. Kazen 2002, 147–150, 211–214). See further below.

[28] Fonrobert 1997, 121–140, here 130–131.

[29] Trummer 1991, 112–113.

[30] Wright 1987a, 189.

[31] Milgrom 1991, 935–936.

same rules are assumed to apply, although some details are missing, due to abbreviation (i.e., touching her, touching items on her bed or seat, and intercourse). This corresponds to how the rules were interpreted and applied in Second Temple times, as we have already seen. Milgrom has suggested that the בָּם of v. 27 should be read בָּהּ, as in two manuscripts.[32] This is supported by the LXX reading (αὐτῆς), and makes the verse read: "And everyone who touches *her* becomes unclean, and must launder his clothes and wash in water and is unclean until evening." If this reading is accepted, the rules about touching a *zavah* correspond to those about touching a *zav* (v. 7).[33] There is still a difference as compared to the menstruant, but as we have already seen this could be explained by menstruation being a recurring process, limited in time, and corresponding to the purification period of other impurities, thus not really considered contaminating as seriously as other discharges.[34] Touching a *zav* or a *zavah* would thus require bathing and laundering, while touching a menstruant would require bathing only. This corresponds to the requirement for the former to bring a sacrifice, which does not apply to the menstruant, as previously noticed.[35]

The case of a discharger touching a clean person complicates the issue further. This is explicitly forbidden only in the case of the *zav*. He is said to contaminate clean persons and vessels by touching them without having first washed his hands (vv. 11–12). Would it not be reasonable to assume such contamination at least in the case of the *zavah* by analogy, and by implication from the fact that the *zavah* contaminates persons via her bed or seat?[36]

A question that is neither discussed explicitly by rabbinic authorities, nor extensively by modern commentators, concerns the definition of touch. The regulations about touching a *zav* (v. 7) talk about his "flesh" (הַנֹּגֵעַ בִּבְשַׂר הַזָּב). This expression could be interpreted as his genitals,[37] but this is unlikely.[38] It rather refers to his body in general. This probably includes his clothes as well, since clothing could be regarded as an extension of a person's body. That "flesh" should not be taken literally could be argued from the parallel passage

---

[32] Milgrom 1991, 943.

[33] Rules about not touching the bed and seat of the *zavah* must then be inferred from those about the menstruant. Cf. Milgrom 1991, 943.

[34] Except for the semen-emitter, who contracts a one-day impurity only. However, the semen-emitter is not discussed in detail here.

[35] Cf. Milgrom 1991, 943.

[36] Wright 1987a, 193. Such an argument ought to apply to the menstruant as well, and appears in Wright's chart on p. 190. Harrington is hesitant, however (1993, 224). Milgrom's stance is somewhat unclear (1991, 953; cf. 936).

[37] Cf. the translation of Elliger 1966, 191.

[38] Wenham 1979, 219. Wright (1987a, 183, n.34) points out that when the *zav* is required in v. 13 to wash his flesh in fresh water, it is clearly a matter of his whole body.

about the menstruant (v. 19) in which the object of touch is simply "her."[39] Milgrom does not accept this explanation, but thinks that direct contact with the body of the discharging person is intended in both cases.[40] Wright conveys another line of argument, however, making use of an analogy with the bed. Since the clothing of the *zav* is in constant contact with his body, it is like the bed upon which he sits. Touching the clothes of a *zav* would thus incur the same impurity as touching his bed, requiring laundering and bathing, as well as waiting until evening. The effect would be the same as that of touching the body of the *zav*.[41]

We have seen that some of the discrepancies may be harmonized, presupposing a basic systemic "redaction" or development that abbreviates instructions for female dischargers, using the *zav* as the model. Regardless of how we figure possible "sources" behind the text, there have been apparent efforts to shape the chapter into a coherent whole.[42] These have been successful to a certain extent. A number of uncertainties still remain, however, especially about the status and purification of the menstruant, and to some degree about the *yoledet*. The various rules for touching and being touched, as well as coming into contact with items which have been underneath a discharger are not phrased simply as model followed by abbreviation. Their complexity suggests the necessity of complementary explanations. Although some discrepancies might be explained by differing origins, it does not suffice to blame the remaining on the inability of the priestly authors to combine disparate rules into a compatible system.

Discrepancies as a gender issue

Gerstenberger suggests that the silence about several issues regarding women (i.e. spitting, touching, saddle) could be explained by a male point of view: women were not to spit, they were not to give men their hands, and they did not usually ride.[43] This is quite possible, but does not explain why instructions about touching vessels occur only in the regulations concerning the *zav*.

One of the most coherent interpretations of discrepancies between rules applying to the *zav* and rules pertaining to female dischargers has been offered by Judith Romner Wegner.[44] She argues from purity being necessary to perform

---

[39] Wright 1987a, 182–183, n.34.
[40] Milgrom 1991, 914, 935.
[41] Wright 1987a, 183, n.34. For this argument Wright refers to Morgan W. Tanner.
[42] The *yoledet* of Lev 12 (probably inserted into the block somewhat later) is repeatedly compared with the menstruant (Lev 12: 2, 5). Cf. Elliger 1966, 157.
[43] Gerstenberger 1993, 187.
[44] Wegner 2003, 451–465.

cultic acts, according to the priestly system. The purifying *zav* is to launder his clothes and bathe after having waited for seven days (v. 13) while the *zavah* is required only to wait for seven days (v. 28). Wegner does not accept Milgrom's explanation that laundering and bathing are implied, but understands this discrepancy to reflect differences in cultic status. Women are seldom involved in sacrifices, and when they are, as in the case of the purifying *yoledet* or *zavah* (Lev 12:6; 15:29), they *bring* (הֵבִיא) their offering to the priest, in contrast to the *zav* (15:14), who comes "before the LORD" (לִפְנֵי יְהוָה) and *gives* (נָתַן) the sacrificial animals to the priest.[45]

According to Wegner, laundering and bathing were necessary only for performing cultic rituals "before the LORD," which women did not do. For the same reason, nothing is said in v. 33 about women lying with unclean men, only about men lying with unclean women, since such defilement disqualified them from cultic activities, while women were never qualified to begin with.[46]

Wegner's analysis should be seriously considered. It does explain certain discrepancies in the text. It is safe to say that the regulations are structured and worded from a male perspective. In spite of this, Wegner's explanation does not account for all inconsistencies discussed above. Even if Wegner were right that the "exclusion of women embodied a fundamental aspect of P's worldview," this would suggest that other views might have existed, both at the time when Leviticus received its final form and during earlier periods.[47] Several observations point to a more complex situation. According to Lev 15:18 both the man and the woman had to bathe after intercourse, and wait for the evening before becoming clean. In Lev 12:4, the *yoledet* is prohibited from coming to the sanctuary, which suggests that she would regularly do so otherwise. And Wegner herself admits one exception which would allow women to come "before the LORD," namely the suspected adulteress (Num 5:16).[48]

Another indication of female participation in the cult, showing possible traces of priestly redaction, is found in 1 Sam 1. Wegner dismisses this piece of evidence, commenting that "the use of the phrase לפני יהוה in that JE text is unconnected with the Aaronide cult in Jerusalem contemplated by P's use of the phrase."[49] It seems, however, as if the Hebrew text has been redacted, possibly out of (priestly) interests similar to those which Wegner discusses. The phrase

---

[45] Wegner 2003, 452–459.

[46] Wegner 2003, 458–459.

[47] Wegner 2003, 90. A different view is found with Gruber 1987, 35–48.

[48] She emphasizes, however, that even in this case the woman is not an active participant in a voluntary cultic act, but rather a passive object, brought before the Lord, rather like a sacrificial victim (Wegner 2003, 459–460).

[49] Wegner 2003, 460.

לִפְנֵי יְהוָה is found in 1:12, where Hannah is praying for a child "before the Lord." Since the expression occurs frequently in the Hebrew Bible, outside of P, without any explicit notion of sacrificial cult, this instance would not be conspicuous even from the standpoint of those advocating a priestly worldview of the kind outlined by Wegner. The LXX provides alternative readings, however, in two other instances, which portray Hannah as partaking in sacrificial activity "before the Lord." In 1:9, she comes, according to the MT, "after she had eaten in Shiloh and after she had drunk (אַחֲרֵי אָכְלָה בְשִׁלֹה וְאַחֲרֵי שָׁתֹה)." The LXX, however, does not read "after she had drunk," but "and she appeared before the Lord" (καὶ κατέστη ἐνώπιον κυρίου) (LXX 1 Kgdms 1:9). Taking אָכְלָה not as the main verb complemented by an absolute infinitive (שָׁתֹה), but as a noun ([sacrificial] meal), the text could be reconstructed with the help of the LXX as: "after a sacrificial meal in Shiloh, Hannah appeared before the LORD." Likewise, in 1:24, after Hannah is described as having brought the boy, together with three bulls, a bag of flour and a wineskin, the MT very scantily states: וַתְּבִאֵהוּ בֵית־יְהוָה שִׁלוֹ וְהַנַּעַר נָעַר.[50] The following sentence reveals a deficiency in the Masoretic text, however, as *they* (plural) are said to slaughter *the bull* (singular), and bring the boy to Eli.[51] The LXX makes more sense, in portraying the boy as accompanying both his parents as they come "before the Lord" to partake in a sacrificial act.[52] These two variant readings are most probably more original than those of the MT, not least in view of the numerous agreements elsewhere between the LXX and 4QSam[a], which suggest that the LXX readings in the books of Samuel are often older than those of the MT.[53] The MT probably reflects a redactional process associated with some sort of priestly interests.[54] A more original reading has survived in the Greek translation, however, implying

---

[50] An English translation becomes wordy: "and she brought him to the house of the Lord in Shiloh and the young boy was a young boy."

[51] וַיִּשְׁחֲטוּ אֶת־הַפָּר.

[52] καὶ εἰσῆλθεν εἰς οἶκον κυρίου ἐν Σηλωμ, καὶ τὸ παιδάριον μετ' αὐτῶν. καὶ προήγαγον ἐνώπιον κυρίου (1 Kgdms 1:24–25). Subsequently, the LXX does state Elkanah as the offerer, but the point is that Hannah is portrayed as taking part in a cultic act "before the Lord."

[53] The first reading is followed by e.g. *The Jerusalem Bible* (1971), and both of them by the Swedish *Bibel 2000*. For a discussion of the agreements between the LXX and 4QSam[a], see Ulrich 1978, 39–93, 257–259. Although the 4QSam[a] version of 1 Sam 1:24 is heavily damaged, a Hebrew reconstruction based on the LXX text fits the available space in the column very well; the 4QSam[a] version must have been much longer than the MT and the remaining letters support the LXX reading. Cf. Ulrich 1978, 40–41.

[54] On the surface, the Masoretic reading (הַנַּעַר נָעַר) could be seen as the result of a haplography due to *homoioteleuton* (cf. Ulrich 1978, 41), but since the numerous discrepancies between the MT and the LXX/4QSam[a] generally cannot be explained by such factors, it is more plausible to posit a different reason for this discrepancy, too.

that women were not consistently excluded from the cult, and not throughout the biblical period.[55]

Returning to the discrepancies in the purity laws on discharges, we conclude that it is reasonable to regard some of the wording being due to the male perspective and cultic interests of the priestly authors, possibly including the phrase לִפְנֵי יְהוָה. The hypothesis of women's exclusion from the cult does not explain the majority of discrepancies in biblical rules about discharges, however. While the legal text is surely shaped from a male perspective, the remaining discrepancies are not necessarily dependent on this. A number of discrepancies may rather be explained by earlier underlying conceptions.

The impurity of discharges

While touching or being touched by any of the four main genital dischargers was later seen as equivalent, it is possible that some of the discrepancies in Lev 15 reflect early conceptions. Certain discrepancies, including those about the touch of the unclean person, might be explained by positing a *distinction between the genital discharger and the discharge itself.*

The widespread fear of and disgust for genital discharges, and in particular menstrual blood, is widely attested in Antiquity.[56] It is reasonable to suggest that the idea of people with discharges being impure was derived from attitudes to the fluids themselves. The remnants of such thinking can be observed in Samaritan *halakah*. Although extant Samaritan texts are relatively late (from around 1000 CE and onwards) they do represent one ancient Israelite halakic tradition, based on an interpretation of the Torah.

In Samaritan *halakah*, a person who comes into direct contact with a menstruant's blood (not only through intercourse, but through touching) is made unclean for seven days, just like the menstruant herself. Likewise, the menstruant has to wash off the first menstrual blood before the count of seven days can start, otherwise it will keep on re-contaminating her. Certain Samaritan rules concerning the *zav* similarly imply that the discharge itself is considered to be the contaminating agent. The idea of impurity being transmitted by the actual flux or blood seems to be strong.[57]

---

[55] Sanders' statement that "at the time of Leviticus women did not actually enter the temple" (1990, 143), is too generalized. Cf. Gruber 1987.

[56] Milgrom (1991, 763–765) gives numerous examples. Cf. Ezek 36:17; Pliny, *Nat.* 7:64.

[57] *Kitâb aṭ-Ṭubâkh* [6–15], *Kitâb al-Kâfi* XI [84–89] and *Kitâb al-Kâfi* XIII [13–18] in Bóid 1989a, 141, 150–151, 154. Cf. Bóid's comments (1989, 199–204, 210, 218–219, 236–237). In Samaritan law, the first menstrual blood (*niddå*), contaminates for seven days, while the subsequent bleeding (*dåbå*), contaminates for one day only (*Kitâb al-Kâfi* XI [84–89], in Bóid 1989a, 141). The left hand with which the woman washes off the *niddå* blood is treated as be-

A similar view at the root of the legislation of Leviticus would explain several traits in Lev 15. It is likely that the risk of direct contact with the discharge itself is contemplated by the text. As underwear was not worn in biblical times,[58] anything situated underneath a *zav*, not only items used for sitting or riding, would run the risk of becoming contaminated by his discharge.[59] This could explain the wording of 15:10, where everything that has been situated *underneath* the *zav* is said to contaminate (כֹּל אֲשֶׁר יִהְיֶה תַחְתָּיו). This is added to the general rules about not coming into contact with the bed or seat of any discharger (15:4–6, 20–23, 26–27). While it could be argued, from a systemic reading, that the specific rule in v. 10 was applicable by analogy to all dischargers, a possible explanation is that this further elaboration would be needed only for the *zav*, since drops of his discharge, which had happened to fall upon something situated underneath him, would not be detectable in the same way as blood.[60]

The fear of contact with the discharge itself could also explain the prescription in v. 11, which requires that the *zav* rinse his hands before touching anything. Since men touch their genitals when urinating, the hands of the *zav* must always be regarded as contaminating, unless recently washed, since they could transfer the unclean substance.[61] This would not apply to female dischargers, and could explain the lack of similar prescriptions for them.

Furthermore, the fear of contact with menstrual blood, as well as its visibility, could explain why touching the bed or anything the menstruant has sat upon requires laundering (vv. 21–22) while touching the menstruant herself does not

---

ing at the same level of uncleanness as the *niddå* blood itself for the whole week, even if there is no longer any blood on it (Marginal note IV in a manuscript of the *Kitâb al-Kâfi*, in Bóid 1989a, 196, 289). Concerning the *zav*, the Samaritan *Book of Insight* (*Kitâb aṭ-Ṭubâkh*) [103–106] considers an animal used for riding by a *zav* unclean, with the capacity for contaminating other people. This is explained by Bóid (1989, 145, 218–219) from the possibility of the animal having got some of the discharge on itself. Similarly, the *Ṭubâkh* considers the ground on which the *zav* has been standing as contaminating [103]. Bóid suggests (218) that the author is thinking of the possibility of some of the discharge having dripped onto the ground.

[58] For the sake of decency, underwear was compulsory for officiating priests (Exod 28:42–43), but this was apparently an exception.

[59] Milgrom 1991, 911. Cf. Samaritan regulations about cleansing the ground, which might have absorbed some moisture from a discharging person, with fire: *Kitâb al-Kâfi* XII [22–34] in Bóid 1989a, 155–156. Cf. Bóid's comments (246–248, 303). This would also apply to any ground on which a woman had walked before having washed off the *niddå* blood (247).

[60] This could also explain the statement about spittle (v. 8) which likewise would be difficult to distinguish from the discharge itself.

[61] Milgrom 1991, 911.

(v. 19).[62] The invisibility of male discharges on the other hand might explain why touching the *zav* necessitates laundering.[63]

When it comes to the contamination of objects for sitting and lying, the explicit rules are similar for both men and women (Lev 15:4–6, 20–23, 26–27). Due to the pressure of the body and the length of the time of contact, these objects could be suspected of contamination by unclean fluids, perhaps through the clothes of the discharging person. These rules were probably originally based on a fear of coming into contact with the unclean fluids themselves.

The idea of pressure subsequently developed into the concept of *midras* impurity, which eventually was not dependent on any kind of physical contact.[64] At its roots, however, we must suppose a fear of coming into contact with the very discharges as such, and when this *could* have occurred, a one-day impurity followed. Since "risky" situations varied with the type of discharge, rules applying to the *zav* and the *zavah* were framed in slightly different ways. The rules about sexual activity fit into this pattern, too. Semen causes a one-day impurity for the semen-emitter. A woman having intercourse with a man under normal circumstances thus incurs (together with the man) a one-day impurity (Lev 15:18). A man having intercourse with a menstruating woman, however, incurs a seven-day impurity, just as menstrual blood causes a seven-day impurity for the menstruant (Lev 15:24).[65]

If a distinction between the impurity of the discharging person and the discharge itself is assumed as underlying the regulations of Lev 15, some of the discrepancies could thus be explained.

Demonic threat

One of the discrepancies difficult to account for is that the menstruant is not required to bring a sacrifice like the other dischargers. To explain this by the frequency of menstruation making sacrifices economically impossible is hardly satisfactory, as we have seen above. We should rather begin with the observation that menstruation is more like the seven-day *purificatory* period of the *zav* or *zavah*, implying a slighter type of impurity.

---

[62] Cf. Milgrom 1991, 936.

[63] Milgrom's reading of v. 27 (בָּהּ instead of בָּם), discussed above (Milgrom 1991, 943), would cause a further discrepancy, which cannot be explained by distinguishing between the impurity of discharges and dischargers. Touching a *zavah* would then require laundering. As the text stands, however, the consequences of touching the bed and seat of a *zavah* are compatible with those applying to the menstruant.

[64] Cf. Neusner 1977, 55, 63–71; Harrington 1993, 239–253; Maccoby 1999, 50–53. The concept of *midras* impurity must be fairly early since it is taken for granted in the Mishnah, even in discussions attributed to the Houses (e.g. *m. Kelim* 20:2; 26:6; *m. Nid.* 10:8).

[65] Cf. Ellens 2003, 39–41.

The dischargers that are required to bring a sacrifice are, with the *yoledet* as an exception, those who according to the separate tradition in Num 5:2–3 should be expelled from the camp during their time of impurity, together with other serious seven-day impurity bearers.[66]

> Order the children of Israel to send away from the camp every *tzarua'* (צָרוּעַ) [= *met-zora'*] and every *zav* and every corpse-impure. Male or female, you shall send away; outside of the camp you shall send them; and they shall not defile their camp, where I live in their midst.

However, the legislation on discharges in Lev 15 contains no signs of expulsion, but detailed discussions about contamination. This suggests a context in which people suffering from discharges were living within their communities. In no other way can we explain regulations concerning the transmission of impurity even via beds and seats, and purifying rites required from people being thus contaminated, or the instruction for the *zav* to wash his hands before touching anyone. All the rules seem to presuppose that clean people are constantly at the risk of coming into contact with discharging persons, directly or indirectly, and when this happens, appropriate purification rites must be carried out. Nothing is even said about permission to enter the camp after initial purification, as in the case of the *metzora'* (מְצֹרָע; Lev 14:1, 8), which again suggests a context where people suffering from discharges were present in their towns and villages throughout their period of impurity.[67]

How are we to explain these discrepant traditions? Wright suggests that Num 5:2–3 reflects conditions of the wilderness camp, which could be regarded as

> a hybrid cross of a regular community and a war camp. It is well known from non-Priestly material that a war camp was under stricter conditions of purity than the normal community. ... God moves throughout the camp so that he might grant victory to the soldiers. The camp must be holy for God's presence to continue there.[68]

As an historical explanation of the presence of conflicting traditions, this does not suffice, however. Which practice was adhered to and when? Milgrom suggests that the tradition in Num 5:2–3 is the more ancient of the two, although he is uncertain as to which layer it belongs.[69] Knohl assigns this text to the Holi-

---

[66] The *metzora'* is required to bring a *chattat* sacrifice just like the *zav* and the *zavah*. The corpse-impure is not required to bring an individual sacrifice, but the burning of the red cow that provides the ashes for the purification water is called a *chattat* (Num 19:9).

[67] Cf. Wright 1987a, 173.

[68] Wright 1987a, 171.

[69] Milgrom is ambiguous about whether this tradition should be assigned to P$_2$ or H. Although he regards the former to be earlier than P$_1$ and the latter subsequent to P, he nevertheless finds the strict tradition itself as the more ancient among the two (1991, 44, 262, 316, cf. 986–1000).

ness School and its tendency to expand the domain of divine holiness beyond the temple and the cult, as compared to the earlier Priestly Torah.[70] While the idea of the Holiness Code being later than the Priestly laws in Leviticus, even leaving traces of redaction and interpolation in other parts of the Pentateuch, is gaining ground, many would doubt a pre-exilic dating of H. Milgrom's early dating for P and H is considered unreasonable by many scholars today and both P and H are generally regarded as exilic or post-exilic strata.[71] Today, H is most plausibly dated in the early Persian period.[72] Moreover, there is a tendency to regard Numbers not as coming from the P source but belonging to the latest stages of Pentateuchal redaction. Achenbach regards the purity laws in Numbers, including Num 5:1–4, as part of a (second phase of) theocratic redaction of the book, belonging to the youngest texts of the Pentateuch. He argues for a context in which the holiness of the Temple community in its entirety was in focus and dates this layer to the 4th century BCE. Achenbach emphasizes that these rules are not of a fictive kind and refers to contemporary apotropaic purity rules in Persian religion, which relate to skin disease and corpse contamination as well as to menstruation.[73]

Even when a late date for Num 5 is deemed the most reasonable, Milgrom may be right that the underlying tradition is old. Expulsion of genital dischargers from the community seems to be an ancient idea, evidenced in ancient Babylonian and Persian texts.[74] Milgrom thinks, however, that P_1 "initiates the long historic process whereby the power of impurity is progressively reduced."[75] He explains this process with the demonic background of the concept of impurity, and the idea of airborne impurity, which threatened the sanctuary from afar. The idea of airborne impurity would have made it necessary to expel all severe impurity bearers, i.e., those suffering a seven-day impurity and required to bring a *chattat* sacrifice.[76] The concept of airborne impurity could not remain as the

---

[70] Knohl 1995, 86, 184–186.

[71] Milgrom's dating of P and H is much too early for most scholars (1991, 998–999; cf. 3–35, 61–63; 2000a, 1319–1367. This applies to Knohl's somewhat later dates as well, although he does envisage a Holiness School active through a long period, stretching into the post-exilic era (1995, 200–229).

[72] Nihan 2004.

[73] Achenbach 2003, 499–528, especially 500–504. Achenbach refers among other things to evidence for Zorastrian practices from Herodotus and from *Vidēvdāt*.

[74] Milgrom 1991, 763, quoting Gudea, Statue B IV.4: "the woman in labor I caused to go forth from the city." Cf. the relative isolation of menstruants in Zoroastrian religion. Boyce 1975, 307–308.

[75] Milgrom 1991, 999.

[76] Milgrom 1991, 999. Cf. Harrington 1993, 223, who accepts Milgrom's theory. Cf. the rabbinic explanation that *zavim* were banished from the camp only after the tabernacle had been built (*Num. Rab.* 7:1; *Lev. Rab.* 18:4).

demonic idea vanished with time, and was finally eliminated in rabbinic Judaism. Hence all but the *metzora'* were allowed to remain at home.[77]

Milgrom's reconstruction, especially the theory about airborne impurity, has been seriously questioned.[78] There is a missing link in the reasoning. If the requirement to bring a sacrifice indicates that the discharging person has defiled the *sanctuary*, although without having been in direct contact with it, why does this sacrifice (Lev 15:14, 29) belong to the rites necessary for purifying the *person*? The wording in Lev 15:31 "And you shall separate the children of Israel from their impurity, so that they shall not die in their impurity by their contamination of my tabernacle which is in their midst," does not necessitate pollution from afar, but בְּטַמְאָם could be translated "when (if) they contaminate," rather than "by their contamination," as Maccoby has pointed out.[79] The issue could thus be contamination by direct contact or entrance, as in the case of the *yoledet*, where it is stated explicitly: "She must not touch anything holy and not enter the sanctuary until the end of the days of cleansing" (Lev 12:4).[80] This becomes the more plausible when we consider that Lev 15:31 looks like an insert that separates the preceding law from the subsequent conclusion and should likely be assigned to H.[81] The need for separating severe impurity bearers from the "camp" in order to protect the sanctuary becomes obvious when a small Temple city state during Persian times is envisaged.

While Maccoby criticizes Milgrom's view of airborne impurity, he shares Milgrom's somewhat evolutionary understanding of the development of Israelite religion[82] and like Milgrom he thinks that the stricter tradition reflects an older stratum of P. In Maccoby's reconstruction, prohibitions against defiling the sanctuary first referred to the whole camp, which was regarded as the outer grounds of the sanctuary. Those with major impurities were expelled, while

---

[77] Milgrom 1991, 999.

[78] Cf. Maccoby 1999, who deals with it in two consecutive chapters (165–192). The idea is not present in rabbinic interpretation, and there is no evidence for it in intertestamental or Qumran literature (184–185).

[79] Maccoby 1999, 172–173. Maccoby takes the interpretation of the "camp" as his point of departure: "If, according to one strand of P, the whole camp is a holy area from which impurity must be excluded, then there may be good reasons for requiring speedy purification without introducing any notion of aerial contamination of the Tabernacle from a distance" (1999, 185).

[80] Cf. Maccoby 1999, 170.

[81] Knohl 1995, 69–70, 195; Milgrom 1991, 945–947 (possible interpolation); Nihan 2004, 118 n. 167 (with question mark).

[82] Cf. Milgrom's suggestion for a continuous development from the time of P₁: "Slowly, then, almost imperceptibly, airborne impurity was progressively eliminated: all impurity bearers, with the exception of the *mĕṣōrā'*, were allowed to remain at home" (1991, 999). It is difficult to imagine how the integration of genital dischargers could have taken place slowly or imperceptibly, which must have been the case if it was dependent upon a gradual vanishing of the concept of airborne impurity.

those with minor impurities remained in the camp, but, because of its holiness, had to seek early purification. At the next stage, holiness was reduced in the camp and restricted to the sanctuary and its surroundings.[83] As a result, all impurity bearers except the *metzora'* were allowed within the camp, but could not enter the sanctuary. They had to seek early purification, to avoid defiling others who might enter the sanctuary. Finally, in rabbinic interpretation, three camps with ascending degrees of holiness were defined, corresponding to different parts of Jerusalem.[84]

These are attempts at generalized descriptions of long historical processes. When it comes to details, there are discrepancies that still defy explanations. Even according to the stricter legislation of Num 5, neither the menstruant nor the *yoledet* is expelled from the community,[85] in spite of the fact that the *yoledet* belongs to those required to bring a *chattat* sacrifice.[86] Although this could perhaps be explained by the normality of their conditions[87] there is nevertheless an inconsistency here that might require other explanations, as we will see in subsequent chapters.

It is probably wise to avoid any ideas about straight lines of historical development. Suffice it to state that divergent traditions are present in the text of the Pentateuch, apparently representing different practices, and that these divergences probably correspond to diverse social and historical contexts. In addition to the main legal tradition concerning discharges (Lev 15), we have a stricter tradition within the Torah itself (Num 5). Such a practice of exclusion could have old roots, as suggested by comparisons with texts from neighbouring cultures, but its expression in Num 5:2–3 probably represents a later redaction or revision at a time of cultic reformation and social reconfiguration in Jerusalem during Persian times. The contradictory texts were actually exploited by later interpreters in times of legal dissension. The two traditions represent what Milgrom and others have called a "minimalist" and a "maximalist" stance that can

---

[83] This actually corresponds very much to Milgrom's idea (Milgrom 1991, 316–317).

[84] Maccoby 1999, 186–187. In Qumran interpretation the holiness of the entire city of Jerusalem required arrangements similar to those of Num 5:2–3. Cf. Kazen 2002, 157–158, 187–189; see also subsequent chapters.

[85] Arguments from etymology (נָדָה meaning "to cast out" or "exclude") are of little value in reconstructing actual practice. In any case the root meaning is probably connected to the flow of blood ("expulsion," "spattering"), not the exclusion of the menstruant. Cf. Fonrobert 1997, 124, n.11. For a different view, see O'Grady 2003, 15–17.

[86] Milgrom discusses whether the two traditions of Lev 15 and Num 5 should be seen as diachronically or synchronically related. Cf. 1991, 995.

[87] In contrast, unnatural discharges were at times regarded as signs of sinful behaviour and/or associated with divine punishment. 2 Sam 3:29. Cf. 4Q270 2 ii; 4Q272 1 ii, 4; *Sifre Numeri*, Parashat Naso 1; *Lev. Rab.* 18:4; *Num. Rab.* 7:1.

be traced throughout the history of early Judaism.[88] This shows that what I elsewhere call an "expansionist current" has its roots in the early Second Temple period.[89]

Regardless of whether Milgrom's theory of airborne impurity is accepted or not, and regardless of how we date the strict tradition, there is enough evidence for positing a social and religious background in which impurity would have been regarded at least partially as some kind of a demonic threat, which could be dealt with by apotropaic means. Those expelled according to the stricter tradition of Num 5 were dischargers and others suffering from pathological, i.e., unnatural conditions, in addition to those having been in close contact with death. Traces of such conditions being understood as resulting from demonic activity, may be preserved in later texts, too.[90]

In particular, several purification rites preserve vestiges of apotropaic rites with strong magical features, as we have already discussed in the previous chapter. Vestiges of demon-belief associated with impurity come to the surface in the bird rite for purifying a *metzora'* (Lev 14:1–7) and in the red cow rite (Num 19:1–10) for obtaining the necessary ashes used for sprinkling corpse-impure persons. The circumstances of these rites suggest a background in which at least *tzara'at* (צָרַעַת) and corpse impurity were considered dangerous independently of the sacrificial cult, and viewed as the result of demonic hostilities, perhaps even as forms of possession, requiring various exorcist riddance rites.[91]

While such vestiges are not as evident in the case of dischargers, the rules about purification periods for the *yoledet* (Lev 12) might contain traces of similar demonic associations. There is a well-known discrepancy between purification periods at the birth of boys (7/40 days) and girls (14/80 days). The purification ritual is the same in both cases, while the length of time before the *yoledet* has access to the sanctuary or before she might touch *sancta* differs. In some sense, the mother of a girl seems to represent a stronger threat or, perhaps, a *lengthier* threat to the divine. This has been explained by the girl being a potential menstruant; hence the mother is responsible for a "double impurity." It has been suggested, however, that the issue is rather a matter of life force, or

---

[88] Harrington 1993, 227; Milgrom 1990, 85–89.

[89] Cf. Kazen 2002, 72–87. This seems to be the view of Milgrom as well (1990, 85–89), in spite of the formulations in 1991, 999.

[90] Much of the evidence for traces in later texts is admittedly ambiguous: 11Q5 xix, 13–16 (a spiritualising interpretation of "impure spirit" is also possible); 1Qap Gen^ar xx, 26; 4Q266 6 i, 5–7; 4Q269 7 1–3; 4Q272 1 i, 1–3 (The nature of the spirit causing *tzara'at* in the 4Q texts is unclear). The clearest rabbinic evidence for impurity being associated with demonic activity is perhaps *Pesiq. Rab Kah.* 4:7. Cf. the associations between impurity and demonic activity in the Synoptic gospels. For a discussion, see Kazen 2002, 300–339; Wahlen 2004.

[91] Cf. Kazen 2002, 305–310.

life-giving capacity, somehow different from God's. As a "life-giver," the mother represents a competing power. This is even more accentuated with the birth of a girl, who will herself become a "life-giver" in due time.[92] While the evidence is inconclusive, it is possible to suggest traces of demonic activity, defined as forces competing with God, in the rules about the *yoledet*. Early conceptions of impurity as associated with demonic threat may thus explain certain of the discrepancies in biblical purity law on genital discharges.

Conclusions

In our search for explanations of the discrepancies found in purity laws on discharges, we have seen that *no single explanation* covers all the ground. A systemic reading at the end of the Second Temple period suggests a *basic* systemic shaping of these laws at least at the final stage of textual development. Taking the instructions for female dischargers as abbreviations of those for the *zav* alleviates some of the tensions, but does not fully explain all differences in wording, even if Milgrom's suggestion that the phrase יִטְמָא עַד־הָעֶרֶב implies bathing is accepted.

While priestly interests in limiting female participation in the cult may probably be traced behind the use or non-use of the phrase לִפְנֵי יְהוָה, this does not explain all differences between rules for males and females. Discrepancies in rules about touching and being touched, as well as the status and purification of the menstruant, are better explained from early conceptions making distinctions between the impurity bearer and the impurity of the discharge itself, i.e., between the person and the fluid, regardless of any association with the cult.

Finally, considering impurity as originally being associated with demonic threat, may explain the discrepancy between the instructions of Lev 15 that aim at integrating dischargers, and the stricter rules of Num 5, according to which they should be expelled together with the *metzora'* and the corpse-impure. While the demonic aspect is not as evident in the case of dischargers as it is in the purification rites of the *metzora'* or the corpse-impure, it might also explain the need for a sacrifice for "long-term" dischargers as opposed to the menstruant (or the semen-emitter), regardless of whether sacrifices are viewed as necessary for averting demonic threat to the sanctuary or to people. It might even relate to the impure periods of the *yoledet* and their difference in length.

The evidence for the systemic and priestly shaping of traditions containing underlying assumptions that are not always spelled out, betrays a long history of development and merging of what might originally have been quite disparate

---

[92] Cf. De Troyer 2003.

practices. This may, of course, have implications for the ongoing debate on how to date and define various strata or reconstruct possible sources. There are, however, implications for other discussions, too, not least from evidence for an underlying differentiation between impurity bearers and their discharges. Discrepancies suggesting a fear of contamination through direct contact with the fluids themselves support our suggestion in the previous chapter about an underlying notion of disgust at the core of some purity rules.[93] It is quite likely that aversion against gory or unnatural discharges, associated with death and decay, lies at the bottom of a number of regulations, not least in view of the contempt with which dischargers are spoken of elsewhere, and the use of נִדָּה as an expression of moral disgust.[94] Discrepancies reflecting a gender issue together with others that seem to suggest fears of demonic activity, remind us that although purity was a cultic issue, it did not exclusively relate to the temple; ideas of contamination operated quite independently of the temple cult. Finally, our results suggest a diversity of preconceptions and interpretations that did not come to an end with the final form of Leviticus, but must be expected to have left visible traces throughout the Second Temple period and beyond. That, however, is a different story, for which there is no room here.

---

[93] See also Kazen 2008.
[94] Cf. 2 Sam 3:29; Ezek 36:17.

Chapter 4

Who Touched Whom?
On Graded Impurity and First-day
Ablutions in 4Q274[1]

Introduction

The fragments numbered 4Q274 and named *4QTohorot A* are usually dated to the first century BCE, due to the early Herodian script.[2] The texts show little signs of dispute, however, and may be pre-sectarian, originating in the second century BCE.[3] The text of frgs. 1–2 discusses contamination by touch, and genital dischargers are prominently in focus. The instructions are often thought to be ambiguous and confusing, and according to Jacob Milgrom, "not a single one of its halakic cases is mentioned in rabbinic literature."[4] In this article I argue that the text deals with the behaviour of impurity bearers in intermediate stages of less or lessened impurity compared to more permanent impurity bearers and that it attests to an early origin for ideas of graded impurity and graded purification. As we will see, the text may be read as evidence that not only the corpse-impure sought early purification, but dischargers also "peeled off" the most virulent layer of impurity through some type of first-day ablution. When further contextual evidence is taken into consideration, this should not be seen as a sectarian development only.

Previous research

The text, including a photograph, was first published by Robert Eisenman and Michael Wise in 1992.[5] It was followed in 1995 by Ben Wacholder and Martin Abegg's reading and reconstruction, mainly based on Milik's transcriptions in the Preliminary Concordance.[6] In the same year, Joseph Baumgarten and Jacob Mil-

---

[1] This chapter was originally published as "4Q274, Fragment 1 Revisited – or Who Touched Whom? Further Evidence for Ideas of Graded Impurity and Graded Purifications." *Dead Sea Discoveries* 17 (2010): 53–87.
[2] Baumgarten 1999, 99.
[3] Harrington 2004, 57.
[4] Milgrom 1995, 59.
[5] Eisenman and Wise 1992, 207–210, plate 18.
[6] Wacholder and Abegg 1995, 79–80.

grom published separate reconstructions and translations of fragment 1 in a volume containing papers from 1989–1990.[7] In 1999, Baumgarten, who had access to Milik's transcriptions, published his own version with a few revisions in DJD 35.[8] Meanwhile, the text was published by Florentino García Martínez, first in his translation, and then, together with Eibert Tigchelaar in the *DSS Study Edition*.[9]

Baumgarten understands the text as referring to various types of dischargers and reads it in light of other texts found at Qumran. He refers to 4Q512 for a "markedly penitential tone" and sees affinities with the *Temple Scroll*'s demand for separated areas for "lepers," *zavim* and semen emitters. Similarly, the *zav* is not only to be kept outside of cities, but, according to 4Q274, also at a certain distance from other impurity bearers. Female dischargers, too, must not contact other impure people. Baumgarten notes that this is more stringent than rabbinic *halakah*. Another stringent ruling is the demand for purification before eating.[10]

In DJD 35, Baumgarten sets 4Q274 in the larger context of expansive purity practices in the Second Temple period. The practice of eating non-consecrated food (*chullin*) in purity together with the application of a first-day water rite to make this possible for impurity bearers whose purification took seven days, is evidenced by texts found at Qumran. Baumgarten finds this comparable to the Pharisaic *tevul yom*, which similarly made eating in purity possible in advance, in this case before sundown.[11]

Although Milgrom agrees with Baumgarten on the penitential tone, he differs on the reference of the first three and a half lines, which he reads as referring not to the *zav* but to the *metzora'*. Milgrom also refers to the quarantine laws of the *Temple Scroll*, although he notes that compass directions are only given for the Temple city. Milgrom argues that the call of the *metzora'* is interpreted as "unclean to the unclean," which explains the need for impure people to keep apart from other impure people, as exemplified in the fragment. This is supposed to be one of Qumran's innovative teachings: any impurity is increased by contact with a stronger impurity. Another innovative teaching is that a purifying *zav* does not transmit impurity by touch, presumably because he has undergone a first-day ablution. He also finds a third new idea in the requirement of purification before eating for people with increased impurity. Milgrom reads the text as divided into three cases and points out that bathing and laundering before eating is required in all three.[12] This is interpreted within the larger context

[7] Baumgarten 1995a, 1–8; Milgrom 1995.
[8] Baumgarten 1999, 99–109.
[9] García Martínez 1994, 88; García Martínez and Tigchelaar 1997–1998; rev. ed. 2000, 628–629.
[10] Baumgarten 1995a, 7. Cf. 11QT[a] XLVI, 16–18.
[11] Baumgarten 1999, 89–90.
[12] Milgrom 1995, 61, 65–68.

of early purification to avoid what Milgrom understands as airborne defilement of the sanctuary.[13]

In 1992, Hannah Harrington discussed the text in her dissertation comparing Qumran and Rabbinic purity *halakah*, based on the reading of her supervisor Milgrom. Some further discussion is also found in a more recent volume on purity texts found at Qumran.[14] Harrington regards fragment 1 as evidence for "the requirement that all Israelites bathe before eating any food," which resulted from "homogenization" in the interpretation of purity legislation. This applied even to impure people, who were not thereby entitled to partake of the communal meal, only to eat at all. Although Harrington takes 4Q274, fragment 1, as referring to "impure persons, who continue in their impurity or purification for an extended period," she specifically mentions purifying persons as a particular threat for contaminating food, since they were no longer isolated outside of the camp, but had to come inside for their purification.[15] Generally, Harrington finds the discharge laws of 4Q274 stricter than rabbinic law, although she follows Milgrom's understanding that a purifying *zav* did not defile by touch unless he had a semen emission, which is strangely lenient.[16] Harrington also notes that menstrual blood is equalled to other discharges.[17]

The text is also discussed by Jonathan Lawrence, using the translation of Wise, Abegg and Cook. According to Lawrence, the fragment is in general agreement with the rules of the Hebrew Bible concerning when washing for purification is required or not. When it comes to details, however, he finds a number of departures. As Lawrence reads the text, the woman who has touched a *zav* or a *zav*'s vessel does not have to wait until sundown, but may eat after bathing. He furthermore claims that the text equates menstrual blood with semen. He also finds it strange that a *zavah* is allowed to eat the food at all. Lawrence finds the text ambiguous as to whether the purity of the woman or that of others who are contacted by her stands in focus. Like Baumgarten, he understands the referent in the first three and a half lines of the text as a *zav* rather than a *metzora'* – an interpretation that is facilitated by the translation of Wise, Abegg and Cook.[18] He also hints at a first-day ablution for corpse-impure being extended to other cases, but this possibility is not followed up in any detail.[19]

---

[13] This is only alluded to in Milgrom 1995, but more clearly spelled out in his discussion about first-day ablutions and intermediate levels of impurity in 1991, 969–976, 991–1000.

[14] Harrington 1993, 48, 61–62, 65, 79–90, 92, 94; Harrington 2004, 57–60, 88, 95–98, 102.

[15] Harrington 2004, 57, 59.

[16] Harrington 2004, 95–96; Harrington 1993, 85–87.

[17] Harrington 2004, 96, 102; 1993, 87.

[18] Lawrence 2006, 89–91. Wise, Abegg and Cook (1996, 281) reconstruct and translate line 3: "Any one of the unclean [wh]o h[as a dischar]ge ..." (this differs from others, see further below).

[19] Lawrence 2006, 99, see especially note 40, referring to Eshel 1997 (= Eshel 1999, 135–139.

In a recent publication on ritual purity in the Dead Sea Scrolls, Ian Werrett deals with 4Q274, too. Werrett relies on the reconstruction and translation of Baumgarten and, like Lawrence, follows Baumgarten in seeing the *zav* as the referent for i,1–4a.[20] Werrett understands the primary interest of fragment 1 as preventing impure persons from contacting other impure individuals. This pre-supposes that "unclean individuals were capable of contracting additional forms of impurity if that form of impurity was greater than their own," something that goes beyond ideas found in the Torah.[21] In addition to the instructions concerning the *zav*, the fragment consists of a series of examples of less serious types of bodily discharge. One detail, however, does not fit into this scheme neatly, according to Werrett: the equalling of menstrual blood and bodily discharge in i, 7–8. Werrett does not regard this as evidence for the *zav* and menstruant being equally impure, but rather as a result of gap-filling the laws of Leviticus. Blood and discharge were considered equally defiling for purifying people, in the sense that contact necessitated bathing before eating. Werrett finds similarities between 4Q274 and the *Temple Scroll* with regard to quarantine regulations and the keeping apart of various impurity bearers. He notes, however, that the instructions of 4Q274 seem to assume that contact actually took place, which suggests a different context with other concerns.[22]

As is clear from this overview, there are a number of common suggestions and questions with regard to this text. While most agree on the penitential note at the beginning, the referent of the first three and a half lines is debated. While some affinity with rules for isolation or segregation in other texts is evident, the extent of the present rules is unclear. The context is certainly one of expansive purity practices, which fits ill with suggestions about lenient practices concerning the *zav*. Bathing before eating is definitely an issue, even for some types of impure people, but on what grounds? Contact between various categories of impurity bearers is found at the heart of the discussion, but does contamination only spread from the more impure to the less? Blood and discharge are somehow equalled, but in what way? And are some sorts of first-day water rites extended to and presupposed for other impurity bearers than the corpse-impure?

Such questions give reason for revisiting the text. A number of ambiguities depend on uncertain readings and reconstructions due to faded or damaged text and tears in the leather. Certain progress can be made by studying high resolu-

---

[20] Werrett 2007, 220–221, 245–246. The translation strangely enough contains a few unexplained deviations from Baumgarten 1999: "(ones)" in line 1, a closing citation mark moved from "out" in line 4 to "unclean!" in line 3, "has lain" instead of Baumgarten's "touched or laid" in line 4, a changed word order in line 5 and two spelling mistakes in line 9.

[21] Werrett 2007, 246–247; citation from 247.

[22] Werrett, 247–248, 280–281.

tion photographs with software applications,[23] but the main options have been laid out before. My suggestions for revisions of previous readings and reconstructions in such cases are modest and frequently limited to an evaluation and a choice between them. Following the reconstruction and translation below, I will first offer notes regarding possible readings and reconstructions, and subsequently a discussion of content and interpretation.

Reconstruction and reading

i,1 יחל להפיל את תחנֿוֿנו מֿשׁכב יגֿוֿן ישכֿ]ב ו[מֿוֿשׁב אנחה ישב בדד לכול הטמאים ישב ורחוק מֿן

2 הטהרה שתים עשרֿהֿ בֿאֿמה בֿאברו אליו ומערב צפון לכול בית מושב ישב רחוק כמדה הזות

3 איש מכול הטמאים]אשֿ[רֿ]יגע[בֿו ירחץ במים ויכבס בגדיו ואחר יואכל כי הוא אשר אמר טמא טמא

4 יקרא כול ימי היותֿ]בו הנ[גֿע והזבֿהֿ דם לשבעת הימים אל תגע בזב ובכול כלי]א[שֿר יגע בו הזב וש]כב[

5 עליו אֿ״ אשר ישב עליו ואֿמֿ נגעה תכבס בגדיה ורחצה ואחר תוכל ובכול מודה]א[ל תתערב בשבעת

6 ימיה בעבור אשר ל]ו[אֿ תֿגֿאל את מחֿנֿיֿ קדֿוֿ]שׁיֿ[ישראל וגם אל תגע בכול אשֿהֿ]זב[ֿהֿ דם לימים רבי[ֿם[

7 והסופר אם זֿכר ואֿמֿ נקבה אל יֿגֿ]ע בזב בזו[בֿו בדוה בנדתה כי אם טהרה מֿ]נד[ֿתֿה כי הנה דֿם

8 הנדה כזוב יחֿשׁבֿ]ל[נוגע בו ואם תֿצֿ]א מאיש[שֿכבת הזרע מגעו וטמֿאֿ הֿ]וא וכו[ֿל נֿוגע באדם מכֿוֿֿל

9 הטמאים האלה בשבעת ימי טהֿ]רתו א[ֿל יוכל כאשר יטמא לנפֿ]ש האדם ור[ֿחֿץֿ וכבס ואח]ר[

ii,1 יא[כל ...

Translation

Col. i

1   He shall begin to lay down his pleading. He shall recli[ne] on a bed of sorrow [and] dwell in a dwelling of groaning. He shall dwell separate from all the unclean and far from

2   what is pure, twelve cubits, in his quarter of mourning, and he shall dwell as far as this distance northwest of any dwelling-house.

3   Any man of the unclean [wh]o [touches] him shall bathe in water and launder his clothes and afterwards he may eat, for this is as it says: Unclean, unclean,

---

[23] For this study, PAM 43.309 in *Dead Sea Scrolls Electronic Library* (rev. ed. 2006) has been used, together with PAM 42.601.

4   shall he cry all the days [the afflic]tion is [on him]. And the woman discharging blood
    (*zavah dam*) for seven days shall not touch the man discharging (*zav*) or any utensil [t]hat
    the man discharging (*zav*) has touched or lain
5   on or that he has sat on. And if she touched, she shall launder her clothes and bathe, and
    afterwards she may eat. And with all her strength she shall not mix during her seven
6   days in order n[o]t to defile the camps of the ho[ly] (ones) of Israel, and also, she shall not
    touch any woman [discharg]ing blood (*zavah dam*) for man[y] days.
7   And the one who counts, whether male or female, shall not tou[ch the man discharging
    (*zav*) in] his [dischar]ge (or) the menstruant in her (initial) *niddah* (bleeding), unless she is
    pure from her [*nidd*]ah (bleeding), for behold,
8   *niddah* blood is considered like a discharge [to] the one touching it. And if a semen emis-
    sion com[es forth from a man] – his touch i[s] unclean. And [anyo]ne who touches a per-
    son from all
9   these unclean ones during the seven days of [his] puri[fication] shall [no]t eat, as if he were
    defiled by [a human cor]pse, [and he shall b]athe and wash (his clothes) and afterwar[ds]
    [Col ii, 1] he shall e[at ...

Notes

Column i, line 1

Milgrom reads תחנונו, and is followed in this by Baumgarten,[24] while García
Martínez & Tigchelaar, following Eisenman & Wise, suggest תיכונו, rendering
the sentence: "he shall begin to lay down his rank."[25] Although three letters are
faded and thus capable of being variously interpreted, a ח is more likely than a י;
the left stroke of the ח is faintly visible.[26] A penitential note also suits the context well. Baumgarten inserts a negation (אל) on the last line of the preceding
non-extant column, arguing that according to the instructions for a *zav* in 4Q512
he "may recite blessings only after his purification."[27] This presupposes, however, that the referent in the present text is *not* under purification. The penitential prayers in 4Q512 for the *zav*'s seven days of purification rather suggest that
the referent in our text could be a *purifying* impurity bearer, too, and that this is
the reason why he is told to begin his penitential activity.

line 2

באברו אליו ("in his quarter of mourning"). This partly follows Eisenman &
Wise's reading,[28] which García Martínez rendered "in the quarter reserved for
him" in his 1994 translation.[29] This translation still remains (by mistake) in García Martínez & Tigchelaar, although the Hebrew is now read as בדברו, like

---

[24] Baumgarten 1999, 100; Milgrom 1995, 59–60.
[25] García Martínez and Tigchelaar 2000, vol. 2, 628–629.
[26] This is clearer in PAM 42.601 than in 43.309, and also suggested by Tigchelaar (personal communication).
[27] Baumgarten 1999, 102.
[28] Eisenman and Wise 1992, 207; "in the designated part of town" (209).
[29] García Martínez 1994, 88, i.e., אבר is taken to mean "separate dwelling" or "(town) quarter" (cf. Jastrow) from "wing."

Abegg & Wacholder, Baumgarten and Milgrom.[30] Both readings have their problems, but the shape of the second letter is rather strange for a ד. If an א, the left downstroke is missing, but there are other examples of this,[31] and a small visible crack in the leather plausibly explains this particular case. The reading בדברו אליו ("in his speaking to him") furthermore causes a problem of reference: who is the "him"? Baumgarten assumes that this refers to persons having pure things in their hands, hence presumably pure persons.[32] According to Milgrom the only possible antecedent is הטמאים ("impure persons") in line 1. The incongruence in number is, however, awkward and seems unnatural.[33]

While the reading באברו אליו is more likely, the use of the preposition אל would be strange and likewise unnatural ("in his town quarter, to him").[34] I suggest that we read אליו as "his mourning."[35] This solves the problem of reference and fits perfectly into the penitential context: אברו אליו would then parallel משכב יגון and מושב אנחה in line 1.

line 3

It is not totally certain which act necessitates the bathing of איש מכול הטמאים. In the phrase [אש]רֹ [יגע] בֹו, which follows Baumgarten and Milgrom,[36] there is hardly one undisputed letter among the few that are at all visible. Eisenman & Wise's reading (בֹ[יו]ם [השבי]עֹי) is unlikely;[37] although a ם would be possible, a ר is more probable, and the ע is doubtful, since the photographs show a faint horizontal upper stroke. Wacholder & Abegg's suggestion, presumably based on Milik (אשֹר זֹו[ב זֹ]בו) is theoretically possible,[38] but redundant, or at least a

---

[30] García Martínez and Tigchelaar 2000, vol. 2, 628–629. A similar translation could, possibly, base itself on בדברו, taking דבר as a deficient reading of דביר, meaning "back-room" or "separate chamber." A "secular" use of דביר is, however, difficult to ascertain; in the DSS as well as in the Hebrew Bible it is commonly used for the Most Holy, or for the shrine(s) of God or the chamber(s) of the king (1 Kgs 6; 4Q400, 4Q402, 4Q403, 4Q405 and 11Q17). Another possibility would be to read בדברו as an infinitive construct of דבר I ("turn aside," pi.), hence "in his turning aside with regard to him," i.e., he must not come closer than this distance before turning aside for the other person's sake (cf. the infinitive construct with a similar meaning in Song 5:6). The context, however, is clearly on living or staying ("sit"); the verb ישב is repeated.

[31] See for example וֹאֹם in line 5.

[32] Baumgarten 1999, 102.

[33] Milgrom 1995, 61–62. For examples of the idiom, see 1 Sam 17:28 and 2 Chr 25:6. The latter is also followed by אליו. The construction בדברו אל- is, however, less common than one might think.

[34] Theoretically, אבר could be read as "penis," hence "with his penis for himself," which would require Baumgarten's identification of the man as a *zav* and taking the expression as some kind of euphemism. I find this very unlikely, however.

[35] I.e. אלי ("mourning") with a suffix. Cf. Jastrow.

[36] García Martínez and Tigchelaar prefer not to conjecture, but leave the phrase as […]…[…]…

[37] Eisenman and Wise 1992, 207.

[38] Wacholder and Abegg 1995, 79. But any possible trait of a ז is only seen in PAM 42.601, and is too tiny for identifying the letter.

roundabout way to define a *zav*. I reluctantly accept the majority reading, although the בו at the end looks more like a ס to me. I find no plausible alternative verb, however, that would not destroy the context altogether.[39]

I read ירחץ with Eisenman & Wise and García Martínez & Tigchelaar, rather than ורחץ with the others. Differences between the letters י and ו are not consistent enough to ensure certainty. Here an imperfect makes a smoother sentence.

line 4

The reconstruction כול ימי היות[בו הנ]גֹע is suggested by Eisenman & Wise, as well as by Milgrom[40] and later followed by Baumgarten.[41]

line 5

I follow Baumgarten who argues against Qimron that תתערב does not refer to intercourse.[42]

line 6

It is tempting to translate את מחֹנֹי קדֹו[שי] ישראל as "the holy camps of Israel," not least in view of Deut 23:15, which can also be regarded as an "extended" purity law. The position of the adjective, however, speaks for "the camps of the holy (ones) of Israel," cf. 1QM III, 5.

line 7

Here one of the two main tears necessitates advanced guess-work. Eisenman & Wise suggest אל י[גע בזבה] או while Wacholder & Abegg reconstruct אל יגֹ[ע בדם זו[בֹו, presumably based on Milik's early transcription.[43] Milgrom reluctantly proposes אל יגֹ[ע בזב זו[בֹו, referring to Milik.[44] Neither of these suggestions really fills the lacuna. Baumgarten, however, reports Milik's restoration as אל יגֹ[ע בזב את זוב[ו,[45] which just fills the lacuna, while his own reconstruction

---

[39] The fragment contains several instances of ס that are similarly shaped, although the present letter is faded. For possible verbs ending on ס, יכבס is impossible, because it returns later on the same line. One could possibly suggest יכנס, hence "any man of the unclean [wh]o [gathers, i.e., food] shall bathe in water and launder his clothes and afterwards he may eat." This does not make sense, however, in view of the subsequent motivation and the recurring sequence of touch, bathing, washing and eating in the following lines.

[40] Eisenman and Wise 1992, 207; Milgrom 1995, 62–63.

[41] Baumgarten 1999, 100. Wacholder and Abegg's reading is less likely (הזוב הֹ[את]הֹ[ז]רֹע), since the second letter is a י rather than a ז, and this reading would make the man in lines 3–4a a semen emitter.

[42] Baumgarten 1995a, 5–6.

[43] Eisenman and Wise 1992; Wacholder and Abegg 1995, 79.

[44] Milgrom 1995, 59, 63.

[45] Baumgarten 1995a, 2.

in DJD 35, ‏א[טמ זוב בזב ע]יֹג אל‏, needs a little more space, despite the same number of letters.[46]

The crucial problem is the letter(s) at the left edge of the tear. If an ‏א‏ it is more or less unique; the left downstroke is too short.[47] Moreover, the photographs suggest that the strokes are not connected, which speaks for two letters. Reading ‏בו‏ is possible, even if not without problems; a ‏ב‏ seldom comes that close to the following letter at the top and when it does, the bottom stroke usually protrudes under the next letter.[48] A plural with a pronominal suffix (ending ‏יֹו‏) would perhaps provide a solution, but is difficult to fit into the context.[49]

Lines 7–8a contain three phrases echoing Lev 15:32–33. Although in reverse order, Lev 15:33 reads ‏והדוה בנדתה והזב את־זובו‏, with pronominal suffixes in both cases. This is very similar to Milik's reconstruction, according to Baumgarten. While it is reasonable to supply ‏זב (את־) זוב‏ from Lev 15:33, none of the allusions are exact quotations, and I would suggest the conjecture ‏אל יִג]ע בזב בזו]בֹו‏, which is enough to fill the lacuna. This phrase would describe an "active" *zav* with language analogous to the subsequent "active" menstruant (‏בדוה בנדתה‏). For further discussion and an interpretation of the initial *niddah* blood, see below.

line 8

The choice between Eisenman & Wise's ‏יחֹשֹב‏ and Milik's ‏ואֹשֹר‏ is difficult; the former is followed by Wacholder & Abegg and García Martínez & Tigchelaar, while Baumgarten and Milgrom follow the latter.[50] However, I think the remnants of the second letter belong to a ‏ח‏ rather than an ‏א‏. What remains of the right stroke is long enough to suggest a straight vertical line, which would be very exceptional in an ‏א‏; hence the reading ‏יחשב‏ ("is considered," ni.). This makes good sense if one follows Eisenman & Wise in inserting the preposition ‏ל‏ before ‏נוגע בו‏. In view of the diversity in size and shape of ‏ל‏ elsewhere in the fragment, the letter may be fitted in along the vertical crack in the leather. The

---

[46] Baumgarten 1999, 100. For the expression ‏זוב טמא‏, see 4Q270 2 ii, 12 and Lev 15:2 (cf. Lev 15:25, 30).

[47] There is a possible exception in ‏אם‏ a bit earlier on the same line, where the ‏א‏ comes rather close but not quite.

[48] This applies even more to a ‏ב‏. The little stroke besides what could be a ‏ו‏ or a ‏י‏ could also suggest another ‏ו‏ or ‏י‏, or a ‏ה‏. Less likely is the left edge of an ‏א‏ which could render ‏אל יִג]ע בזב‏ ‏זוב [אֹו...‏, resulting in smooth syntax and good sense, but the lower left stroke of an ‏א‏ in this fragment almost always protrudes further to the left than its upper corner and of this we find no trace.

[49] We would then need something like ‏בזב או בכליו‏ or ‏בזב ובגדיו‏. While clothes figure elsewhere in the close context they do so mainly as objects to wash. However, fragment 2 ii 4–7 discusses touching semen as well as clothes and vessels in contact with it.

[50] Eisenman and Wise 1992, 207; Wacholder and Abegg 1995, 80; García Martínez and Tigchelaar 2000, vol. 2, 628; Milgrom 1995, 59; Baumgarten 1995a, 2; idem. 1999, 100.

lack of any remaining traces may be explained by this crack, which has caused a total erasure of several letters on other lines as well.

For the next phrase, שֶׁכבת הזרע [מאיש]א תֹּצֵ [ואם, I follow Baumgarten's modification in DJD 35 of Milik's reconstruction (מאיש instead of ממנו).[51] Although the phrase is another echo from Lev 15:32 (ואשר תצא ממנו שכבת־זרע), the semen emitter is introduced in Lev 15:16 as איש כי־תצא ממנו שכבת־זרע. None of the three allusions to Lev 15:32–33 in lines 7–8a are precise quotations, for example, שכבת הזרע is used rather than the biblical שכבת־זרע. We should thus expect a pragmatic paraphrase of the biblical expression when the semen emitter is introduced in this text. Reconstructing ממנו furthermore causes problems of reference, since there is no suitable person around.[52] The phrase, however, introduces a new figure, the semen emitter.

Although the following words are differently reconstructed, most interpreters end up with similar translations. The letter before the lacuna is most probably a ה and to the left of the tear the extant וגע is preceded by a small dot at the bottom of the ו, which has been taken as a trace of a preceding נ, and by the likely remains of the top of a ל. This makes Milik's reconstruction (מגעו וטמא [ה]וא וכו[ל נֹוגע) plausible[53] and Baumgarten's unlikely (מגעו יטמא [ה]איש [ה]וגע(הנ).[54] The syntax of Milik's suggestion is not smooth (a conditional clause followed by a nominal clause) but possible. The use of הוא may be inspired by the introduction to the biblical discharge laws (Lev 15:2).

line 9

Milgrom suggests טה]רתם instead of טֹה]רתו, which would eliminate the ambiguity regarding whose purification period is in question and refer to "all these unclean ones." With טֹה]רתו the ambiguity remains, however. The reference could either be "*anyone* who touches" or "*a person* from all these unclean ones." It is preferable to keep the ambiguity and let the context decide.

---

[51] The latter is adopted by almost everyone else, except Eisenman and Wise, whose conjecture (1992, 207) is too long for the lacuna.

[52] It cannot be the hypothetical one who touches blood or discharge, but must either refer to the one who is counting or to the *zav* in line 7. The latter has been suggested by Milgrom (1995, 66–67) as well as by Harrington (1993, 86–87), and has caused undue speculation about whether the *zav* defiles only when he has had a semen emission. Milgrom even makes a major point of this, understanding this surprisingly lenient rule as the "second innovation" of the text. This discussion is unnecessary, however, if we supply איש, as pointed out by Baumgarten (1999, 102–103).

[53] Cf. Wacholder and Abegg 1995, 80; Baumgarten 1995a, 2. Milik's suggestion is also followed by García Martínez and Tigchelaar (2000, 628). Milgrom's reconstruction ignores the ה and lacks letters enough to cover the lacuna.

[54] Baumgarten 1999, 101.

Column ii
While only two letters remain on the first line, the context from i, 9 demands
יאכל. Apart from this, the only remains of column ii are found on line 2 (ישׂ or
ושׂב) and line 7 (ו).

Discussion

According to Milgrom, the text of the fragment describes three cases, each in
which bathing and laundering is required after contact with a more severe kind
of impurity (lines 3, 4–5 and 8–9).[55] While I differ in details, a general division
in three main sections is practical (i, 1–4a; i, 4b–6; i, 7–9 & ii, 1).

Baumgarten suggests that the referent in the first section (i, 1–4a) is a *zav*,
because of the mention of bed and seat, as well as the following context. The
cry "unclean, unclean" (Lev 13:45) is extended from the *metzora'* to the *zav*,
who is to be kept outside of the city and at a certain distance from other impurity bearers.[56]

Milgrom claims that the *metzora'* is the subject, suggested by scriptural allusions to Lev 13 and by the requirement to live separate from others.[57] He admits that the thought of pure food coming as close as 12 cubits from a banished
"leper" makes no sense when he is supposed to be banished from towns altogether. Also, the demand for "lepers" to dwell north-west of habitations is
thought to contradict the *Temple Scroll* explicitly, according to which "lepers"
are assigned a special area *east* of the Temple city, similarly to dischargers
(*zavim*) and semen emitters (11QT^a XLVI, 16–18).[58]

Since Baumgarten thinks that all this refers to the *zav*, these objections are
less relevant to him. Nevertheless, with his reading, "at a distance of twelve
cubits from the purity when he speaks to him," it is not clear who is supposed to
be speaking to whom (see note to line 2 above). And what is the point of stipu-
lating a minimum distance to הטהרה (pure food?) during *conversation*?

I suggest that the text speaks of a purifying "leper," i.e., what the rabbis
called a *mittaher*. It is not a matter of expelling a "leper" to an area east of the
city, as in the *Temple Scroll*. This text is about something entirely different; it
gives instructions for how to handle a healed "leper" in the precarious in-
between state subsequent to the bird rite and initial shaving, bathing and laundering, but prior to his final shaving, bathing and laundering on the seventh day

---

[55] Milgrom 1995, 65–68.
[56] Baumgarten 1995a, 6–8; cf. idem. 1999, 87–88, 101–102.
[57] Milgrom 1995, 61, 65. Not least the use of "affliction" (נגע) in line 4, so frequently used in
Lev 13 for symptoms of *tzara'at*, indicates that this is about the "leper."
[58] Milgrom 1995, 61–62.

and the *asham* and *chattat* sacrifices on the eighth day, i.e., during his seven-day purification period. Scripture rules that he can enter the camp, but not his "tent" (Lev 14:8). A number of unanswered details remain, however, for example, where is this person supposed to stay? In lines 1–2 we learn that a purifying "leper" must no longer come in contact with "all the impure," nor yet come closer to what is pure than 12 cubits.[59] He is not allowed into inhabited houses but is allowed to "sit" in a separate place associated with penitential activity, at this minimum distance from his house during the purifying period.[60]

The text provides important clarifications as to the status and behaviour of the purifying "leper." An interpretation of באברו אליו as a special area, quarter or shelter associated with penitence, fits this general understanding, although even without it the instruction to live twelve cubits from any ordinary dwelling-house (בית מושב) speaks for itself. Scripture's general requirement that the purifying "leper" should stay within the settlement but out of his house is thus specified to a set distance. The point of alluding to Lev 13:46 (כול ימי היות בו הנגע) is that this text provides an argument for an interpretation that severely restricts the "leper" during his purification period; in spite of being admitted into the "camp" he is considered unclean *all* the days of his affliction, i.e., until the eighth day.

A similar concern with the status of the purifying "leper" is found in 4QMMT B 64–72. In that text the focus is solely on preventing purifying "lepers" from contact with what is *pure*, from entering their house and from eating holy things until sunset on the eighth day.[61] In 4Q274, continued contact with what is *impure* is considered just as problematic.

It is not clear, however, who the unclean people in line 1b are. Here we find the first of three occurrences of the expression כול הטמאים. While the most immediate understanding would be the fully impure, this interpretation fits the next occurrence (line 3) less well, where the expression איש מכול הטמאים more likely refers to *other purifying* impurity bearers. In lines 8–9 the reference is again ambiguous. We should not presuppose absolute consistency, but the context will have to decide. In line 1b it is reasonable to read the injunction to dwell separate from all the unclean to mean that the purifying "leper" should avoid contact with any impurity bearer, whether "full" or purifying.

However, the following reference in line 3 to any man of all the unclean (איש מכול הטמאים), can hardly refer to *any* impurity bearer if בו in "who touches

---

[59] It is possible that טהרה here as in some other texts found at Qumran refers to pure *food* (cf. 1QS V, 13; VI, 16; VIII, 17). It is, however, not certain, and I prefer to leave the issue open, especially since it is not of crucial importance for my argument.

[60] In rabbinic idiom, the *yoledet* in her second stage impurity is called a "sitter" (יושבת).

[61] Cf. Himmelfarb 2001, 24–25.

him" is supposed to refer to the purifying "leper." Why would a fully impure need to bathe after having touched a purifying person, in order to eat? Such an interpretation seems very unlikely, suggesting a context in which the fully impure were supposed to eat their food in purity. Unless we propose a different reconstruction of line 3 (see comment to line 3 above), we should understand איש מכול הטמאים as referring to any of the *other purifying* impurity bearers discussed in this fragment. A purifying *zav*, *zavah*, or menstruant is not supposed to touch a purifying "leper" and if this happens the person touching must bathe and wash his or her clothes before eating. The rationale would be that being almost pure, a purifying person would be supposed to eat food in relative purity. At the same time, not yet being fully pure such a person would still transmit a minor impurity by contact. With these presuppositions, one would need to address the situation that is presented here. The "leper" was generally considered to be the most severe case among the impurity bearers mentioned in this fragment.[62] A similar logic is applied to the relative impurity of *purifying* impurity bearers. Purifying *zavim* or menstruants that are subsequently mentioned, are thus to be prevented from contacting a purifying "leper," lest their intermediate state be affected. While the purifying "leper" is in an intermediate state, too, his impurity is slightly higher than that of purifying dischargers.

In the following section (i, 4b–6), the woman discharging blood (הזבה דם) is discussed. Baumgarten and Milgrom agree that this refers to the menstruant, pointing to the similar terminology in Lev 15:19.[63] This may also be argued from the order in which various impurity bearers are mentioned in the version of the *Damascus Document* (4QD) represented by the group of fragments 4Q266–273.[64] In spite of the damaged text of 4Q266 6 i–ii, complemented by 4Q272 1 i–ii, which partly overlap, it is clear that the "leper"[65] and the *zav*[66] are

---

[62] Cf. the rabbinic hierarchies of impurity collected in *m. Kelim* 1. Milgrom also assumes a hierarchy of impurities in 4Q274, with the effect that any impurity is increased by contact with a stronger impurity, but he takes the text as referring to the fully impure.

[63] Baumgarten 1995a, 5; Milgrom 1995, 62. It is true that the text of Lev 15:19 may be subdivided in different ways; it is possible to read ואשה כי תהיה זבה (and when a woman is discharging), followed by דם יהיה זבה בבשרה (her discharge in her flesh is blood). This cannot be the reading presupposed by the text in 4Q274, however, since it keeps together הזבה and דם in alluding to Lev 15:19.

[64] Cf. Himmelfarb 2001, 16–26. For overviews of the 4QD documents and their relationship to the CD, see Hempel 2000; Wassén 2005, 19–44. For a recent new reconstruction and translation of these texts, see Wacholder 2007. Wacholder understands the sequence of the categories here to follow the order of the *Temple Scroll* (11QTᵃ XLVIII, 15). See pp. 269–274.

[65] הצרעת (4Q266 6 i, 13); see 4Q266 6 i, 1–13 and 4Q272 1 i, 1–ii, 2.

[66] הזב את זובו (4Q266 6 i, 14); see 4Q266 6 i, 14 and 4Q272 1 ii, 3–7.

followed by the menstruant[67] and then by the *yoledet*.[68] While this is persuasive the evidence is not conclusive. Our text does not necessarily follow the same order, nor does it have the same focus.[69] The expression might possibly include a *zavah* during her seven-day purification period,[70] but since the purifying *zavah* is addressed together with the purifying *zav* in the following section, the most reasonable conclusion is that the menstruant is in focus in lines 4–6. During her seven-day purification period, which begins at the onset of menstruation, she is not allowed, according to the text, to touch any type of *zav* or *zavah* impurity, since that would incur a more severe type of impurity. At the same time, the purifying menstruant may not mingle with pure people but must avoid contaminating them. Her intermediate state of impurity is lower than that of other purifying dischargers, but she still contaminates the fully pure.

In the subsequent section (i, 7–9 & ii, 1) the purifying discharger, whether *zav* or *zavah*, is specifically addressed. Although the wording on several points alludes to the summary in Lev 15:32–33, it is clear that those in focus here are *purifying* dischargers, or possibly any purifying impurity bearers. "One who counts" may neither touch a *zav*, nor a *zavah*. However, the prohibition is given a condition that may seem strange. Baumgarten translates: "unless she was purified of her [unclean]liness."[71] Milgrom's rendering is similar: "unless she is purified from her me[nses]."[72] But why does anyone want to add "unless she is purified"? It should be self-evident that a menstruant who is purified is no longer a menstruant, but clean, and could thus be touched.

Although reconstructed in part, the reconstruction is supplied from Lev 15:33 and close attention should be paid to the details of the text. In the sentence אל יג]ע בזב בזו[ב̇ו בדוה בנדתה the *zav* is *not* a purifying *zav*, but an "active"

---

[67] הזבה דם שב]עת ימים (4Q272 1 ii, 8); see 4Q266 6 ii, 1–4 and 4Q272 1 ii, 7–17. It is possible to argue that the *zavah* is discussed between the menstruant and the *yoledet* (4Q266 6 ii, 2a–4; cf. Himmelfarb 2001, 20–21), but this rather seems as an occasional case of irregular bleeding outside of normal periods, included in the instructions about menstruants.

[68] אשה אשר] תזרי[ע וילדה (4Q266 6 ii, 5); see 4Q266 6 ii, 5–13.

[69] I.e., it does not provide general rules for impurity bearers, but special rules for intermediate states of impurity.

[70] In Lev 15:25 the latter is called זוב דמה ימים רבים אשה כי־יזוב, which reminds of אשה זבה דם לימים רבים in line 6 of our text. At first sight, then, the two categories seem to be kept apart, but we should perhaps allow for the possibility that הזבה דם could be used generically for all female dischargers, only that it is supplemented by ימים רבים in line 6 to indicate an irregular condition. The phrase הזבה דם לשבעת הימים of line 4 could thus be taken to *include* a purifying *zavah* during her seven-day purification period together with the menstruant. From a perspective of graded impurity and purification the two share a similar status; both are in a sort of in-between state. The syntax of line 4 is ambiguous, however, since the words לשבעת הימים may be taken together with the following injunction not to touch; in Lev 15:19 these words most probably belong to what follows.

[71] Baumgarten 1995a, 101.

[72] Milgrom 1995, 60.

discharger. Purifying people, purifying dischargers in particular, who count off their seven days before full purity, must not touch an "active" *zav*, i.e., one who is still discharging an unclean emission. Such a person is fully impure and should not be contacted by purifying people. He will not begin his purificatory seven-day period until his discharge has ceased. If the subsequent phrase (בדוה בנדתה) is understood in analogy, it would refer to a "full" or an "active" menstruant. The menstruant differs, however, from the *zav*, by entering her purificatory period immediately. In what sense, then, could we envisage a menstruant that has not yet begun to purify? Is there a difference between a menstrual state of "full" impurity and an intermediate one during the purificatory period?

In Samaritan *halakah* a clear difference is made between *niddå* blood and *dåbå* blood. The former refers to the initial bleeding, which is considered more virulent, and has to be washed off before the counting of days can start. It contaminates with a seven-day impurity and continues to do so if the woman does not wash. The latter refers to continued bleeding after washing and contaminates with a one-day impurity, i.e., one that can be dealt with by bathing and waiting until evening.[73] While Samaritan texts as we have them are relatively late, there is reason to believe that the *halakah* often has more ancient roots. During the Second Temple period an initial first-day ablution for the corpse-impure, peeling off one layer of impurity, is attested. Evidence for such a practice comes not only from texts found at Qumran, but from a number of Jewish sources of various origins. It is reflected in Tobit and in Philo. Both Josephus and the Gospel of John imply that people came to Jerusalem one week in advance of Passover for purification, which fits with a requirement for an additional first-day ablution.[74]

An additional first-day ablution made it possible for corpse-impure people to remain within towns, even in the eyes of those following a strict practice. Historical evidence suggests that menstruants were similarly allowed within ordinary cities. While the *Temple Scroll* seems to include them with other dischargers outside of settlements in general, Josephus envisages menstruants within Jerusalem, although in some kind of seclusion, which means that he cannot think of them as expelled from ordinary towns. Rabbinic texts seem to ex-

---

[73] *Kitâb aṭ Ṭubâkh* [2–15]; *Kitâb al-Kafi* XI [48–60, 84–87], XIII [13–18], in Bóid 1989a, 141, 149–151, 154. Cf. Bóid's comments, 198–205, 231, 235–236.

[74] 11QTᵃ XLIX, 16–21; L, 13–16; 1QM XIV, 2–3; 4Q414 2 ii, 3, 4, line 2; Tob 2:5, 9; *Spec. Laws* 1:261; 3:205–206; Josephus, *J.W.* 6.290; John 11:55; cf. 12:1. A first-day purification rite may even be implied in Ezek 44:25–26. Some of this evidence will be discussed in more detail below. For further discussion and references to secondary literature, see Kazen 2011a, forthcoming.

clude the menstruant from the Temple mount only.[75] These pieces of evidence stretch over a long time period and represent varying degrees of strictness, but for a historical picture of actual practice at the end of the Second Temple period, we must in this case give priority to Josephus.[76] Without some kind of analogy to a first-day ablution for the corpse-impure, the inclusion of menstruants would have been an inconsistency. I suggest that 4Q274 attests to an initial purificatory practice similar to what is later attested in Samaritan *halakah*, i.e., a first-day ablution for menstruants.[77] The idea of some sort of initial purification for dischargers in addition to the corpse-impure has been suggested both by Milgrom and Baumgarten and will be discussed further below.

Since the purification period of the menstruant was counted from the *beginning* of her bleeding, not from the *end*,[78] as in the case of the *zav* and the *zavah*, it was only logical to assume that the initial bleeding had somehow contaminated her with a seven-day impurity and that its contamination potential was higher than the bleeding during subsequent days. If so, this bleeding needed to be removed. In 4Q274, purifying people are thus warned not to touch a menstruant unless this initial purification has been carried out.[79] The juxtaposition with an "active" *zav* suggests an analogy, which is made explicit in the motiva-

---

[75] 11QT[a] XLVIII, 14–17; *Ant.* 3.261; *J. W.* 5.227; *Ag. Ap.* 2.103; *m. Kelim* 1:8. See below for further discussion of some of this evidence.

[76] While Josephus is sometimes thought to talk of an ideal at the time of Moses rather than reflecting contemporary practice (Sanders 1990, 157; Maccoby 1999, 36), or to reflect legal interpretations of the aristocratic priesthood (Sanders 1990, 160), I am more inclined to trust Josephus than the fairly utopian *Temple Scroll* or the schematic lists in *m. Kelim* for actual practice. Although I have no problems in envisaging more lenient practices, especially in ordinary towns and villages, Josephus probably reflects a general "expansionist" tendency that did not lack influence and sometimes was able to set the agenda.

[77] In Samaritan *halakah* we encounter a further peculiarity: the left hand used for washing off the first blood is seen to remain in a more virulent state of impurity than other parts of the body, i.e., transmitting a seven-day impurity like the first blood (*Kitâb al-Kafi* XIII [19–21, 29–30] in Bóid 1989a, 154). While the context is one of childbirth, the text has – at least by some – been understood as a reference to a general principle regarding the hand used for washing off the *niddå* blood (marginal note IV to the text, in Bóid 1989a, 196). Cf. Bóid's comments, 244, 281. Possibly, some similar notion may lay behind 4Q272 1 ii, 17, where in a context of purification of *zavah* and menstrual impurity "her hand" (ידה) is mentioned. The text is fragmentary, to say the least, and no decisive reconstruction and interpretation is possible. Line 17 cannot, however, reasonably refer to a general washing of hands (plural) as in the case of the *zav*, but must be a special case, because "her hand" is mentioned in the singular.

[78] In later rabbinic practice the seven days were *added* to the menstrual period. The beginning of this development can be seen in *b. Nid.* 66a. While this increased stringency was neither self-evident, nor generally accepted in Talmudic times, the menstruant in the end came to be equalled with the *zavah gedolah*. For details, see Meacham (leBeit Yoreh) 1999a, 29–32; 1999b, 255–256.

[79] Some similar understanding is possibly indicated by the translation of García Martínez and Tigchelaar (2000, vol. 2, 629): "And the one who counts (one's seven days), whether male or female, should not to[uch ...] ...at the onset of her menstruation."

tion that follows: "for behold, *niddah* blood is considered like a discharge [to] the one touching it." While the menstruant is below the *zav* and the *zavah* in an ordinary hierarchy of graded impurities, the first blood is an exception. To touch such a person for one who is purifying, is just as contaminating as touching an "active" *zav*.

In the following sentence the semen emitter is suddenly introduced. The comment is very short, only stating that when semen goes forth from a man his touch is defiling. One possible reason why the semen emitter turns up at this point is that he, too, could be thought of as the bearer of an intermediate type of impurity, just like all the preceding categories. 4Q274 1 lists purifying "lepers," the menstruant who begins her purification period at the onset of her menstruation when she washes off the first blood, *zavim*, whether male or female, during their period of purification and, also, the semen emitter, whose impurity lasts for one or three days only.[80]

I do not think, however, that the purpose here is to discuss the semen emitter as a new category. His case and the way he defiles is discussed at length in fragment 2 i. In the context of fragment 1, however, the semen emitter should rather be understood as a complement to the two previously mentioned cases of unclean persons that must not be contacted by those in an intermediate purifying status. The semen emitter should in particular be compared to the menstruant who has not yet purified herself from her initial *niddah* bleeding. The text states that one who is counting will be just as defiled by contact with a menstruant in her initial impurity as by contact with an "active" *zav*, since the initial blood is just as contaminating as a discharge. This begs for one further question: what about the semen emitter who does not require a seven-day purification period? He is clearly below the other dischargers in a hierarchy of impurities. Does he still defile a purifying person as much as the previous two cases? The answer is yes, he does.

It may be objected that in the previous cases people are warned not to touch someone that might contaminate them, whereas in the case of the semen emitter the perspective is reversed; the text explicitly talks of *his* touch as defiling. Re-

---

[80] According to biblical law, the semen emitter is impure for one day only (Lev 15:16–17). The utopian *Temple Scroll* (11QT[a] XLV, 7–8) prohibits the semen emitter from entering the Temple area for three days. The same time limit applies to a man who had intercourse (XLV, 11–12), and concerns the whole Temple city (עיר המקדש). This extension of biblical law is probably based on Exod 19:10–15 and is modelled on ideas of the war camp. We cannot conclude from this that semen emitters were generally considered impure for three days by the circles responsible for this text, although this is possible. Cf. Harrington 1993, 91–94; Werrett 2007, 156–159. In any case, the semen emitter and the way he contaminates is elsewhere compared with or adapted to the rules regarding the *zav* or the menstruant (4Q272 1 ii, 4–5; 4Q274 2 i), which makes Werrett suggest that "the defiling power of semen has been intensified beyond that of the Torah" (283).

versibility is, however, implied for the purifying "leper," too, since he must keep at a distance, and the menstruant must similarly avoid mixing with others that are more pure than she is. One implication of our interpretation of the text's argument is that no distinction is made between touching and being touched. Although such distinctions are sometimes resorted to in order to explain seeming discrepancies in the text, this is not necessary.[81] To the rabbis, touching and being touched was basically regarded the same.[82] In the previous chapter it was argued that this is best explained as the result of an equalizing tendency in Second Temple Judaism, in which systemic readings and interpretations were sought for.[83] While we cannot and should not expect systemic consistency in all purity texts found at Qumran, as they may be of diverse origin and reflect an extended period of development,[84] the equalling of touching and being touched is likely a general development towards the end of the Second Temple period.

In the last part of the third section we find another occurrence of כול הטמאים (lines 8–9). Here we have to decide whether אדם מכול הטמאים האלה refers to the *purifying* or to the *fully* impure. Furthermore, the ambiguous טהרתו (line 9) could either refer back to "anyone who touches" or to "a person from all these unclean ones." We are faced with four possible meanings: 1) *Any person* (a pure person) must not touch a *purifying* impurity bearer during *the latter's* period of purification; 2) A *purifying* impurity bearer must not touch *another purifying* impurity bearer during *the latter's* period of purification; 3) A *purifying* impurity bearer must not touch *another purifying* impurity bearer during *the former's* period of purification; 4) A *purifying* impurity bearer must not touch a *fully impure* during *the former's* period of purification.

Although the expression "all the impure" (כול הטמאים) in lines 8–9 is ambiguous, it is qualified with the demonstrative האלה, reasonably identifying "all the impure" with those cases that were just discussed: the "active" *zav*, the not-yet-purifying menstruant and the semen emitter. This speaks for the fourth alternative. The end of line 8 together with line 9 summarize the third section, which addresses "the one who counts." "Anyone who touches" during his purification refers to the same category that is introduced in line 7, i.e., purifying impurity bearers during their seven-day period, in particular purifying dischargers. Our interpretation thus fits the structure of the text.

It is admittedly precarious to talk of a text's structure when dealing with a fragment. We can only guess as to what preceded fragment 1. Fragment 2 i deals with purification, in particular cases of semen contamination. Fragment 2

---

[81] Cf. Harrington 1993, 86.
[82] *m. Zabim* 5:1, 6.
[83] Chapter 3 above, or Kazen 2007, especially 350–353.
[84] Cf. Werrett 2007, particularly the concluding discussion, 302–304.

ii and 3 seem to be focused on impure foodstuff. It has become clear, however, that fragment 1 deals with various types of lessened or intermediate states of impurity: the purifying "leper," the menstruant, and those who count, presumably purifying dischargers. These people must avoid contact with that which is pure as well as that which is impure. The text implies a hierarchy also of intermediate impurities in which contact must be avoided with impurities higher than one's own. This is in line with the first of the three "innovative teachings" claimed by Milgrom.[85]

It is possible to argue that the real focus of each of the three sections in the text is on purification and eating, i.e., on what Milgrom calls the "third innovation" of this text. The requirement to bathe and wash one's clothes is repeated with regard to the one who touches a purifying "leper," the menstruant who touches a *zav* and a *zavah*, and any purifying person who touches any of the three "active" categories in lines 7–8. People in an intermediate state of purity are clearly expected to eat their food in some sort of supposedly intermediate purity. To eat in purity is apparently the primary, although not the sole, reason for the careful and detailed rules in this text. Not defiling "the camps of the holy ones of Israel" is one reason for not mixing with pure people, but the warning against contracting further impurity is motivated by the purity of food.

First-day ablutions and graded impurity

In 4Q274 1 i, 9, the prohibition against eating before initial purification is compared to the rules for corpse-impure persons. As already mentioned, an initial ablution for the corpse-impure seems to have been widely practised during the Second Temple period and probably served the function of allowing the corpse-impure to stay within settlements during their purificatory period.[86]

According to i, 9, however, early purification had a further function for the corpse-impure; it made it possible to eat food in purity. Since the text of 4Q274 1 requires other purifying impurity bearers to bathe and wash their clothes, too,

---

[85] For Milgrom's suggestions, see above under "Previous Research." Cf. Milgrom 1995, 66.

[86] In a recent review of the archaeological evidence from *miqvaot* adjacent to burial grounds, Yonatan Adler (2009) argues that these were not used for first-day ablutions in cases of a seven-day corpse impurity, but for mourners who had contracted a one-day impurity from contact with other corpse-impure people. Adler somewhat confusingly talks of a first-degree and a second-degree impurity for a seven-day and a one-day corpse impurity respectively, in spite of the fact that in rabbinic terminology as well as in modern scholarly discourse, a numbering of degrees or "removes" is often employed for one-day impurities only, and not including the "fathers of impurity." While Adler may be right that these *miqvaot* were (also) used by many mourners who had contracted a one-day rather than a seven-day impurity, he simply omits or disregards the full range of textual evidence relevant to the Second Temple period, in his dismissal of a first-day immersion as a merely sectarian phenomenon.

when they had *acquired* a further impurity, in order to be able to eat in purity, we might be justified to expect similar purificatory water rites as they *entered* their period of purification.

Several interpreters have suggested an understanding of impurity as consisting of multiple layers that may be "peeled away" one by one through various purification rites. Milgrom discussed a graded understanding of impurity in an early study on the *Temple Scroll*, with a view to admission to and exclusion from the temple city and ordinary cities.[87] He later repeated part of the study with a complement, this time with a focus on early purification as a requirement for eating.[88] Milgrom finds his earlier conclusions confirmed by 4Q514, which he claims "deals exclusively with the *zāb*,"[89] and suggests that he, too, was obliged to bathe and launder his clothes at the beginning of his purification in order to eat, although not yet the pure food, but the common food of the community. This would have been done in emulation of the "leper" (Lev 14) and taking Lev 22 (prohibiting the eating of sacred foods in a state of impurity) as a precedent.[90]

Baumgarten has similarly dealt with the issue. In a study of 4Q512 and 4Q514 he suggests that at least the latter text indicates that dischargers were supposed to begin their purification in order to eat non-sacred food in purity. "Immersion was required before meals even during a person's period of impurity in order to remove the primary degree of ritual uncleanliness."[91]

In DJD 35, Esther Eshel suggests that the mention of the first, third and seventh days in 4Q414 2 ii, 3, 4, line 2, reveals the same outlook as 11QT[a] regarding immersion on the first day, but she argues that 4Q414 might deal with other types of impurities than corpse impurity.[92]

It is reasonable to follow Milgrom and suggest that a graded understanding of impurity, including a first-day ablution for corpse impurity, in part developed from the biblical legislation concerning the "leper."[93] According to Lev 14, the purifying "leper" goes through three stages: the bird rite followed by washing of clothes, shaving and bathing on the first day, a second shaving, washing of clothes and bathing on the seventh day and, finally, sacrifices together with the

---

[87] Milgrom 1978, 512–518.
[88] Milgrom 1992, 561–570.
[89] Milgrom 1992, 566.
[90] See also Milgrom 1991, 969–976, 991–1000, for further discussion about first-day ablutions and intermediate levels of impurity.
[91] Baumgarten 1992, 208.
[92] Eshel 1999.
[93] Cf. Tobit, who enters his courtyard but sleeps outside of his house after having contracted corpse impurity and subsequently undergone a first-day ablution (Tob 2:9), similarly to the purifying "leper" in our interpretation of 4Q274. Manuscript evidence exhibit a number of variant readings here, perhaps due to varying halakic practices; cf. Bóid 1989a, 321–322.

rite of smearing oil and blood on the former "leper" on the eighth day. These stages were recognized by the Rabbis and defined and associated with corresponding grades of impurity (*m. Neg.* 14:2–3).[94] They are then said to be similar to three stages of purification for the *yoledet*.

It is also reasonable to see a graded understanding of impurity and purification as a general framework towards the end of the Second Temple period.[95] Such a framework may explain why the corpse-impure are not expected to stay outside of settlements according to a number of texts from the Second Temple period that otherwise assume or require the expulsion not only of "lepers," but also of dischargers, in line with the strict tradition of Num 5:2–3. In *Ant.* 3:261, Josephus makes a difference between "lepers" and *zavim* on the one hand whom Moses expelled (ἀπήλασε) from the city (i.e., Jerusalem), and menstruants and the corpse-impure on the other, whom he set aside (μετέστησε) until day seven after which they were allowed to live in their place (ἐνδημεῖν).[96] Philo, when discussing purification after contact with a corpse, suggests that while the corpse-impure were excluded from the temple for seven days, mere bathing and washing of clothes sufficed for other purposes (*Spec. Laws* 1:261; 3:205–206). Even the *Temple Scroll* that takes a "maximalist" stance and excludes the corpse-impure from the Temple city (עיר המקדש) for the whole period (11QTᵃ XLV 17),[97] does not require their expulsion from ordinary cities, but allows them within, after a first-day ablution, which is described as part of the standard procedures (11QTᵃ XLIX 16–21).[98] Although the *Temple Scroll* is partly uto-

---

[94] I.e., טמא בביאה (impurity of entry), טמא כשרץ (impurity like a "swarmer"), and טבול יום (*tevul yom*). The third stage is then further specified: after shaving and immersing on the seventh day the purifying "leper" may eat second tithe, after sundown he may eat *terumah* and after the final sacrifice he may eat *qodashim*.

[95] Cf. Regev 2000, 177–86. Regev talks of "gradual purification" (179).

[96] While it is true that μεθίστημι could be taken to mean "remove from one place to another," Josephus elsewhere expresses a difference between "lepers" and dischargers, for whom the whole city was closed, and menstruants, who were only excluded (ἀπεκέκλειστο) from the temple (*J. W.* 5:227). Also, in *Ag. Ap.* 2:103 he says that women could not enter the outer court during menstruation.

[97] Although in 11QTᵃ XLV, 15–18 only the *zav* is explicitly said to have to count seven days before entering the Temple city, the subsequent instructions concerning the "leper" and the corpse-impure (לוא יבואו לה עד אשר יטהרו) must be understood as abbreviated and implying the same requirements as those applying to the *zav*. The phrase cannot be taken to mean that only a first-day ablution was needed for entrance, since for the "leper," the concluding sacrifice is said to follow the act of purification (11QTᵃ XLVIII, 18); it must thus refer to the full seven-day ritual.
There are a number of competing interpretations of the "temple city" and the problem partly depends on how the temple area was defined by various groups and at various times. The outline of ten degrees of holiness in the land of Israel that is attested later (*m. Kelim* 1:6–9) suggests a complicated development.

[98] Cf. 11QTᵃ L, 10–16; 1QM XIV, 2–3.

pian, it is not a sectarian text; it represents ideals that belonged to a wider expansionist tendency.[99] Later, the rabbis of the *Mishnah* seemingly think of the corpse-impure as even allowed within the court of gentiles (*m. Kelim* 1:8). Here, we must reckon with a first-day ablution, lessening the power of corpse impurity, as taken for granted, just as such a rite may explain the presence of the corpse-impure person within the ordinary city of the stricter *Temple Scroll*.

Thus there is every reason to regard a first-day water rite for the corpse-impure as common practice at the end of the Second Temple period. This rite did not shorten the duration of their seven-day impurity, but somehow lessened its strength. Without it, the presence of corpse-impure people would be an anomaly in any context that otherwise followed the strict tradition of Num 5 with regard to *zavim* and "lepers," since they are the third category that should be expelled from the "camp." Josephus is not alone in placing *zavim* together with "lepers" outside, while the corpse-impure are envisaged within; the *Temple Scroll* does so, too, although not for Jerusalem, as in Josephus, but with regard to the ordinary city (11QT^a XLVIII, 14–17).[100]

First-day ablutions for dischargers

Josephus' differentiation between "lepers" and *zavim* on the one hand and menstruants and the corpse-impure on the other is significant.[101] It does fit with suggestions about an initial first-day water rite not only for the corpse-impure but also for purifying dischargers, at least for menstruants. I am inclined to include the *yoledet* here as well; she is in many respects likened to the menstruant in biblical as well as in rabbinic legislation, and her stages of purification are likened to those of the *mittaher* (purifying "leper"), which include a first-day ablution (*m. Neg.* 14:2–3). Since a homogenizing tendency is at work towards the end of the Second Temple period, we might even expect all impurity bearers with a similar (seven-day) contamination potency, i.e., all those "counting," to have been treated alike.

---

[99] Cf. Crawford 2008, 88, 92–93.
[100] The text of 11QT^a XLVIII, 14–17 is admittedly ambiguous. The preposition ב may point to the presence of both "lepers" and dischargers within ordinary cities (ובכול עיר ועיר), but this cannot be the case for "lepers," since the purpose of making special places for them is to prevent them from *entering* the cities and defiling them (אשר לוא יבואו לעריכמה וטמאום). "In every city" must hence include the surrounding country. The purpose with a similar treatment (גם ל-) of male and female dischargers, menstruants and parturients is, however, to prevent them from "defiling in their midst" (אשר לוא יטמאו בתוכם). This could possibly mean that these dischargers were supposed to be secluded *within* settlements, but the most natural reading is that they, too, were supposed to stay outside.
[101] Cf. Noam 2008.

This seems to be implied in the fragment 4Q514 1 i, referred to both by Milgrom and Baumgarten:

1	...[...] a woman [...]
2	he must not eat [...] for all the im[pu]re [...]
3	to count for [him seven days of ablu]tions; and he shall bathe and wash (his clothes) on the d[a]y of [his] purification [... And]
4	who[ever] has not begun to purify himself of "his spri[ng]" is not to eat, [nor shall he eat]
5	in his original impurity. And all the temporarily impure, on the day of their pur]ification, shall bathe
6	and wash (their clothes) in water and they will be pure. *Blank* Afterwards, they shall eat their bread in conformity with the regulation of [pu]rity.
7	He is not to eat insolently in his original impurity, whoever has not started to cleanse himself from "his spring,"
8	nor shall he eat any more during his original impurity. All the temporarily [im]pure, on the day of
9	their pu[rification,] shall bathe and wash (their clothes) in water and they will be pure and afterwards they shall eat their bread
10	in conformity with the reg[ulation. No-]one is to [e]at or drink with anyo[ne] who prepares
11	[...] ... in the [ser]vice [...][102]

The text is repetitive and one may suspect "extensive dittography."[103] According to Milgrom, "the first day ablution allows the person to eat from the common food of the community."[104] There is some uncertainty as to the interpretation of the text, however. While the "temporally impure" (טמאי הימים) refer to purifying impurity bearers during their seven-day purification period (including dischargers), and the "original impurity" (בטמאתו הרישנה) of which a person must begin to purify himself before eating must refer to the beginning of the seven-day purification period, bathing takes place on "the day of his/their purification" (ביום טהרתו/ם). The meaning of this phrase is unclear; does it refer to the first or the final day of the purificatory process? Since washing and eating are linked here as in many texts found at Qumran, it is plausible to take "the day of purification" as the first day of the seven-day period, not least in view of this text's emphasis on beginning purification.[105]

---

[102] Translation in García Martínez and Tigchelaar 1998, vol. 2, 1043. In the 2000 pbk ed. "original" is replaced by "primary" in lines 5 and 7, although not in line 8. The variation between "begun" and "started" (lines 4 and 7) for החל in both editions is inconsistent.

[103] Baumgarten 1992, 204.

[104] Milgrom 1995, 67.

[105] It might be possible to understand the initial purification that is necessary for the temporally impure in order not to eat in their original impurity as something else than a first-day water rite (but what would it be then?), separate from a bathing on the "the day of purification." This seems too far-fetched, however.

It is best to understand the one who has not begun to purify from his spring as a semen emitter,[106] who is distinct from "all the temporally impure" (טמאי הימים).[107] The text seems to address two categories; both semen emitters and every other purifying impurity bearer (which includes purifying dischargers in general) must undergo an initial first-day ablution before they can eat. It may be necessary to specify this, since semen emitters are lower in the hierarchy of impurities than other dischargers.

The text is thus evidence for an initial purificatory rite for dischargers in general, to enable them to eat in some intermediate state of purity during their seven-day purificatory period, and most probably this is what is referred to as bathing and laundering on "the day of his/their purification."

With 4Q514 in mind we can return to 4Q274 1. In both texts dischargers are particularly in focus and in both texts the special case of the semen emitter is deemed necessary to address separately. While the point in 4Q514 is that purifying people must bathe *at the beginning* of their period of purification in order to eat, 4Q274 1 states that such people must also bathe *during* their period of purification, if they happen to contact someone with a higher degree of impurity, in order to eat. This is said to be similar to what applies to the corpse-impure (i, 9) and it is difficult to believe that the comparison is valid only for bathing *during* one's purificatory period and not *at the beginning*.

Moreover, the phrase "whoever has not begun to purify himself from 'his spring'" (אשר לא החל לטהור ממקרו) in 4Q514 1 i, 4, 7 is somewhat comparable to the phrase "unless she is pure from her *niddah* bleeding" (כי אם טהרה מ̇נד[ת̇ה) in 4Q274 1 i, 7. The former explicitly refers to an initial purification of the semen emitter.[108] I have argued that the latter refers to an initial purification of the menstruant. One is relative and the other conditional, but their intent is similar: purification (טהר) from (מ-) contamination by semen and *niddah* blood respectively. A parallel reading of 4Q514 1 i thus supports my interpretation of 4Q274 1 i.

Baumgarten has argued for a general use of "purification water" (מי נדה) in Qumran, not only for removing corpse impurity but for all sorts of impurities.[109]

---

[106] The term מקור ("source," "spring") is elsewhere found in the war camp regulations of the *War Scroll* (1QM VII, 6) and definitely alludes to Deut 23:9–11, which prohibits a semen emitter from staying inside the war camp. The allusion is certain since the subsequent line (VII 7) about the location of latrines corresponds to the following verses (23:12–14) in Deuteronomy.

[107] In biblical legislation, מקור is used with regard to the menstruant and the *yoledet*, but not for irregular bleeding (Lev 12:7; 20:18). Similarly, the term is used positively for the source of male seed in Prov 5:18.

[108] Cf. the use of the same verb (חלל hi.) for the beginning of penitential prayers belonging to the initial stage of the purifying "leper" in 4Q274 1 i, 1.

[109] Baumgarten 1999, 83–87. This text is repeated in idem., 2000, 481–485.

He refers to 4Q277 1 ii, 8–9, where the sprinkling of purification water is said to effect purification from corpse impurity and "any other impurity," which is followed by a discussion of the *zav* (lines 10–12).[110] The translation "any other impurity" is uncertain, however, due to the fragmentary state of the text (...] ומכל טמאה] אחרת) and although Baumgarten suggests that it is the sprinkling that effects purification from corpse impurity *and* other impurities, an alternative reading would be that other impurities must be removed by immersion *before* sprinkling can effect purification from corpse impurity. Another piece of evidence is 4Q512 1–3, where sprinkling water is envisaged on the "temporarily impure," which would include all sorts of purifying impurity bearers, but here the term מי נדה is not used. Baumgarten also refers to 4Q284 1, where "sprinkling water for purification" (מֹי נדה להתֹ[קד]ש[)[111] is followed by "seminal discharge" on the next line.[112] A similar juxtaposition is found in 4Q274 2 i, where a first sprinkling (possibly on the third day?) and the seventh day are mentioned, followed by a discussion of semen emission.[113]

None of these texts are, however, unambiguous enough to conclude with any degree of certainty that the מי נדה was used for dischargers, and they do *not* refer particularly to an initial first-day water rite.[114] Together with other, stronger evidence, however, they do suggest an "expansion of ritual washing to new uses not known in the Hebrew Bible."[115]

Conclusions

In this article I have argued that the text of 4Q274 1 does not discuss contact between impure people in general, but primarily deals with purifying people in intermediate states of impurity, and their contact with what is clean and unclean. The text presupposes a graded understanding of impurity and reflects the ambition to prevent people who are lower on the scale from contacting people who are subject to a higher degree of impurity. The text is thus evidence for developing hierarchies of impurities. I have given special attention to the status of the menstruant and suggested that the text expects her initial impurity to be

---

[110] Baumgarten 1999, 83.

[111] Baumgarten 1999, 84. García Martínez and Tigchelaar reconstruct מי נדה להזֹ[ת]ש אי[ש (2000, vol. 2, 638). In fact, in this phrase, only six letters are clearly visible in the fragment (...נדה לה ש...), but מי is a likely conjecture although the remains are minimal.

[112] Baumgarten 1999, 83–84.

[113] Cf. Baumgarten 1999, 104.

[114] This is even less the case with the list in 1QS III, 4–5, which Baumgarten understands as indicating that sprinkling was used not only for corpse impurity. This passage may be read as thoroughly metaphorical, emphasizing that no possible purificatory rite can ever purify the wicked man.

[115] Cf. Lawrence 2006, 189.

mitigated by a first-day purificatory water rite, analogous to the biblical rule for purifying "lepers" and the developing practice of a first-day ablution for the corpse-impure.

I have argued that the referent in the first section is the purifying "leper" rather than the *zav* and that the penitential note suits such an interpretation well. The reason for the strict rules against contacting him is the biblical statement that he remains unclean *all* the days the affliction is on him.

I have also tried to demonstrate that the *zav* in i, 7 is not to be understood as a surprisingly lenient case, only defiling if/when he has a semen emission, but that the semen emitter in i, 8 is a different case from the *zav* and that the point of the argument is that all three – the "active" *zav*, the menstruant before she has washed off her initial *niddah* blood, and the semen emitter – contaminate any purifying impurity bearer alike.

There is convincing evidence that a first-day ablution for corpse impurity developed and became wide-spread practice during the Second Temple period. As has been pointed out before, this rite should be understood as mitigating the status of the corpse-impure, which explains the acceptance of such people within settlements and even within Jerusalem (except for the views of the stricter *Temple Scroll*). In view of Josephus' accounts and their relationship to the strict tradition in Num 5, it would be logical to expect a similar first-day water rite for menstruants; it could almost be seen as a "systemic necessity." Some scholars have argued that certain texts from Qumran suggest that the use of water rites for the corpse-impure were being extended to dischargers. In particular, 4Q514 gives evidence for a first-day ablution being employed for all purifying impurity bearers, i.e., not only "lepers" and the corpse-impure, but also various types of dischargers. I have suggested that this is not a sectarian development only, but that the menstruant (and probably the *yoledet* as well) employed a first-day water rite in order to lessen her initial state of impurity and that this represents a developing expansionist practice during the Second Temple period. It is attested in 4Q274 1 i, 7–8, as I read it, and the date and character of the text give no reason for restricting this practice to a narrow sectarian environment only. Whether the practice of a first-day ablution was being extended to *all* purifying dischargers (as suggested in 4Q514) also outside of sectarian circles, may remain an open question.

When the developing practice of initial purification in general is considered, it is usually related to questions of inclusion within and exclusion from society. The relevant texts from Qumran, however, have a different focus on *eating* in purity. The requirement even for purifying people to eat common food in relative purity seems to be particular for the type of expansionist trajectory that finds expression in these texts, but a preoccupation with pure food is found elsewhere, too, in Second Temple society. The rabbinic solutions of *tevul yom* and hand-washing for secondary impurities, which presumably go back to Pharisaic developments, serve a similar function, and express increasing aspirations for purity not only among small circles of "associates," but in larger segments of Second Temple society – an issue to be further dealt with in subsequent chapters.[116] The extension of first-day ablutions for initial purification, first to corpse-impure people and then to dischargers, not only in sectarian circles, but to some extent in other parts of society, thus served double purposes: social integration and eating in purity. A graded understanding of impurity not only caused halakic elaboration, but also provided solutions.

---

[116] See below, especially chapter 6. See also Kazen 2011a, forthcoming.

Chapter 5

The Status of the *Zavah* and the Jesus Tradition

Introduction: the discharge rules

In the present chapter I discuss the status of female dischargers at the end of the Second Temple period, in particular the woman with an irregular bleeding, the *zavah*, and relate this discussion to the narrative of the woman with a blood flow in Mark 5:24b–34.

The status of the *zavah* at the end of the Second Temple period is a contested issue that has been much discussed.[1] The rules in Lev 15 dealing with the *zav*, the *zavah*, the menstruant, and the semen emitter indicate that all dischargers are thought of as remaining within their own homes. While this is not explicitly stated, it is implied by the fact that contact leading to defilement is assumed and means are provided for the purification of both dischargers and those who have contacted them.

During biblical and early rabbinic times, the seven-day purification period prescribed for *zavim* and *zavot* was counted *after* the cessation of their symptoms, while menstruants counted their seven days from the *onset* of menstruation, not from its end, as later became common practice.[2] In contrast, the period of impurity for the semen emitter is only one day, just like that of people contracting a secondary impurity by contacting one of the primary impurity bearers. Although the *Temple Scroll* extends this period to three days,[3] the semen emitter is not subject to a seven-day purification period according to any known Jewish movement. When compared to *zavim* and *zavot*, we have to think of the semen emitter and the menstruant as subject to a lesser or an intermediate type

---

[1] For a few examples from the last two decades, see Cohen 1991; Sanders 1990; 1992; Fonrobert 1997; Maccoby 1999; Baumgarten 1999; Kazen 2002; Haber 2003 (reprinted in Haber 2008); Wassén 2008.

[2] The beginning of this development can be seen in *b. Nid.* 66a. Eventually, the menstruant was equalled with the *zavah gedolah*, although this was not self-evident in Talmudic times. Cf. Meacham (leBeit Yoreh) 1999a; idem 1999b, 255–256.

[3] 11QT^a XLV, 7–8. The extension is probably based on Exod 19:10–15 and modelled on ideas of the war camp. Due to the utopian and non-sectarian nature of the *Temple Scroll* we cannot conclude that semen emitters actually were considered impure for three days in Qumran, although this might be possible. Cf. Harrington 1993, 91–94; Werrett 2007, 156–159.

of impurity. In their case we could in fact think of the *discharge itself* as the primary contaminant, as I have suggested in previous chapters.[4]

In addition we find rules for the *yoledet* (post-partum woman) in Lev 12. These rules seem to depend on, or presuppose at least in part, the legislation of Lev 15. This is clear from the way in which the first period of her purification (7 days in the case of a boy and 14 in the case of a girl) is compared with the rules concerning menstruation (Lev 12:2, 5). While the second stage of the purification period of the *yoledet* is much longer than that of any discharger, it has little to do with the cessation of "symptoms." The first stage is not dependent on the length of the bleeding either, but consists of 7/14 days, counted from the birth of the child and modelled on the menstruant. The state of the *yoledet* is, like that of the menstruant, a regular and recurring situation. For a number of reasons, then, *zavim* and *zavot* stand out in their character as "irregular" dischargers.

In stark contrast to the legislation in Leviticus, the strict tradition of Num 5:2–3 requires the expulsion of all "chronic" impurity bearers: "lepers," *zavim* and the corpse-impure. The menstruant and the *yoledet* are not mentioned here and most probably are not thought to be included in the list either. The strict tradition thus singles out "irregular" dischargers and treats them just like Lev 13–14 treats "lepers": they are to be expelled (Lev 13:46). Hence nothing is said in Lev 13–14 of contamination by touch or purification from contact with a "leper." Such rules were later deduced from the rules of "leprous" houses in Lev 14.[5] The corpse-impure are never dealt with in Leviticus; the general legislation concerning corpse impurity is found in Num 19 and from this passage we cannot say for sure whether they are envisaged within or outside the "camp." Only a short sentence (Num 19:22) states that their touch defiles items and people with an impurity that lasts until the evening. Nothing like the elaborate details of the discharge laws is to be found in the biblical texts on corpse impurity.

Discrepancies within and between

Regardless of how we try to structure the biblical purity legislation discrepancies abound. In chapter 3 I discussed discrepancies *within* the laws on discharges. Some of these details are particularly relevant for discussing the historical status of female dischargers towards the end of the Second Temple period. It is often asserted that the discharge laws of Lev 15 are to be read systemically and that the laws of female dischargers are modelled on those of the

---

[4] I.e., as in Samaritan interpretations and in 4Q274. See chapters 3 and 4 above. For Samaritan texts, see Bóid 1989a, 236–238, 335.

[5] Cf. *m. Neg.* 12–13; Maccoby 1999, 141–148; Kazen 2002, 112–116.

zav. This is true to a large extent and particularly valid for the purification of the *zavah* by washing her clothes and bathing. Although this is never explicitly said, it is probably to be assumed from the rules for the *zav.*[6] No difference is acknowledged in rabbinic interpretation, but the immersion of all dischargers is taken for granted.[7] Other differences with regard to contamination by contact may have been intended in the text but are nevertheless read systemically and harmonized towards the end of the Second Temple period; touching and being touched were apparently seen as equally contaminating.[8] Does a basic systemic shaping of the text then suggest a complete harmonization of *every* detail? I do not believe so. While some assume that the exception to the rule of contamination by touch, that a *zav* contaminates other people *unless his hands are washed*, would have been equally valid for the *zavah,*[9] we have no evidence of such an understanding or practice. Although the text of Leviticus is to some extent shaped with systemic considerations in mind, these rules are not of a piece. As I have indicated in chapter 3, some of the underlying differences between the rules for the *zav* and the *zavah* might for example be explained by the fact that the male discharge is not as visible as female blood. Others could be due to different social roles of men and women respectively. While most rules were read and interpreted systemically, some details and discrepancies could also be exploited in ways that cannot be anticipated by moderns.[10] We thus cannot presuppose that discharging women at the end of the Second Temple period could mitigate their impure status by washing their hands, too. Although hand-washing before meals became a means to lessen *secondary* impurities in this period, this proves nothing concerning the use of hand-washing for female discharging *impurity bearers.*[11]

In addition to discrepancies *within* the discharge laws there are a number of discrepancies *between* rules relating to dischargers and to other types of impurity bearers, which are of interest in trying to map out the status of dischargers

---

[6] This requirement is spelled out only for the *zav* (Lev 15:13) but not for the *zavah* (15:28). Cf. Milgrom 1991, 923–924, 934–935.

[7] *m. Nid.* 4: 3; *m. Miqw.* 8:1, 5.

[8] *M. Zabim* 5:1, 6; 4Q274.

[9] Cf. Haber 2008, 128.

[10] Two examples: in *m. Nid.* 8:1–3, R. Aqiva appeals to the word "blood" (not stain) in Lev 15:19 for disregarding bloodstain from a *zavah*; in *b. Ker.* 8b, the occasional use of "man" in Lev 13 taken to mean that certain rules are not applicable to women but they are only included when the text talks of "the leper."

[11] The scant evidence we have talks only of hand-washing for the *zav.* Cf. the fragmentary text of 4Q277. The hand of a female discharger (... שבֿ] הזבה דם שבֿ – a menstruant or possibly a *zavah* during her seven-day purification period) is probably mentioned in 4Q272 1 ii, 17, but in the singular. This does not suggest the washing of hand*s* as in the case of the *zav* but, if one may be allowed to speculate, possibly has to do with washing off the first (*niddah*) blood, as part of a first-day purification procedure. See further below, and Kazen 2010a.

at the end of the Second Temple period. We find, for example, obvious differences with regard to the required purificatory rites: dischargers (*zavim* and *zavot*) offer doves as *chattat* and *olah* sacrifices on the eighth day,[12] while the corresponding sacrifices for the purifying *metzora* should consist of lambs, or doves if the offerer is poor, and also include an *asham* sacrifice, which in any case must be a lamb, as well as food offerings. Such differences could be understood to reflect a gradation of seriousness of these two types of impure conditions, associated with the expulsion of "lepers" but not of dischargers. This does not provide sufficient explanation, however. While these rules have clearly been redacted and adapted to fit into a priestly system, they still carry a number of disparate traits that are probably due to different origins. The obviously apotropaic bird rite initiating the purification of a *metzora* has no equivalent when we look at other impurity bearers, except that it resembles the red heifer rite (Num 19) that provides the purification water necessary for removing corpse impurity.

What interests us here, however, is not so much discrepancies relating to differences in background or origins, nor the order or number of varying rites of purification, but practices of inclusion, isolation or expulsion of certain categories of impurity bearers at the end of the Second Temple period. The two rites just mentioned are both carried out "outside the camp." Those involved have to bathe and wash their clothes before they can enter the settlement.[13] The idea of keeping some impurities out of settlements and not allowed in again until certain purification rites have been carried out is expressed in a variety of traditions. The briefest but strictest mention, with the most extensive consequences, is Num 5:2–4, which requires the expulsion of all corpse-impure people, "lepers" and dischargers (apparently *zavim* and *zavot*, but not lesser impurities). This stricter tradition could be associated with the war laws in Num 31:19, 24, requiring soldiers who had touched corpses to stay outside of the "camp" until

---

[12] Just like the corpse-impure (see below), the semen emitter and the menstruant (*niddah*) are not required to offer any sacrifices according to biblical law. This is often explained by the frequency and normality of these conditions. The parturient (*yoledet*), however, is required to offer a lamb as *olah* and a dove as *chattat* sacrifice (two doves if she is poor) after the purification period of 40 (boy) or 80 (girl) days (Lev 12). While birth is as frequent as death and as normal as menstruation, the childbirth law represents yet another variant, which at least in the biblical text is only partially harmonized with the discharge laws.

[13] This is actually stated as an explicit requirement only for entering the camp of the priest, but the priest in this passage (Num 19:1–10) is clearly inserted by the priestly redactors in their attempt to integrate this rite into the official sacrificial system, bringing it in under the category of *chattat* sacrifices, in spite of it having little to do with a normal *chattat*. The role of the priest is marginal, but his participation associates the rite with the sanctuary. Cf. Milgrom 1981. The requirement to bathe before entering the camp may lie behind the first-day ablution for the corpse-impure that had apparently become standard practice at the end of the Second Temple period.

the end of the seven-day purification period. The strict legislation of Num 5 is motivated by the divine presence in the camp,[14] and although it is a much-contested issue whether the stricter practice in fact has more ancient roots than the lenient one, or perhaps represents an alternative contemporaneous tradition, as discussed in chapter 3 above, it seems to be phrased as an additional commandment and in my view reflects ideas current in the early Persian period.[15]

Harmonization and criteria

As already mentioned several times, we have indications that purity laws were at least to some extent harmonized and interpreted systemically. At the same time, discrepancies remain whatever practices we assume to have been followed at a given time. Is it possible to explore the logic behind practices of inclusion and expulsion and thereby get a clearer understanding of available options and solutions? What criteria can we envisage for allowing certain impurity bearers within settlements and keeping others out?

Does the requirement of some impurity bearers to bring a *sacrifice* give us some clue? While this could be argued for dischargers and "lepers," the *yoledet* is required to bring a *chattat* sacrifice but is *not* expelled even according to the stricter tradition. The corpse-impure person, on the other hand *is* expelled, but *not* required to bring a sacrifice. If we use the requirement to bring sacrifices as a criterion indicating how serious the impurity was considered, the *zav* and the *zavah* should be expelled, together with the *metzora*, but *also* the *yoledet* and *not* the corpse-impure.

Alternatively, as a second possibility, we might consider the *length* of various impurities as our point of departure. Then the *metzora* together with the *zav* and the *zavah* ought to be expelled, since they will be impure for an indefinite period of time until their symptoms cease. From this perspective, the burial of corpses outside of settlements is logical; dead bodies contaminate for an extended period. Again, however, the *yoledet* ought to be a more serious case than the corpse-impure, since her impurity lasts 40 or 80 days, while corpse impurity only lasts for seven days, and from this perspective must be considered analogous to the impurity of a menstruant.

The third possible criterion would be *normality* as against permanent status or chronic disease. In this case, the *metzora* would again have to be expelled, but *not* the corpse-impure. The *zav* and the *zavah* would, however, be a more tricky case. Their impurity could in theory be of indefinite length, like that of the *metzora*, but in actual practice we would expect most cases of unnatural

---

[14] אֶת־מַחֲנֵיהֶם אֲשֶׁר אֲנִי שֹׁכֵן בְּתוֹכָם
[15] See chapter 3 above for further discussion and references.

discharges to be *temporary* conditions.[16] Judging from the type of cases and questions that are discussed in rabbinic literature this seems reasonable.[17] While these are discharges outside of normal semen emission or menstruation they are not necessarily permanent conditions. A criterion of normality thus yields ambiguous results: either we could expect a lenient stance that only requires the expulsion of "lepers" or we might suppose a stricter or at least ambiguous stance towards "irregular" dischargers. Neither variant of a criterion of normality ought, however, to require the expulsion of the corpse-impure.

Finally, let us consider the *contamination potency* of various impurities as a fourth possible criterion. Now the picture changes somewhat. The corpse-impure, "lepers" and dischargers all transmit a one-day impurity to persons, items,[18] food and drink. If rabbinic systematization is allowed to be taken into account we see that this transmitted impurity is understood to be in the "first remove," i.e., all of the above-mentioned impurity bearers transmit (mainly by contact) a first degree impurity to others, which may be transferred[19] to profane food (*chullin*) and liquid at one further (i.e., a second) remove, to priestly rations (*terumah*) at a third, and to sacrificial food (*qodashim*) at a fourth remove. It would be only logical to treat all these impurity bearers alike. This comes close to the strict ruling in Num 5, but still does not account for excepting the *yoledet* and the menstruant.

As we can see, most perspectives or criteria attempted so far would not require the expulsion of corpse-impure people, except for the last one, and *all* attempts to find a logical principle leave us with anomalies or ambiguities when it comes to the category of genital dischargers. While this should count as strong evidence for diverse origins of different parts of the purity legislation, and warn us against looking for a consistent system *behind* this mixed bag of ideas of impurity, our main interest here is first century practice and the logic

---

[16] Sanders suggests that most irregular bleedings were caused by miscarriages (1992, 219). To some extent, "leprosy" (today often translated by "skin/scale disease") might also be regarded as a temporary condition, since it had nothing to do with Hansen's disease, and legislation deals at length with procedures of re-integration. Possible causes would, however, suggest that symptoms of "leprosy" were generally of longer duration than irregular discharges.

[17] Many of the discussions concern how to define these discharges and distinguish them from normal semen or menstrual blood, and how to count days when defining which discharges should be seen as normal or as causing *zav/zavah* impurity. This becomes immediately evident from a quick glance at the tractates *Niddah* and *Zabim* in the *Mishnah* as well as in the *Tosefta*.

[18] In rabbinic discussion, susceptible items are mostly limited to rinsable utensils formed as receptacles; see *m. Kelim*. Cf. Wright 1987a, 94.

[19] This is never stated or implied in the biblical text. Wright states (1987a, 220) that "*a person or object that receives impurity which lasts only one day cannot pollute other persons or objects in the profane sphere*" (Wright's italics); cf. 179–219. Rabbinic texts, however, take for granted that persons with a one-day impurity may contaminate ordinary food, liquid and hands at one further remove (cf. Harrington 1993, 141–260).

behind the developments of the late Second Temple period. As we have seen in previous chapters, there is an ongoing harmonization and systematization, beginning already in the biblical text, which in one sense reaches its fulfilment in rabbinic literature, but in another sense is simultaneously undermined by rabbinic tendencies towards an increasing leniency as time goes by.[20] We thus find several principles guiding rabbinic systematization of impurity: the contamination potency of various contaminants, the degree of susceptibility (i.e., differences in capacity to receive contamination corresponding to various degrees of holiness), and a system of removes in which contamination is envisaged as a chain of contacts. These are neither clear-cut, nor clearly differentiated, but interact, and other types of systematizations are used, too.

Temple Scroll theory

Our next step is to relate this theoretical discussion of possible criteria for inclusion or expulsion to known texts and customs from the Second Temple period and see whether things get clearer by this. We begin with the *Temple Scroll*, which is known for its strict rules for the Temple city: after intercourse a man must not enter it for three days (XLV, 11) and all three categories of purifying impurity bearers (dischargers, the corpse-impure and "lepers") must stay out until the seven days of purification are over (XLV, 15–18). Three places are to be made east of the city for "lepers," dischargers and semen emitters (XLVI, 16–18). This rule is even stricter than that of Num 5.[21]

The following column (XLVII) makes it clear that the purity of the Temple city is higher than that of ordinary cities. Further on, ordinary cities are discussed: special burial grounds are prescribed for every four cities, apparently to limit the areas defiled by graves (XLVIII, 10–14). Then comes an ambiguous passage, dealing with "lepers" and dischargers (XLVIII, 14–17).[22] At first sight

---

[20] See Kazen 2002, 54, 155–156; Poirier 2003, 259–265. Although the fall of Jerusalem and the cessation of the temple cult did influence subsequent rabbinic reflection on purity, we should not, however, think that the interest in and importance of purity automatically decreased. For a nuanced critique, see Miller 2003; 2007.

[21] Several interpreters, following Yadin, suggest that the *Temple Scroll* with its strong utopian traits gives no room whatsoever for women living within the Temple city, since entrance after sexual intercourse is prohibited (XLV, 11; cf. Haber 2003, 177), but strictly speaking the restrictions would apply to women of fertile age and married couples (cf. Wassén 2008, 649–650). The extent of the "Temple city" (עיר המקדש) is crucial for interpretation: does it refer to the Temple proper (Schiffman, following Levine) or to the city in its entirety (Milgrom, following Yadin)? Sidnie White Crawford (2000, 49) attempts a compromise, suggesting that the Temple city "is not envisioned by the author/redactor of the Temple Scroll as having permanent residents, but as a place of *temporary* residents." The whole city would thus be looked upon as a Temple area for visiting pilgrims and cultic personnel, with God as the only permanent resident.

[22] This text is quoted and discussed in detail in Kazen 2002, 157–159.

the preposition ב seems to indicate the presence of these two categories within cities (ובכול עיר ועיר), but this cannot be the case, since the purpose of making places for "lepers" (תעשו מקומות למנוגעים בצרעת ובנגע ובנתק) is explicitly stated to be to prevent them from *entering* the cities and defiling them (אשר לוא יבואו לעריכמה וטמאום). "In every city" must thus be taken to include the surrounding country. While a similar treatment (גם ל-) is indicated for male and female dischargers, menstruants and parturients (לזבים ולנשים בהיותמה בנדת טמאתמה ובלדתמה), the purpose in their case is expressed as preventing them from "defiling in their midst" (אשר לוא יטמאו בתוכם).[23] This *could* possibly be read as if dischargers were supposed to be *secluded within* settlements rather than expelled, like "lepers." The most *natural* reading, however, is that both categories were supposed to *stay outside*. This rule comes close to that of Num 5 but is stricter since it explicitly expels menstruants and parturients, too. In the next column (XLIX), however, we find the rule more lenient, since the corpse-impure are not supposed to be expelled but assumed to stay within cities.

When we relate the instructions of the *Temple Scroll* to the four criteria discussed above, we find all those who are required to offer a sacrifice (first criterion) expelled from the ordinary city – but also the menstruant. We find all seven-day impurity bearers expelled (second criterion) – except for the corpse-impure. A distinction between normality and chronic disease (third criterion) gives no explanation. Contamination potential (fourth criterion) seems at first not to account for the omission of the corpse-impure. I would, however, claim that it did in the thought world of the authors and recipients of the *Temple Scroll*. The secret lies in the post-biblical requirement of an initial first-day ablution (and washing of clothes), which is clearly outlined in the *Temple Scroll*:

> And as for persons, anyone who was in the house and anyone who entered the house shall bathe in water and wash his clothes on the first day; and on the third day they shall sprinkle over them water of impurity, and they shall bathe, and was their clothing and the vessels that are in the house. And on the seventh day they shall sprinkle a second time, and they shall bathe and wash their clothes and their vessels, and by evening they will become clean of the dead, (and may be allowed) to touch all their pure stuff.[24]

> And he shall wash his clothes and bathe himself on the first day; and on the third day he shall sprinkle and wash his clothes and bathe himself; and on the seventh day he shall sprinkle for the second time and wash his clothes and bathe himself, and at the going down of the sun he will become clean.[25]

---

[23] The concluding נדת טמאתם in the full phrase אשר לוא יטמאו בתוכם בנדת טמאתם must be understood generally as "defilement of their impurity" rather than as referring specifically to menstruation.

[24] 11QTᵃ XLIX, 16–21, transl. Yadin 1983.

[25] 11QTᵃ L, 13–16, transl. Yadin 1983.

This extra rite was somehow thought to "peel away" the most aggressive layer of corpse impurity, although it did not shorten its duration, and provides some explanation for the position of the *Temple Scroll.*[26]

We cannot know to what extent any of the detailed requirements of the *Temple Scroll* were practised in actual societies at the end of the Second Temple period. The exclusion of dischargers cannot be dismissed by arguments from common sense, however; a number of groups through history, known from texts but also from living examples, did adhere to strict rules of isolation and/or expulsion of such people.[27] Poverty or practical considerations (from our perspective) seem not to have caused any obstruction to strict practices. When it comes to first-day ablutions for the corpse-impure, there is compelling evidence from other sources, as we will see below.

The *Temple Scroll* is at least in part idealist or utopian. Although not sectarian, but representing one type of a more general expansionist viewpoint,[28] its many rules on sacrificial matters could not have been realized unless its adherents were in power in Jerusalem. This does not, however, exclude the possibility that purity rules regarding the ordinary city might have represented more general practices of a larger segment of Second Temple society and could have been applied where these views were in favour.[29]

Philo and corpse impurity

A first-day ablution after corpse impurity seems to have been generally practised during Second Temple times.[30] In a section about those offering sacrifices, Philo discusses necessary purifications.

> Regarding the body, as I said, it [the law] purifies it by washings and sprinklings (λουτροῖς καὶ περιρραντηρίοις), and does not allow one who has sprinkled or bathed himself once (περιρρανάμενον εἰς ἅπαξ ἢ ἀπολουσάμενον) to immediately (εὐθὺς) pass inside of the temple enclosures, but it orders him to wait for seven days and be sprinkled twice (δὶς περιρραίνεσθαι) on the third and seventh, and after that, when he has bathed (λουσαμένῳ), it allows him both to enter and do his service without fear.[31]

---

[26] Milgrom 1978, 512–518. Cf. Baumgarten 1992, 205–206; Eshel 1999, 138; Regev 2000, 177–181. Regev calls this "gradual purification."

[27] In addition to evidence from Qumran texts, these include among others Samaritans, Karaites and Falashas. For further references, see Milgrom 1991, 765; Kazen 2002, 72, n.187, 159–160.

[28] The date of the *Temple Scroll* before the founding of the Qumran community and its affinity with other pseudepigraphic literature point to a general expansionist or "maximalist" stance. See Crawford 2008, 88, 92–93.

[29] Milgrom 1991, 968–971; Harrington 1993, 55–58.

[30] Kazen 2002, 185–189.

[31] *Spec. Laws* 1:261.

In another context, discussing injury to the point of possible murder, Philo touches on the same issue:

> ... so that even those having touched a dead body that admittedly had died naturally, cannot presumably become clean immediately (εὐθύς), before they are purified by sprinkling and bathing (περιρρανάμενοι καὶ ἀπολουσάμενοι καθαρθῶσιν). He did not even allow the very clean (τοῖς σφόδρα καθαροῖς) to enter into the temple within seven days, having ordered them to sanctify on the third and the seventh. Further, he ordered even those entering a house in which someone had died to touch nothing until they had bathed themselves (ἀπολούσωνται) and washed the clothes they were wearing.[32]

It is clear from the first of these texts that Philo thinks of an initial cleansing, whether by sprinkling or bathing, which does not suffice for a temple visit. It is also clear from the second that immediate full purification from corpse impurity is impossible; although one can apparently become "very clean" (σφόδρα καθαροῖς) at once, this does not qualify for a temple visit. Even entrance into a house of a deceased person renders a person unclean and necessitates bathing and washing of clothes, presumably as soon as possible, since touching anything would have been prohibited until this rite had been carried out. This certainly implies a first-day rite also for those who have touched a corpse directly, which is also assumed in the first text.

It has been argued that by λουτροῖς καὶ περιρραντηρίοις Philo is describing a domestic diaspora ritual of sprinkling, which developed from pagan influence and was used independently of any temple visit. Those having undergone such a ritual would have been considered pure, although not allowed into the temple. Still, such a rite was practised, because Jews in general saw purity as part of piety.[33] Although I have no problem with the idea that Jewish purity practices were shaped and developed by influences from surrounding cultures, I find that Philo gives evidence for more than a domestic diaspora rite. It rather seems to me that Philo attests to a widespread practice of an extra first-day ablution.[34] To what extent such a first-day ablution might have been practised independently of subsequent purifications on the third and seventh day in Alexandria may remain an open question. I cannot see, however, that this first-day ablution is being separated from the rest of the rite in the two passages above.

What the terminology does suggest is that both sprinkling and bathing were involved, and at least the first passage indicates that *neither* sprinkling *nor* bathing on the first day were considered sufficient for entering the temple *immediately*; a full seven-day period was required. The alternatives for an extra first-day ablution – sprinkling or bathing – are highly interesting, not least in view of

---

[32] *Spec. Laws* 3:205–206.
[33] Sanders 1992, 263–271.
[34] Cf. Regev 2000, 177–181.

the fact that rabbis, Karaites and Samaritans at times disagree on whether immersion is required or mere washing suffices.[35] While we may expect varying practices at the end of the Second Temple period, some sort of first-day ablution must be assumed, and the second passage from Philo suggests bathing. Such a practice may be implied already in Ezek 44:25–26, and in Tob 2:5, 9 it is definitely presupposed.[36] In addition to the *Temple Scroll*, the fragmentary 4Q414 mentions it explicitly, and the idea is implied by 1QM XIV, 2–3.[37] Samaritan texts take it for granted.[38] Together with Philo, these texts represent a broad variety of traditions. We should consider a first-day water rite neither particularly sectarian, nor only a diaspora invention. It could have developed through outside influences and it may have been applied in various ways. It fits with evidence for people coming to Jerusalem one week in advance of Passover.[39]

For our present purpose we need not decide whether the ashes of the red heifer were available outside of Jerusalem[40] and to what extent the full seven-day rite could have been employed in Galilee or in the diaspora. The point is to show that a first-day ablution was generally practised (whether in view of temple visits or not), and considered somehow to mitigate or lessen corpse impurity. Such a practice makes it possible to explain how a tradition of containing the corpse-impure within settlements and a relatively strict stance, related to the command in Num 5, could be mitigated at the end of the Second Temple period. From a perspective of contamination potency a first-day ablution could make it possible for the corpse-impure to remain, without compromising a strict understanding of the command.

Josephus and the menstruant

As argued above, a focus on contamination potency would result in the exclusion of *all* genital dischargers, as the *Temple Scroll* seems to demand according to the most probable interpretation. Josephus, however, seems to come closer to the alternative reading of the *Temple Scroll*. In *Ant.* 3:261 Josephus states that

> [Moses] expelled (ἀπήλασε) from the city both those who were sick with *lepra* and those with genital discharges; also the women who the natural flux came over, he set

---

[35] Bóid 1989a, 332–336.
[36] A discussion of differences between various Hebrew, Aramaic and Greek versions, suggesting that they are due to differences in opinion concerning sunset and bathing, is found in Bóid 1989a, 321–322.
[37] Here the context is that of battle. The idea of a first-day washing is probably present in 4Q514 as well, this time with reference to dischargers. See below for further discussion of this text.
[38] *Kitâb al-Kâfi* III [43]; XIII [11-13]; Bóid 1989a, 153–154, 242–243, 324.
[39] Josephus, *J. W.* 6:290; John 11:55. Sanders (1992, 132–135 and notes) explains how Josephus' counting is evidence for the same waiting period.
[40] Cf. Baumgarten 1995b.

aside (μετέστησε) until the seventh day, after which he allowed [them] to live in their place (ἐνδημεῖν) as already pure. Similarly also for those attending a dead [person], after so many days [he allowed them] legitimately to live in their place (ἐνδημεῖν).

It is quite clear that Josephus makes a difference between "lepers" and *zavim* on the one hand (expulsion) and menstruants and the corpse-impure on the other (seclusion, isolation). Sanders points to this distinction when discussing this and other passages from Josephus,[41] but in the end he concludes that "Josephus here probably reflects the rules which he and his kind – the aristocratic priesthood – followed" while "[p]eople who occupied small houses could not have lived in the same way."[42] The argument is mainly practical. Other arguments against Josephus describing contemporary practice claim that he is only commenting on the text, thinking of the time of Moses or talking of an ideal.[43] Of this, however, I am not easily convinced.

While a certain amount of idealization must be expected from Josephus, I find his statement here fully in line with other passages where he deals with this issue, such as *J. W.* 5:227: "to dischargers and 'lepers' the whole city on one hand (μὲν) and to menstruating women the temple on the other hand (τὸ δ᾽ ἱερὸν) was closed (ἀπεκέκλειστο)." This evidently means that menstruating women were not allowed into any of the temple courts and fits with the statement in *Ag. Ap.* 2:103 (only preserved in Latin) that the outer court was open to everybody, including foreigners, but excepting menstruants.

All of these references from Josephus, including *Ant.* 3:261, should be understood as referring to Jerusalem.[44] Menstruants and the corpse-impure are envisaged *within* the city, but subject to restrictions. "Lepers" and *zavim* are kept *out*. This comes close to the rules of the *Temple Scroll* for the *ordinary* city, although in the *Temple Scroll* the same rule applies to *all* dischargers, whether we understand them as supposed to be expelled from or secluded within cities. Deviating opinions probably depend on how different spheres of holiness are understood and how the temple city is defined; *m. Kelim* 1:6–9, outlining ten degrees of holiness, is evidence for this. The first degree is the land of Israel (1:6). The second degree consists of cities surrounded by a wall; they are considered more holy than the land, because lepers are not allowed inside (1:7). While the wall of Jerusalem demarcates a third degree, it is not associated with any further exclusion of impurity bearers. The fourth degree,

---

[41] Sanders 1992, 157–160.
[42] Sanders 1992, p 160.
[43] Sanders 1992, 157; Maccoby 1999, 36; cf. Kazen 2002, 113–114, 156.
[44] In *Ant.* 3:261 this is not explicitly stated, but Josephus talks of the "city" in the singular.

however, is defined by the Temple mount, where no discharger, whether *zav*, *zavah*, menstruant or parturient, is allowed (1:8).[45]

We cannot trust the schematized and systematic lists introducing the *Seder Tohoroth* to provide an accurate picture of first century practice. They do, however, give us clues as to the kind of logic that might have been involved. It should be noted that all extant texts discussed so far suggest *stricter* practices of exclusion and/or seclusion than those implied by *m. Kelim* 1. The *Temple Scroll* assumes ascending degrees of holiness, too, but seems to have moved holiness "one step forward" or impurity "one step back," depending on the stance we prefer to take.

Coming back to Josephus, we noted that he seemingly placed the corpse-impure and menstruants on the same level, within Jerusalem, but subject to restrictions. The *Temple Scroll* thinks of both outside of Jerusalem, but when it comes to the ordinary city the corpse-impure person is allowed within, while the menstruant is probably placed outside, together with other dischargers. The rabbis seemingly think of the corpse-impure person as even allowed within the court of gentiles (*m. Kelim* 1:8)! In the latter case we must definitely reckon with a first-day ablution, lessening the power of corpse impurity, as taken for granted; just as such a rite explains the presence of the corpse-impure person within the ordinary city of the stricter *Temple Scroll*, it is needed to explain his presence in the court of gentiles, according to much more lenient rabbinic views. We must ask, however, whether Josephus' *equal* treatment of the corpse-impure and menstruants may be similarly explained by systemic reasoning.

A mitigating water rite?

Looking at the four possible criteria discussed earlier, we find that according to the first three, sacrifice, length and normality, corpse impurity and menstruation are equal: both require no sacrifice, both last for seven days from their inception, and both are parts of the natural cycle of life and death. Remains the fourth criterion, contamination potency. The obvious question to ask is whether a mitigating rite for menstruants, similar to that of a first-day ablution for corpse-impure, may have existed.

The suggestion has been raised before by Milgrom and Baumgarten, who suggest the presence in Qumran of a first-day purificatory rite not only for corpse impurity but for other cases, too.[46] Milgrom refers to 4Q514, which is quoted and discussed in detail in chapter 4. As I have argued above, this text

---

[45] This is quite different from the view of 4QMMT B 60–62, which seems to regard the whole of Jerusalem as the innermost camp, the head of the camps of Israel, as compared to other cities.
[46] Milgrom 1995, 67; Baumgarten 2000.

gives evidence for an initial purificatory rite for dischargers in general, to enable them to eat in some intermediate state of purity during their seven-day purificatory period. We have also mentioned Baumgarten's arguments from other texts for the general use of purification water (מי נדה) in Qumran, not only for removing corpse impurity but also for all sorts of impurities, not least those caused by discharges,[47] although these texts do not refer particularly to an initial first-day water rite. Baumgarten also provides a few non-Qumran references supporting an extended use of sprinkling for general purification.[48]

Although some of the evidence just mentioned is capable of varying interpretations and may be disputed, the "expansion of ritual washing to new uses not known in the Hebrew Bible"[49] was a general expansionist phenomenon during the Second Temple period, not at all restricted to Qumran, and this development served the purpose of mitigating impurity through graded purification. Several texts from Qumran reflect a broader expansionist movement and even sectarian texts often reveal presuppositions that were more generally held. This can be seen especially in 4Q274 1 i, 1–9, which has been the focus of discussion in chapter 4. As I have argued there, this fragment is further evidence for ideas of graded or intermediate impurity being present throughout the Second Temple period. The text suggests, similar to what is found in Samaritan *halakah*, some sort of first-day water rite for menstruants, in order to wash off the first (*niddah*) blood, which is considered to contaminate by contact with a seven-day impurity. This would have been equivalent to the first-day ablution for the corpse-impure that became common during Second Temple times. We thus have some evidence for practices of graded purification, which would have made it possible to equate menstruation and corpse impurity from a first century perspective focused on contamination potency.

Dischargers in real life

What conclusions are we to draw so far? What practice was adhered to at the end of the Second Temple period? To what extent were dischargers expelled or restricted?

The answer partly depends on who were in charge. Those behind the *Temple Scroll* were hardly in power in Jerusalem, so we should not expect their views to have been in force there. It is entirely possible, however, that all dischargers

---

[47] 4Q277 1 ii, 8–9; 4Q512; 4Q284, frg. 1; 4Q272 1 ii; 1QS III, 4–5. Baumgarten 2000.

[48] I.e., from *Sifre Zuta*; Philo, *Spec. Laws* 3:63 (Philo uses the same terminology that he does when he discusses corpse impurity); *Baraita de Maseket Niddah*; 4Q272, 277 and 278 (where *zav* impurity and corpse impurity are juxtaposed).

[49] Cf. Lawrence 2006, quote from p. 189.

were required to stay out of some other towns or villages where such strict views were dominant. It is also quite probable that groups of people adhering to such rules tried themselves to implement them even if others did not. Such diversity would, of course, cause problems that had to be met by extra precautions, and this is exactly the kind of situation we find at the end of the Second Temple period. Practices such as immersion before meals, hand-washing, and voluntary associations may be partly explained by the fact that people lived by differing standards or according to differing degrees of consistency within one and the same society. While agreeing on basic facts and rules, diversity in interpretation and application necessitated special arrangements by those most concerned.

There is no reason to regard Josephus as more utopian or idealist than the *Mishnah*, especially in view of a notable tendency towards increasing leniency on the part of the Rabbis after the fall of the temple. Menstruants would in any case have been allowed inside Jerusalem, although according to Josephus they were somehow quarantined, and we have suggested one possible explanation that could have made this acceptable even for those taking a strict stance.[50] Concerning the *zav* and the *zavah* I am more inclined to trust Josephus for first century practice than *m. Kelim* 1, but this also depends on which area of Jerusalem the city was thought to embrace.[51] If nevertheless within the city walls, *zavim* were probably subject to severe restrictions, in view of the stance reflected by Josephus that they should not really have been there.

In other places the *zav* and the *zavah* probably lived inside the town or village, but subject to restrictions; in places where expansionists such as those behind the *Temple Scroll* dominated, they may even have been expelled, or their presence would at least have been questioned. The evidence of *m. Nid.* 7:4, suggesting the existence of a special place for seclusion should not be too easily disregarded; there is no room to discuss it here, but I have dealt with the manuscript evidence and *Tosefta*'s misinterpretation elsewhere.[52] As I have indicated above, evidence for seclusion or restriction should not be dismissed by arguments from poverty, especially not when analogies can be found.

Where dischargers receive a fuller differentiation, the *zavah* appears near the top of the list, above the *zav* and next to the "leper," bone and corpse (*m. Kelim*

---

[50] The *yoledet* (parturient) should be included with the menstruant, although not mentioned by Josephus. She is in most respects likened to the menstruant: in Lev 12 her case is modelled on that of the menstruant, her discharge is natural and, like the menstruant, her contamination potency lasts for seven days (after the birth of a boy), although this is followed by a further period of lesser potency (and doubled in the case of a girl).

[51] Cf. 4QMMT B 60–62; see above, n. 45.

[52] Kazen 2002, 160, see especially n. 371. Cf. Sanders 1990, 155–156.

1:4). The *zav* seems to have one advantage: according to Lev 15:11 he contaminates others by touching them with unwashed hands. This implies that he might touch others without contaminating them if his hands have been washed. Nothing, however, is explicitly stated anywhere about mitigating the touch of a *zavah*. While systemic reading and equalization at the end of the Second Temple period usually meant that touching and being touched by any discharger was considered all the same in principle,[53] the *zav* who had washed his hands may have been the exception in actual practice; although heavily damaged, 4Q277 seems to confirm Lev 15:11.[54] This would have left the *zavah* as the most vulnerable among all the dischargers. As long as irregular bleeding continued, her contamination potency could not be lessened by any first-day rite, as suggested in the case of the menstruant. I am not arguing that the *zavah* was expelled from ordinary towns, only that she must have been subject to restrictions and that she was "worse off" than any other impurity bearer, except for the "leper."

The *Zavah* in Mark

In Mark 5:24b–34 Jesus is pictured as being approached and touched by a *zavah*. The narrative is sandwiched into a healing story in which Jesus revives the dead daughter of Jairus. While some have tried do deny a purity issue in the text,[55] the particular expressions alluding to the LXX text of Leviticus exclude any doubts concerning a relationship between the Markan narrative and purity legislation.[56] The expression ῥύσις αἵματος for "blood flow" (Mark 5:25; Lev 15:19, 25) is not ordinary Greek for vaginal bleeding, and the frequent use of ἅπτεσθαι both in Mark 5 and Lev 15 is also conspicuous, as is the expression ἡ πηγή τοῦ αἵματος (Mark 5:29), which comes from Lev 12:7 (cf. Lev 20:18). Judged from the language, the Markan narrative intentionally alludes to Lev 15, but in spite of this Mark makes no explicit point of it.[57]

Why does Mark fail to address the purity issue explicitly when he does so elsewhere? In the narrative of the "leper" (1:40–45), purity language is used similarly, but the purity issue is *explicit*, even including instructions for purification and references to the Law of Moses. The additional instruction about

---

[53] For further discussion and references, see chapter 3 above, or Kazen 2007. This is different from Wassén 2008, who argues for harmonization but claims a distinction between touching and being touched by an impurity bearer.

[54] 4Q277 1 ii, 10–11: "And anyone touched by [a man who has] a flux [   ] [and whose] hand[s were not] r[in]sed in water becomes [unclean]" (tr. Baumgarten 1999, 116).

[55] Kahl 1996; D'Angelo 1999. Arguments against a purity issue in the Markan texts are often arguments against particular feminist interpretations with anti-Jewish nuances.

[56] See further Kazen 2002, 132–136.

[57] Haber 2008, 132–133.

bringing the sacrifice "for your purification which Moses stipulated" (προσένεγκε περὶ τοῦ καθαρισμοῦ σου ἅ προσέταξεν Μωϋςῆς) would not be necessary if the recipients were able to grasp the details of Jewish purity law without assistance. Since, however, the purity issue is unavoidably constitutive for this narrative – an understanding of "lepers" as impure would have been common knowledge, and purification is used synonymously with healing – this is the sort of information that an author would need to provide for a not-too-well-informed audience, mainly consisting of gentiles with little understanding of the legal details of Jewish law. Similarly, in the hand-washing narrative in Mark 7, to which we will turn in the following chapter, the author explains legal details for the sake of his audience. He has hardly begun his story before he interrupts himself to explain the expression "with unclean hands" (κοιναῖς χερσίν) by "unwashed." Then he inserts a lengthy explanation about Pharisaic and Jewish or Judean purificatory water rites before eating (7:2–4) as if his audience would be more or less unaware of these. Later in the same narrative the author finds it necessary to explain *qorban* (7:11). In the narrative of the *zavah*, nothing like this is present. The reason is that Mark's primary concern in the text lies elsewhere, and is intent on healing and christology.[58]

We always have to ask ourselves at what level we envisage different traits of a text. While it is safe to say that allusions to Lev 15 exist in the Greek text, we should not thereby suppose that they would be apparent to *Markan* readership, or to *Mark's* audience that elsewhere needs to be informed about Jewish practices and Jewish laws. A plausible explanation will be found by considering the *zavah* narrative a pre-Markan tradition, incorporated by Mark. This would explain why a number of traits and details are clearly present while not exploited by the author. Furthermore, the tradition must have reached Mark in written form and in Greek. There are good arguments for assuming this. It has long been observed that the language of this narrative is somewhat exceptional; participles abound in a way that is unusual for Mark.[59] While it might be argued that this could be due to Mark's formation of a sandwich construction, the language of the middle sections of other Markan sandwiches do not support this idea. Mark's composition technique alone cannot satisfactorily explain the Greek of the *zavah* narrative. The different character of this narrative as compared to the surrounding narrative of Jairus' daughter strongly suggests that the

---

[58] Kazen 2002, 132–136, 172–174; D'Angelo 1999, 91–102; Haber 2003. These aspects are being developed in Kazen 2011c, forthcoming.

[59] Cf. Taylor 1966, 289. Taylor points out that in vv. 25–27 we find a rare example in Mark of a longer Greek period, with several subordinated participles. In addition to this, the intercalation uses the past tense in contrast to the Jairus narrative, which is mainly in the present tense except for the transition passages. Cf. Theissen 1983, 180–182.

sandwich construction is not pre-Markan but a Markan trait. This judgement is further strengthened by the frequency of such constructions in Mark. Had Mark received this narrative as an oral tradition in Aramaic we would neither have expected this Greek, nor these allusions to purity legislation that seem redundant and risk blurring Mark's focus.

This would mean that the purity issue, including the allusions to Lev 15 (LXX), belonged to and were grasped by an *earlier* audience to a Greek pre-Markan tradition, but not necessarily by the *Markan* audience. While a pre-Markan audience would have been able to relate the narrative of the "leper" with the narrative of the *zavah* – although we do not know whether they would have had access to both in close proximity to each other – a Markan audience would rather have understood other points concerning faith and healing. Mark in facts sandwiches two narratives that both have implicit purity issues, but only for the purpose of letting the *faith* of the since-twelve-year sick woman spill over onto the father of the twelve-year-old daughter, all within a christological framework. The question of what happened to the purity of Jesus when touched by the *zavah* is thus to be seen as a hypothetical *pre-Markan* question, which is not further discussed or answered on the *Markan* level.

While the pre-Markan tradition can be used as a small piece of evidence for tracing the behaviour of the historical Jesus, it says little about Mark and his audience. When he wishes them to consider purity issues he tells them – and then usually for the explicit purpose of bringing out theological and christological points. We may even question whether he really wishes his audience to consider such issues at all, or whether it is rather the details of his tradition that force him to provide necessary explanations for his relatively uninformed recipients?

It is true that there is an implicit purity issue in the enveloping narrative, too. The dead daughter of Jairus would transmit corpse impurity to anyone entering the house, which is precisely what Jesus does. This is not commented on by Mark, however, who portrays Jesus and his disciples as entering together with the parents. In Luke's version one might even get the impression of the mourners being inside, while Matthew has carefully redacted the story so that only Jesus goes in after having dismissed the mourners. At the risk of over-interpretation, I would suggest that Matthew is sensitive to purity issues in a way that Mark is not. While Mark must be aware of the potential question concerning corpse impurity – since he displays a certain knowledge of purity law elsewhere for the benefit of his readers – it is of no concern to him here, since his audience would not raise it and his own focus is elsewhere. While the two narratives in the sandwich construction are brought together by Mark, this is not because of the purity issue that can be found in both of them, but because of the motif of faith. The purity issue could have been relevant at a pre-Markan stage, but then the two narratives would most likely not have been intertwined in this way.

If an underlying Greek pre-Markan *zavah* narrative is accepted, it must have originated in a Greek-speaking Jewish-Christian diaspora context where the LXX was used and purity laws were known, and it probably had earlier roots. While the Markan narrative emphasizes the miraculous aspect of touch, it is difficult to avoid the impression that an underlying narrative assumed that the woman's behaviour was unacceptable particularly in view of her status, which would then explain her fearful reaction. While this narrative gives us no details about the precise halakic status of women with long-term discharges, it does confirm the general picture of the *zavah* as a most vulnerable category at the end of the Second Temple period.

Conclusions

In this chapter I have argued that the *zavah* became one of the most problematic categories in Second Temple Judaism. Although she was supposed to be expelled from settlements according to the strict tradition of Num 5, she would, like other dischargers, in reality most often have lived within towns and villages, but in contrast to the others with few means to mitigate her impurity.

We have seen that the exclusion of "lepers" is a fairly clear issue; it is demanded both by Lev 13–14 and Num 5 and as we have seen above the practice is attested by numerous texts from the gospels, Qumran and Josephus.[60] Later rabbinic leniency cannot automatically be claimed for first century practice.[61] The call of the "leper" had the intent of no contact whatsoever[62] and even the purifying "leper" must keep a certain distance to what is pure during the seven-day purification period.[63]

The question of corpse impurity is a bit more complex. The very fact that a purification rite is described in Num 19 suggests that people are expected to become contaminated, and in spite of Num 5, we have seen that although

---

[60] Mark 1:40–45; Luke 17:11–19; Josephus *Ag. Ap.* 1:281; *Ant.* 3:264; 4QMMT B 64–72; 4Q274 1 i, 1–4; 11QT[a] XLVI, 16–18; XLVIII, 14–17.

[61] *m. Kelim* 1:7. A walled city then became defined as one surrounded by walls from the time of Joshua, *m. 'Arak.* 9:6. A development towards an even greater leniency (restrictions only applicable during the Jubilee) is suggested by *b. 'Arak.* 29a.

[62] Lev 13:45; 4Q274 1 i, 3–4; *b. Soṭah* 32b; *b. Šabb.* 67a; *b. B. Qam.* 92b; *b. Ḥul.* 78a; *b. Nid.* 66a; *b. Mo'ed Qaṭ.* 5a. Many of the talmudic references apply Lev 13:45 secondarily to other issues.

[63] Lev 14:8–9; 4QMMT B 64–72; 4Q274 1 i, 1–2.

corpses were removed from settlements, corpse-impure people were generally not expelled during the Second Temple period.[64] This is natural, in a sense, since most people died at home, which by necessity caused a number of other people within that settlement to contract corpse impurity. Even the very strict and somewhat utopian *Temple Scroll* allows the corpse-impure within ordinary cities.[65] This is made acceptable by a first-day ablution, which lessened the virility of corpse impurity and became common practice in late Second Temple Judaism, as reflected in, or suggested by, texts from Ezekiel, Tobit, Qumran, Philo, Josephus and the Gospel of John. In spite of conflicting views, all sources agree on the presence of the corpse-impure within ordinary cities or settlements.

The status of dischargers constitutes the most difficult case. We have seen that according to the most probable reading, the *Temple Scroll* follows Num 5 in demanding a similar treatment of dischargers as it does of "lepers," even for the ordinary city, including menstruants and parturients.[66] This is the most extreme among the positions found in contemporary texts, and cannot represent general practice. Josephus' picture of long-term dischargers not being allowed in Jerusalem, while menstruants (and probably parturients) were accepted under certain circumstances, has more to speak for it. As for the ordinary city I have suggested that dischargers were usually allowed within, but they would have been circumscribed by restrictions.

As we have noted, healed "lepers" were allowed into settlements after an initial purification and the corpse-impure could stay thanks to an initial ablution, although in both cases there are indications that they were not supposed to stay inside their homes. As I have argued in the previous chapter, it is quite possible that menstruants similarly employed a first-day water rite, washing off the first menstrual *niddah* blood, similar to what is described in Samaritan *halakah* and indicated by 4Q274 1 i, 7–8a. As for the *zav*, we have mentioned the biblical provision of temporarily lessening his contamination potency by handwashing. We have also noted the lack of evidence for this provision being extended to the *zavah*. While it is reasonable to think of an initial ablution for *zavim* and *zavot after* the cessation of symptoms, analogous to that of menstruants, hand-washing for a *zav during* his indefinite period of full impurity seems

---

[64] Cf. Kazen 2002, 177–179.

[65] As we have seen above, the corpse-impure are not mentioned among those quarantined outside of ordinary cities (XLVIII, 13–17) although they are envisaged outside of the Temple city (11QT^a XLV, 17). Similarly, Philo thinks of the corpse-impure staying out of sacred areas (*Spec. Laws* 1:261; 3:205–206), while Josephus suggests that they were somehow isolated within Jerusalem during their purificatory period (*Ant.* 3:261).

[66] See above for the possible but less probably reading of XLVIII, 14–17 that dischargers were supposed to be secluded within settlements rather than expelled.

to have allowed for temporary and limited contact, facilitating social interaction although not affecting his *general status.*

Without this kind of possibility, the *zavah* would have been the most vulnerable and serious case of all the dischargers, as indicated in the list of impurities in *m. Kelim* 1:4, where she is mentioned towards the end, only next to the "leper," the bone and the corpse. The status of the *zavah* towards the end of the Second Temple period is thus to be understood as more severe than that of other dischargers, close to that of a "leper." She was certainly subject to restrictions, in many instances probably isolated,[67] and in some locations where strict interpretations were favoured perhaps even excluded – although I think this would have been exceptional. She could probably not take recourse to a mitigating water rite to lessen her contamination potency even temporarily.

---

[67] The evidence for and arguments against a special place of seclusion for impure women cannot be discussed here. Cf. Kazen 2002, 160, especially n. 371.

Chapter 6

Hand-washing, Pure Food and Graded Purification: *Mishnah*, Mark and Jesus

Introduction

In previous chapters we have touched upon hand-washing as a way to mitigate the contagion of an impurity bearer, in particular the *zav*. The *zav* is actually the only example in the Pentateuch of a layperson washing hands separately for the sake of purity, as pointed out by Booth.[1] This is, however, a different practice with another purpose than hand-washing before meals. The latter became a means to lessen secondary impurities in order to make it possible for people to eat ordinary meals in purity. To this issue we will turn in the present chapter.

The issue of hand-washing before meals in order to eat ordinary food (*chullin*) in purity has received much attention through more than a century of scholarship and opinions vary considerably.[2] The motives behind hand-washing before eating *chullin* are obscure. I will not attempt a history of research but only mention the most common positions. The supposition that the *Mishnah* reflects first century custom was questioned already by Büchler, who suggested that hand-washing for ordinary food was practised only by a few at the time of the temple.[3] Alon, on the other hand, claimed that hand-washing was fairly common before the destruction of the temple, although the eating of defiled *chullin* was not forbidden.[4] Neusner's opinion that the Pharisees ate ordinary food in purity in emulation of priestly practice has become influential.[5] This has been a point of dissent between him and Sanders who, in spite of opposing this view, comes very close by admitting that Pharisees made minor symbolic gestures towards living like priests.[6]

---

[1] Booth 1986, 157.
[2] See Büchler 1906; Alon 1977 (English translation of a Hebrew collection of articles published during the 1950's in Hebrew after the death of the author. The articles relevant here were first published in *Tarbiz* in 1937–1938); Neusner 1971; 1979; Westerholm 1978; Hübner 1986; Booth 1986; Tomson 1988; Sanders 1990; 1992; Harrington 1993; Deines 1993; Maccoby 1999; Regev 2000; Kazen 2002; Poirier 2003; Crossley 2004.
[3] Büchler 1906, 96–157.
[4] Alon 1977, 190–234.
[5] Neusner 1974–1977, 22:106, 108; Neusner 1971, 3:288; Neusner 1979, 14.
[6] Sanders 1990, 131–254, see particularly 192.

One of the key issues is whether hand-washing before eating *chullin* had developed and become accepted among ordinary people, or was even practised commonly among Pharisees, at the end of the Second Temple period. The evidence for a contemporary view on the separate impurity of hands is not unambiguous; arguments in any direction have to depend on reconstruction through a discriminate use of sources that is not primarily geared towards answering the question that lies in the back of the minds of at least a good number of participants in the debate: in view of Mark 7, was hand-washing practised at the time of Jesus?

In his 1986 study, after having provided a possible historical and legal context for hand-washing at the time of Jesus, Booth first seems to end up with conclusions similar to those of Sanders: such a practice before the eating of *chullin* would have been of no use unless people practised regular immersions, which we cannot assume, i.e., the ordinary Jew was usually unclean. Hence the question of the Pharisees concerning hand-washing is not credible at the time of Jesus.[7] Since then, however, truth has moved and we have come to learn that regular immersions were part and parcel of everyday life for not an insignificant segment of the population, even though Mark's enumeration of practices applying to "all Jews" must be an exaggeration. Evidence is provided not least by archaeology: *miqvaot* and stone vessels attest not only a wide-spread practice of regular immersions in Herodian days, but also high ambitions for keeping purity laws in everyday life.[8] Evidence also comes from comparisons between rabbinic texts and texts from Qumran, showing that the defiling force of liquids and the concept of *tevul yom* were live issues and causes for dissent between various groups in Second Temple times.[9] To this we will return below. Within such a picture there is room for a practice of separate purification of hands, although the identification of certain stone vessels with measuring cups used for hand cleansing and presumably conforming to rabbinic standards, has been seriously questioned and should not be pressed as an argument.[10] While it is true that these vessels diminished in use after the destruction of the Temple, this is

---

[7] Booth 1986, 185–187. Booth admittedly does not stop there, but then considers hand-washing as a supererogatory act, practised by the *chaverim*, and concludes that the Pharisaic question is credible provided that the Pharisees in question were *chaverim*.

[8] Some of the important publications are Mazar 1975; Avigad 1984 (1980); Sanders 1990, 214–227; 1992, 222–230 (on *miqva'ot*); Deines 1993 and Magen 2002 (on stone vessels); not to speak of Reich, who has written numerous articles, in addition to his Hebrew dissertation 1990 (e.g., 1988; 1989; 1993; 2000; 2002). However, a large number of participants have joined the debate. For an overview with references, see Reed 2000, especially 43–55; Miller 2003; 2007; Adler 2009.

[9] Baumgarten 1980; Sanders 1990, 36–37; Schiffman 1994; Kazen 2002, 72–85; Crossley 2004, 193–200.

[10] Reed 2003, 388–389.

probably more due to the demise of stone and building industry after the fall of Jerusalem than to a change in purity practices; purity in no way lost importance in the period after 70 CE, as sometimes suggested.[11] This is no argument, however, against the practical function of stone vessels for preventing impurity and this probably contributed to their original spread.[12]

In recent years, a number of scholars have combined archaeological and textual data to argue that purity was increasingly observed towards the end of the Second Temple period, including purificatory rites such as immersion and hand-washing.[13] In this chapter I will argue, as I have done previously,[14] that it is reasonable to suppose that the practice described by Mark in 7:1–5 was advocated by expansionist groups at the time of Jesus. I have elsewhere suggested that what distinguished expansionists from ordinary people was not necessarily observance as compared to non-observance, but the former's consistency and strict interpretation.[15] I would also like to suggest that the description of eating ordinary food in purity as "priestly" is an anachronistic interpretative description. The practices in question rather result from a general ambition for as high a degree of purity as possible, which was promoted by expansionist interests and won increasing acceptance among people at large.

Hand-washing for secondary impurities

As we have seen in previous chapters, first century Jews were able to combine a high degree of concern for purity with common sense practical solutions, by mitigating or lessening the contamination potency of *impurity bearers* in a number of ways. In addition to restrictions, we have noted various first-day ablutions (for purifying "lepers," corpse-impure, and as I have argued, purifying dischargers), hand-washing (for the *zav*), and the employment of stone vessels.

Similar arrangements are found when we look at *secondary impurities*, i.e., one-day impurities acquired by *contact with the primary impurity bearers*. The most conspicuous of these devices is the probably pharisaic innovation of *tevul yom*, which meant considering an impure person pure immediately after immersion rather than at sunset. This idea, allowing for early purification, is assumed in rabbinic literature but was not accepted by the Sadducees. Since the discovery of 4QMMT we know for sure that this was commonly practised during the

---

[11] Miller 2003; 2010.
[12] Cf. the comments of Reed 2003, 384–385.
[13] Regev 2000; Kazen 2002; Poirier 2003; Crossley 2004; Strange 2007; Furstenberg 2008.
[14] Kazen 2002, 60–88.
[15] Kazen 2002, 71–72, 86–87, 272.

Second Temple period, since those behind the halakic letter protest against it.[16] The practice of *tevul yom* for a one-day impurity must be regarded as in a sense functionally equivalent to a first-day ablution for a seven-day impurity, since both remove one layer of impurity immediately, in advance of full purification. (In the case of a one-day impurity, the remaining impurity would then have been considered so weak that it generally did not affect the profane sphere, only *sancta*.) The other two methods, hand-washing and stone vessels, seem to have been used for lessening the contamination potency of one-day impurities, too.

While the use of stone vessels is largely deduced from interpreting material evidence, hand-washing before common meals is well evidenced in rabbinic texts. It is taken for granted and the purpose is evidently to prevent food from becoming impure in the second remove. The necessary presuppositions for hand-washing before common meals to be meaningful at all are the hands being separately susceptible to impurity, as well as the susceptibility of liquids, always becoming impure in the first remove and interposing between the eater and the food.[17] The necessary presuppositions concerning hands and liquids are included in the list of ten items making *terumah* unfit, which we find in *m. Zabim* 5:12. The *Talmudim* count these ten among the eighteen decrees that were passed in the upper room of Hanina/Hananiah, when the Shammaites outnumbered the Hillelites.[18] In a detailed and speculative reconstruction Booth has suggested that this event, including the decree on the separate impurity of hands, took place in 51 CE.[19] Others have dated it to a Zealot synod in 66/67 C.E. that passed a number of anti-Gentile decrees.[20] Peter Tomson has shown, however, that although the ten items from *m. Zabim* 5:12 might have been formulated at some tumultuous gathering towards the very end of the Second Temple period, they cannot possibly have belonged to the eighteen decrees. Rather, the core of *m. Zabim* 5:12 was formulated by R. Joshua, it belongs to the oldest layer of the *Mishnah*, and had then already existed for some time in Pharisaic tradition.[21]

---

[16] The concept of *tevul yom* and its practice and function is a much discussed issue; see for example Baumgarten 1980; Sanders 1990, 36–37; Schiffman, 1994, 285–299; Kazen 2002, 72–85; Crossley 2004, 197–200.

[17] Kazen 2002, 81–84; Furstenberg 2008, 184–186.

[18] *y. Šabb.* 1, 3c–d (V. 1, 7); *b. Šabb.* 13b–17b. Cf. *m. Šabb.* 1:4; *t. Šabb.* 1:16–21.

[19] Booth 1986, 162–173.

[20] See Tomson 1988, for references.

[21] Tomson 1988. Furstenberg refers to the Babylonian Talmud's reconstruction as unreliable and suggests that the hand-washing custom belonged to pre-70 Pharisaic *halakah* (2008, 183–184, especially n. 19).

Was hand-washing a priestly practice?

As already mentioned, Neusner claims that the Pharisees were a pure food association emulating priestly practice. Partly following Alon, Neusner suggests that the Pharisees tried to keep priestly purity laws outside of the temple, applying them to their own meals.[22] To this Sanders objects, pointing among other things to the fact that 1) a number of rabbinic post-70 sayings do *not* require the eating of *chullin* in purity, 2) the "houses" distinguished between priests' food and their own, 3) prohibitions against impurity-bearers touching pure food are absent in the *Mishnah*, 4) we find no discussions about eating other types of food prohibited to priests, 5) biblical purity laws did not apply to priests and the temple only, and 6) Neusner's full analogy between the altar and the table "is neither implied in Leviticus nor specified in pharisaic material."[23] To this could be added Yair Furstenberg's observation that Neusner's interpretation seems to rest on a *midrash* in *Sifre Numbers* from the time of R. Judah, which makes an analogy between hand-washing before Temple service and before eating as part of a "tendency to confine hand-washing and other purity regulations to priests."[24]

I find Sanders and Furstenberg absolutely right in their criticisms, although I think Sanders makes unnecessary concessions. Neither Pharisees, nor any other non-priestly expansionists for that matter, pretended to live like priests.

Trying to live like priests would entail much more than eating *chullin* with washed hands. Priests would have had to avoid corpse impurity for all but next of kin.[25] Neither Pharisees nor other non-priestly expansionists seem to have followed this. Pharisees did not even *eat* like priests, since priests when having been contaminated could *not* eat after immersion, but only after sunset, because a *tevul yom* contaminated *terumah* (priestly food).[26] Qumranites followed this rule for their ordinary food, because they did not accept the innovation of *tevul yom*, but Pharisees did not.[27]

Several scholars have pointed to the crucial significance of Lev 11:32–38 for the idea of eating *chullin* in purity, which is not particularly aimed at priests, but is framed as a general law.[28] In my opinion the idea of living or eating like priests could just as well be completely abandoned. It is sufficient to note that many people at the end of the Second Temple period, Pharisees included, as-

---

[22] Neusner 1974–1977, 22: 106, 108; Neusner 1971, 3: 288; Neusner 1979, 14.

[23] Sanders 1990, 173–176.

[24] Furstenberg 2008, 191. Furstenberg considers hand-washing in the Temple as a preparation ritual rather than a rite of purification (n. 38).

[25] Lev 21:1–3; Sanders 1990, 187.

[26] Maccoby 1999, 209–210; cf. Booth 1986, 201.

[27] See especially 4QMMT B 13–16; cf. 11QTᵃ XLIX–LI; *m. Parah* 3:7; cf. *t. Parah* 3:7–8.

[28] Sanders 1990, 148, 163–166, 200–205. Cf. Furstenberg 2008, 195; Crossley 2004, 193–197.

pired to as high a degree of holiness and purity as possible. Their behaviour could at times look similar to priestly custom, especially in hindsight, but this was neither its *rationale* at the end of the Second Temple period, nor an explanation of its origin.

The key for Sanders' admission that the Pharisees made minor gestures towards living like priests is his interpretation of *m. Ḥag.* 2:7.[29] If we take *midras* literally here, as referring to impurity transmitted by pressure from any of the main dischargers, this passage can easily be misunderstood. It does not, however, describe various degrees of scrupulousness among different groups of people, as Sanders suggests. It rather provides one among several outlines for contamination potency or susceptibility.

> Clothes of an *am ha-aretz* are *midras* to *perushim*;
> clothes of *perushim* are *midras* to those eating *terumah*;
> clothes of those eating *terumah* are *midras* to [those eating] *qodesh*;
> clothes of [those eating] *qodesh* are *midras* to [those handling] *chattat* [water].[30]

The point is *not* that ordinary people were less scrupulous than Pharisees, who were less scrupulous than priests, and so on. This is clear from the two examples immediately following in the *Mishnah*, which are added to prove that even the most scrupulous person makes no difference in this chain of ascending degrees. The preceding section similarly emphasizes that purification with regard to one level is never valid for higher levels, only for lower. Sanders seems to affirm such a perspective when he states that *m. Ḥag.* 2:7 provides "a sequence of ascending purity"[31] but if this is true it cannot mean that Pharisees were necessarily less careful than priests in avoiding impurity from dischargers via pressure. *Midras* is here used representatively to *exemplify or illustrate contamination via an interposing source* and how contamination potency depends on the susceptibility of various categories. Our neat charts with four levels or removes of secondary impurities were not available;[32] hence the need to express this idea in a number of ways. The *Mishnah* suggests that *perushim* – whether understood as Pharisees, a sectarian fringe group, or expansionists in general – reckoned with a (second level) one-day impurity acquired via ordinary people (not of course from people as such, but from ordinary people impure with a secondary, one-day, impurity at the first level). Priestly rations (*terumah*), however, could be defiled at one further (third) remove, sacrificial meat (*qodashim*) at a

---

[29] Sanders 1990, 205–206, 232, 234, 258.
[30] *m. Ḥag.* 2:7.
[31] Sanders 1990, 205.
[32] For examples of such charts, see Wright 1987a; Milgrom 1991; Harrington 1993; Kazen 2002. See also the Appendix.

fourth and, according to this passage, (the one handling) the water mixed with ashes used for purifying the corpse-impure could be defiled at a fifth remove.[33]

As I read the previous *m. Ḥag.* 2:5–6, purification before eating could always be achieved by immersion, but only *qodashim* required it; for eating *chullin*, tithe and *terumah* hand-washing was sufficient. While priests could wash their hands, too, they specifically had to immerse before eating sacrificial food. There is nothing particularly priestly in hand-washing, however. It is rather to be understood as an evolving purificatory practice aimed at mitigating or lessening contamination potency. With regard to impurity-bearers, it was practised by the *zav* and had analogies in various types of first-day ablutions. It apparently became instrumental with regard to secondary impurities, too.[34]

The rationale behind hand-washing

This, of course, does not tell us to what extent hand-washing was practised at the time of Jesus. The portrayal of the *ammei ha-aretz* in the *Mishnah* is a contested issue,[35] as is the identity of the rabbinic *perushim*.[36] While the use of these expressions may indicate a second century *shaping* of the sayings in *m. Ḥag.* 2:5–7, this does not tell against the antiquity of the *ideas* reflected. I suggest that an understanding of some sort of a second level impurity acquired from ordinary people with a one-day impurity at the first level is early and that the separate impurity of hands as well as the susceptibility of liquids are attached to such a conception and best understood as pre-70 pharisaic or rather general expansionist ideas. A number of scholars today would accept or argue

---

[33] A fifth remove is not generally acknowledged in the various scholarly reconstructions. As I have repeatedly pointed out, rabbinic texts do not have their origin in a fully systematized scheme but reflect a number of perspectives. The difference made between an *am ha-aretz* and *perushim* admittedly makes one think of degrees of scrupulousness, but when interpreted in view of the rest of the chain it should rather be understood to indicate that expansionists reckoned with a one-day impurity at a further level even for non-priestly matters, which is a necessary presupposition for second remove impurity of food, hands and liquids.

[34] Yair Furstenberg has recently suggested that hand-washing originated "in alternative concepts of purity, closely related to the Greco-Roman custom of hand-washing and absorbed through popular practice into the Jewish laws of purity" (2008, 200, cf. 192–194). This interpretation has some affinities to both Sanders (1990, 228, 260–263) and Poirier (1996, 217–233). Furstenberg argues that hand-washing originated *outside* of the priestly purity system, not as an expansion of it (199). Even if this reconstruction of the *origins* of hand-washing before ordinary meals were accepted, it need not invalidate my discussion, which is focused on the analogous *function* of hand-washing for the purpose of limiting the spread of secondary impurities as compared to limiting the contamination of certain impurity bearers.

[35] Büchler 1906; Oppenheimer 1977; Kazen 2002, 269–273; Miller 2006.

[36] Finkelstein 1938; Neusner 1971; Bowker 1973; Rivkin 1978; Stemberger 1995; Sievers 1997; Lightstone 2007; Neusner 2007a; 2007b. Cf. Kazen 2002, 44–48. For a history of research about the Pharisees, see Deines 1997.

for hand-washing being practised relatively widely, at least among certain parts of the population, at the end of the Second Temple period.[37] Besides being presupposed in rabbinic discussions,[38] hand-washing practice is mentioned in Mark 7. Although the numerous findings of stone vessels from the time of Herod to Bar Kokhba cannot be used as direct evidence for hand-washing, as already mentioned above, these vessels from all over Palestine beg for an explanation that fits with a high degree of consciousness regarding purity. At least a reconstruction is plausible in which expansionist purity practices were gaining ground among the general population.[39] The practice of hand-washing fits well into this framework and the framework provides the necessary presuppositions for hand-washing to be functional, as we will see.

In what contexts, then, would hand-washing be of use for avoiding secondary impurities? While direct contact with primary impurity-bearers (or with objects for sitting or lying subject to pressure from a discharger) resulted in a first-degree impurity, and required immersion, contact with secondary impurities (i.e., persons or items, such as food or "vessels," including clothes), if impure in the first remove, caused an impurity in the second remove. Mark's picture of Pharisees and "all" (a fair number of?) other Jews (Judeans?) immersing after visiting the market and washing their hands before meals makes rather good sense at the end of the Second Temple period, although the number of people envisaged must be doubted. The motives behind such a practice would not have been limited to a wish to protect *terumah*, but should be understood as part of an increasing aspiration for a high level of purity among the general population.

Hand-washing before meals must be understood within a general view of graded impurity and graded purifications. The idea of graded purification is obvious – although perhaps not always spelled out clearly – in a number of rabbinic texts. Concerning the purification of the "leper," *m. Neg.* 14:2–3 states that after the bird rite and an initial immersion he is clean of the "impurity of entry" (into a town) but defiles like a "swarmer"; after immersion on the seventh day he is clean from impurity like a "swarmer," but defiles like a *tevul yom*.[40] At sundown he could eat *terumah* and after the eighth-day sacrifice he could eat *qodashim*. This, of course, neither suggests that the rule applies only

---

[37] Tomson 1988; Regev 2000; Poirier 2003; Crossley 2004, 183–205.

[38] For a recent overview and discussion of evidence, see Crossley 2004, 183–184.

[39] Cf. Strange 2007.

[40] Here, the reference to a reptile and a *tevul yom* may be understood representatively, indicating a certain level of impurity, similarly to the reference to *midras* impurity in *m. Ḥag.* 2:7, discussed above. At the same time, the reference to specific sources or types of impurity suggests a context in which neat four- (or possibly five-)level schemes were not available or had not been spelled out.

to priests (who eat *qodashim*), nor that a dead lizard would be involved, but the phrasing is schematic, outlining levels of purification apparently corresponding to levels of secondary impurity.

This is similar to but does not completely correspond to the standard charts with four removes. Other categories are used in *m. Nid.* 10:6–7, which is discussed by Sanders on several occasions. A *yoledet* "sitting out the purification blood" (i.e., waiting for the final 33 or 66 days to pass) was according to the School of Hillel considered as one who had touched a corpse-impure. This is another way of defining a secondary impurity that can be further transmitted to food.[41] According to the "standard scheme" this ought to mean that she would be impure in the first remove, but the saying is further defined: she is like one who had touched a corpse-impure person with regard to *qodashim* (כְּמַגַּע טְמֵא מֵת לַקֳּדָשִׁים). One possible way to interpret this is that she is understood to defile sacrificial food only, but neither *chullin*, nor *terumah*. The School of Shammai disagreed: she is considered as unclean as a corpse-impure person. The style and *genre* of the *Mishnah* require, however, that we supply "with regard to *qodashim*" from the preceding statement. Using another terminology, a *yoledet* in her second stage impurity would make *qodashim* unfit according to Hillelites, but unclean according to Shammaites, i.e., according to the latter she contaminates *qodashim* at two further removes. This fits with their disagreement on immersion: only Shammaites claim that this is necessary at the end of the period. So how is it that they agree that she might separate *terumah*? Here we must presuppose hand-washing. Passages like *m. Tehar.* 10:4 show that while the Schools disagreed about the point at which hand-washing should be done, they agreed that it should at least be done before separating *terumah*.[42] This would have made the task possible for a second stage *yoledet* even according to the stricter Shammaite view.[43]

In the first example above (*m. Neg.* 14:2–3), a "leper" after immersion on the seventh day is likened to a *tevul yom*. The second stage impurity of a *yoledet* could, according to the Shammaite view (*m. Nid.* 10:6–7), also be considered somehow equivalent to that of a *tevul yom*. Pressing these categories into the standard scheme, we could talk of them as in the second remove. This might help our thoughts for a while, but in the end it becomes a forced exercise, not to speak of the fact that when the terminology of removes is being used, the sec-

---

[41] The reference to touching a corpse-impure person must likewise be understood representatively; see previous note.

[42] Sanders 1990, 197.

[43] If the second-stage *yoledet* was considered by the Shammaites to contaminate *qodashim* at two further removes, she would only make *terumah* unfit, i.e., contaminate it in one further remove. Hand-washing should then suffice for preventing contamination in handling *terumah*.

ond remove is never applied to persons, only to food, liquid and hands. We find
that the standard scheme is often too simple and too systematized to explain
many of the details, even if it serves the good purpose of general orientation.

In actual fact, a basic idea of graded impurity and graded purification is present and manifest in a number of variants in the texts. For example, in *m. Zabim*
5:10 the idea that anything which has been in contact with a "father of impurity"
contaminates at two further removes is expressed as a general principle. This is
not, however, related to varying degrees of susceptibility. When these are taken
into account, qualifications like those of *m. Nid.* 10:6 above ("with regard to
qodashim") are needed. Something similar is visible in the *Tosefta*, too (*t.
Ṭehar.* 1:4–6): a *tevul yom* as well as (unclean) hands are said to be *the beginning* with regard to *qodesh* (תחלה לקדש), i.e., both are secondary impurities
contaminating *qodashim* in two further removes. This is explicitly spelled out,
together with the concomitant result that *terumah* is defiled (made unfit). This is
a different terminology and a slightly different logic as compared to the rest of
the discussion in the same context, where the first to the fourth removes are
numbered with regard to various items. In this case, however, the end result for
the *tevul yom* and (unclean) hands becomes the same.

The idea of unclean hands and the *tevul yom* at the same or a similar level is
expressed in several texts. We have already discussed *m. Zabim* 5:12 where
hands and the *tevul yom* are both included in the list of ten items that contaminate *terumah*. According to *m. Ṭ. Yom* 2:2, however, a *tevul yom* who touches a
pot with liquids contaminates them if they are *terumah*, although the pot remains clean.[44] If the liquids are *chullin* all is clean. Then it is added that if (his?)
hands were unclean all becomes unclean. The passage is difficult to interpret. If
the hands of the *tevul yom* are referred to, one possibility would be that separately washed hands are *presupposed* for the *tevul yom*, indicating that at least
for some purposes he could lessen his impurity even further by washing his
hands to the point of becoming all but fully clean. He would then be able to
touch ordinary liquid and *terumah* food, but not *terumah* liquid. This is speculative, however, and I would prefer an alternative reading according to which the
comparison is principled; it is not a matter of the hands of a *tevul yom*, but a
principled comparison between unwashed hands and a *tevul yom*. The passage
compares the contamination of a *tevul yom* with that of unwashed hands, claim-

---

[44] It is a difficult point whether the *tevul yom* is thought to touch the liquid while the pot itself is
not susceptible to impurity at a "third remove," or whether he is thought to touch the pot, which
is not itself susceptible, but nevertheless transfers impurity via moisture to the liquid. While it
could be argued that the exception (if hands are dirty) only refers to recontamination (a *tevul
yom* would normally be supposed to be clean by virtue of immersion), it is more likely that a
difference between a *tevul yom* and hands in general (not *his* hands) is intended. See below.

ing a slight difference. In spite of the two *generally* being equated, *m. Parah* 8:7 makes an exception for the *tevul yom*: whatever makes *terumah* unfit also makes ordinary liquid unfit – except for a *tevul yom*. This cannot mean that a *tevul yom* could touch *terumah*, but that, in spite of being basically at the same level as unwashed hands, hence defiling *terumah*, he does *not* (like hands) contaminate ordinary liquid. This fits with *m. T.Yom* 2:2, which ends in a comparison between a *tevul yom* and hands: both are judged more leniently *and* more stringently as compared to each other, suggesting that they are basically at the same level, yet subject to different rules in certain cases. This explains the need for the very detailed *halakhot* concerning the touch of a *tevul yom*, which follow immediately; his category is an extremely complicated intermediate one, similar to hands, but yet not quite.

Rabbinic texts such as these indicate that extra immersions and hand-washing were part of a multi-levelled and elaborate web of graded impurities and graded purifications with roots stretching deep back into the Second Temple period. A number of impurities could be lessened or mitigated by various purificatory practices, through which a high level of concern could be combined with practical aspects. Just as various first-day ablutions and early purifications were increasingly made available for impurity-bearers, secondary impurities were handled by similar means. We cannot explain every custom from a systematic standard chart with fathers of impurity and four levels or removes of secondary impurities, however we elaborate the details, since the purity paradigms from the end of the Second Temple period and beyond were immensely complex and only superficially homogenized.

Hand-washing and the date of Mark

Based on the arguments so far it is fair to conclude that ideas of hands as separately susceptible to impurity build on suppositions that are clearly anchored in the Second Temple period, and that it is reasonable to expect the practice of hand-washing before meals to have roots as far back as the first century CE. From here, however, there are no straight lines to the issue of hand-washing in the Jesus tradition. Although the halakic presuppositions of the basic issue of conflict in Mark 7 would have been present at the time of Jesus, this neither solves the questions concerning the Markan narrative with regard to its tradition and redaction history, nor with regard to its interpretation.

Most interpretations of Mark 7 take a traditional dating of Mark around 70 CE for granted. The dating inevitably plays a crucial role for how underlying traditions and processes of redaction are envisaged. A different view has been presented by James Crossley, who has argued for an early dating of Mark's gospel, based primarily on the antiquity of the halakic practices reflected in a number of Markan narratives. Three of these are discussed in detail: the corn-field incident, the *Streitgespräch* over divorce and the hand-washing incident; the latter receives a chapter of its own.[45] I find Crossley's halakic analyses more convincing than his early dating, which depends on a misreading of the redaction of the text. It is crucial in a text like this to successfully separate textual levels and identify audiences in order to draw proper conclusions about the concerns of the author.

It is easy to agree with Crossley when he claims that the gospel of Mark is "edited in light of gentile ignorance of Jewish purity laws." He also stresses that the underlying assumptions "only make sense in a Jewish context."[46] Crossley, however, goes on to claim that Mark's editorial comments in 7:3–4 display a good understanding of purity law, and suggests that this betrays an interest on the part of Mark for the expansion of purity *halakah*, all of which can help us to understand Mark's motives.[47] At first sight, it may seem that Crossley differentiates between Mark and the traditions that are being used, but as we will see, this is not the case.

By a strange twist of argument, Crossley claims that Mark writes before any conflict regarding the keeping of biblical purity laws emerged in the early Christian movement. Mark's wish, says Crossley, would not have been to question purity law in general. Mark only questions the *expansion* of biblical law or, more precisely, the idea that secondary impurities could contaminate food through contact via hands and liquid. Crossley understands Mark to consistently portray Jesus as faithful to biblical law; hence his editorial comment in 7:19 about declaring all foods clean (καθαρίζων πάντα τὰ βρώματα) means according to Crossley that all foods permitted in the Torah are clean and therefore hand-washing is unnecessary.[48] *Mark's* point would have been the same as Jesus' in 7:15: one can eat food with unwashed hands. It had nothing to do with what foods Jews would eat or not.

Matthew changes Mark, according to Crossley, because in his time food laws had become a source of conflict and were no longer observed by all Christians. In that context, Mark's editorial comment in 7:19 was prone to misunderstanding and could be read to justify negligence of these laws. Hence Matthew changes Mark's comment to "but to eat with unwashed hands does not defile man" (Matt 15:20), which corresponds to Mark's meaning, and by talking of

---

[45] Crossley 2004, especially 159–205.
[46] Crossley 2004, 200.
[47] Crossley 2004, 200.
[48] Crossley 2004, 192.

"the mouth" Matthew restricts the possible meaning of Mark 7:15 to the issue of hand-washing before eating.[49]

Redactional levels and audiences in Mark 7

There are several flaws in Crossley's arguments for dating Mark before any dissension concerning food or purity laws. My focus will be on the question of audience. Together with most scholars I agree with Crossley that this narrative is "edited in light of gentile ignorance of Jewish purity laws."[50] But if Mark's primary audience is gentile, and in addition to that a type of gentile audience that would *need to be informed in detail* of current halakic practices among Palestinian or Judean Jews, why would Mark go to such pains in order to convince them that hand-washing is unnecessary? What could be at stake here, since the audience seems even *unaware of the practice*? I agree with Crossley that there are assumptions in this text that belong to a Jewish context and that the traditions may be very early. I think, however, that Crossley has confused Mark with his source and Mark's audience with an earlier one.

In the previous chapter we saw that in the narrative of Jesus and the *zavah* in Mark 5, there are clear allusions in the Greek text to the purity legislation of Leviticus (LXX) that Mark seems to ignore. There is an undeniable purity issue in the text that probably had relevance on a pre-Markan level, to a pre-Markan audience. In Mark 7, however, Mark cannot ignore the purity issue in the hand-washing incident, because that is precisely why he is using this tradition. To the contrary, he *brings out* the purity issue in the narrative. Mark's redactional comments (7:3–4, 19) are necessary because *his* audience would otherwise understand neither the details and purposes of hand-washing, nor the relevance of this story for their own quite different problems. Furthermore, the two answers given by Jesus (7:6–8, 9–13) before he actually addresses the subject matter of the accusation, both have the same point: Jesus is criticizing his opponents for replacing the commandment or word of God with human *paradosis* (7:8, 9, 13). The former consists of a quotation from Isaiah 29, a passage frequently used by early Christians.[51] While a prophetic critical stance is in line with the historical Jesus, this quotation of Isaiah in a version closer to the LXX than to the MT is likely to represent the work of Mark, or at least a pre-Markan tradition in Greek. The *qorban* section that follows is juxtaposed to the Isaianic citation with little

---

[49] Crossley 2004, 200–202, 208.
[50] Crossley 2004, 200.
[51] Cf. Westerholm 1979, 76. Westerholm mentions Rom 9:20; 11:8; 1 Cor 1:19; Col 2:22. Note also how "this people" (οὗτος ὁ λαός) is used as an accusation against Jews in general. The Isaianic passage was easily understood as predictive of the Jewish people.

redactional effort; it begins with a new introductory formula (καὶ ἔλεγεν αὐτοῖς). It could represent a separate tradition possibly going back to the historical Jesus and it clearly places the commandment of God against human tradition. From an editorial point of view, however, this makes it a very suitable parallel to the hand-washing story, since the latter *lacks* this opposition once the Isaianic reply is removed. We could thus easily think of both of these answers as separate pieces of early polemics, inserted into a likewise pre-Markan hand-washing tradition by the author. Through his redaction Mark has achieved a clear opposition between divine command and human practice, but this does not mean that he has created the material himself.

In the *qorban* section, Mark again finds it necessary to translate the meaning of *qorban* for the sake of his ignorant audience. Matthew, however, needs such explanations neither in the *qorban* section, nor in the primary hand-washing story. Instead he reverses the order of the *qorban* section and the quotation from Isaiah, reworking the material into a counter-question by Jesus and integrating the two with the hand-washing incident into a coherent narrative. This says something about Matthew's indented audience: they are supposed to be familiar with Jewish *halakah* and enjoy the support of Jesus as a responsible teacher of law for their own practice of not observing hand-washing before meals.

Matthew's version fits a Jewish audience better and it is tempting to think of it as more original.[52] This is a false impression, however, and there is firm evidence of Matthew's version being secondary, resulting from his redaction of Mark. He not only shapes the Markan fragments into a coherent narrative, but also introduces "mouth" as a central concept, which is clearly secondary.[53] Mark 7:15 can be given a broad application, but Matthew talks of that which enters and exits through the *mouth* (Matt 15:11). In the subsequent Markan explanation, the focus is on the heart and the issue is moral purity. Matthew, however, retains the focus on mouth in addition to the heart, which causes a somewhat awkward formulation in v. 18: τὰ δὲ ἐκπορευόμενα ἐκ τοῦ στόματος ἐκ τῆς καρδίας ἐξέρχεται. The list that follows is complemented with one more *spoken* sin (ψευδομαρτυρίαι) in addition to the Markan "blasphemy," which would otherwise have been the only one associated with the mouth.

Matthew may well have had access to oral tradition to complement his written sources, but here his text is nevertheless secondary in comparison to that of Mark. Matthew is actually trying to achieve what Crossley suggests for Mark: convince his audience that hand-washing before meals is unnecessary. Perhaps

---

[52] Cf. Dunn 1990, 42–44, 51. Dunn's arguments concern the original form of Mark 7:15, not the entire narrative.

[53] This is one reason why I consider Svartvik's interpretation of this saying as focused on "evil speech" quite unlikely (Svartvik 2000, 375–411).

he is also reacting to Mark and, assuming that his audience knew a Markan version of this narrative, Matthew might imply that it would be a misinterpretation to take this story as an argument for neglecting food laws or purity rules. This does not place the Markan audience in the late thirties or early forties, as Crossley would have it.

I do not find it reasonable to envisage Mark's gentile audience as following every "biblical" command regarding Sabbath, food and purity, at a time before any conflicts on legal issues had yet appeared. First, conflicts on legal issues belong to the default setting of Second Temple Judaism. To think of an early "Christian" movement consisting of Jews and gentiles at a time without legal dissensions is naïve. Secondly, if Crossley's suggested context for Mark's gospel was true, why would the author bring up the hand-washing issue at all? It only makes sense if his audience was pressed to accept this practice? But could they then have been so ignorant about halakic custom that Mark had to explain its basics to them? Thirdly, the point that hand-washing before meals is unnecessary would have been more relevant to Jesus' original audience, and to pre-Markan audiences at a time when the idea of an opposition between human tradition and divine command was being developed. But the redacted text of Mark has to explain two halakic practices to an unknowing gentile audience in order to bring out a slightly different point from given Jesus traditions, which unexplained would otherwise remain puzzling: that inner purity is more important than outer (Mark 7:15).

Although I do think that the historical Jesus expressed something similar, Mark would not need to teach his gentile audience this by elaborate explanations of foreign practices unless he had a further purpose. That purpose is revealed in the "in-house" section (Mark 7:17–23), which is Mark's typical way of expounding the meaning and contemporary relevance of the Jesus tradition for his present audience.[54] This passage suggests that his audience does know of outer (ritual) and inner (moral) impurity, although they were perhaps ignorant of the halakic details previously explained, and that Mark invites them to re-contextualize the Jesus tradition and apply it to their own situation, meaning that food impurity is now irrelevant. This interpretation is supported by the subsequent narrative of the Syrophoenician woman, suggesting that the present inclusion of gentiles – their purity – was foreboded already during Jesus' ministry, too.

It is not necessary to suppose that the Markan audience was discussing whether to eat pork or not; the issues at stake could have been other food- and

---

[54] Mark 7:17 uses εἰς οἶκον. See Mark 2:1; 3:20; 9:28, and the similar ἐν τῇ οἰκίᾳ in 9:33 and 10:10; cf. Hooker 1991, 180, 225, 227, 236.

purity-related conflicts that had to do with commensality between Jewish and gentile Christ-believers.[55] But we must suppose *some issue related to eating* as the context of the audience for which the hand-washing narrative is shaped in its Markan form, and this issue is *not identical* with the historical hand-washing issue behind the original tradition, since that issue has to be explained for the Markan audience. The Markan context is one in which the Jesus tradition is being re-contextualized and re-applied for a later gentile audience who had experienced conflicts and dissensions concerning issues of food, most probably with Jewish Christ-believers.

It is thus reasonable to assume an earlier stage for some of the traditions in Mark 7, and that these would have been previously shaped in Greek with the opposition between human *paradosis* and divine command as the main point. Such arguments are most viable in contexts in which a general adherence to the details of Scripture is being presupposed and the issues at stake revolve around differences in interpretation and which of them that is truest to Scriptural intent. Mark's focus is, however, elsewhere; moral matters are given priority over purity concerns and sweeping generalizations are being made. Trying to disentangle the motives in the background is hazardous but will be attempted next.

Torah and tradition

I do not believe that Mark felt bound to relate every Jesus tradition available for the mere sake of it. We must suppose that he used and shaped the traditions he chose with a view to their relevance for his intended audience. This is true of the hand-washing tradition, too, and his audience consisted of predominantly gentile Christ-believers that needed explanations for halakic details.

We may also get a glimpse of the opponents of Mark's audience through his polemics. The polemics accuses "this people," i.e., Jews *in general*, of giving priority to human traditions over divine commands, thus repeatedly exhibiting lip-service rather than an inner disposition (καὶ παρόμοια τοιαῦτα πολλὰ ποιεῖτε). By this description, Mark generalizes the behaviour of the opponents of his audience, implying that *they* of course do or should do the opposite: give priority to divine commands, by focusing on *inner* purity. Except for the example of honouring one's parents, the contents of the divine word are typically not identified, but can be understood negatively as the opposite of the vice list (7:21–22) that characterizes the "others." This does not tell the Markan audience how to discriminate between Scripture and Scriptural interpretation, i.e., *halakah* or *paradosis*. It is true that the rabbis distinguish between Scriptural

---

[55] Such as the conflict in Antioch referred to by Paul (Gal 2:11–14) or discussions about sacrificial meat (cf. 1 Cor 8; Rom 14).

law and tradition.[56] This distinction was, however, not easy to make, since tradition is often interpretation, attempting to spell out what is ambiguous or implicit in the law.[57] Scholarly opinions differ as to how early a clear awareness of the difference between written text and its interpretation developed.[58] There are no indications that Mark expects his audience to have developed a skilled competency in this regard. They are simply assured that they do nothing wrong in not adhering to Jewish details that they do not fully understand, and that their behaviour is more pious than that of their opponents.

While Mark utilizes the opposition between Torah and *halakah*, it is not his invention but part of pre-Markan tradition. But does it really capture the historical conflict between Jesus and the Pharisees? In a recent article, Friedrich Avemarie argues that Jesus would have regarded the washing of hands not as divine law but as *paradosis*, a scribal innovation, since a widespread practice was fairly recent. While the idea of unclean food *contaminating the eater* is found in rabbinic law and may well go back to the Second Temple period, it is not of biblical origin. Furthermore, Avemarie claims that neither Scripture, nor "rabbinic teaching ... consider[s] the impurity of hands as strong enough to impart itself on foodstuffs."[59] Jesus would thus have claimed that hands *never* contaminate ordinary food and that contaminated food in any case *never* contaminates a person; only things coming out of the mouth defile (v. 15). Ave-

---

[56] Cf. Sanders 1990, 97–130.

[57] This subject is an art of its own and cannot be further discussed here. Cf. Hedner Zetterholm 2006, 209–230; Jaffee 2001, 84–99; Berger 1998, 16–25. The rabbinic concept of an oral Torah probably arose among the Pharisees at the end of the Second Temple period, but its prominence seems to be late, when it played a role in promulgating the Babylonian Talmud, supporting central rabbinic authority. The idea that opposing groups like Sadducees or Samaritans (and later Karaites) were literalists who did not accept any halakic interpretations is over-simplified – at times others could accuse rabbinic interpretations of being literalist, too – but they did not accept what they understood as Pharisaic or rabbinic novelties without basis in their own tradition (cf. Josephus, *Ant.* 13:295–298). See Bóid 1989b, 624–649; Bóid 1997, 101–115. Bóid regards the washing of hands together with the other items mentioned in Mark 7:2–4 as belonging to the seven Rabbinic commandments that were added as new *mitzvot*, not to interpret the Torah but in order to assert Rabbinic (Pharisaic) authority to actually institute new practices on the same level as the Torah (1997, 104–106 and personal communication). The seven rabbinic *mitzvot* are summarized in Maimonides' *Book of Commandments* (washing hands before bread, *eruv*, blessing before food, sabbath candles, *purim*, *chanukhah*, and *hallel* on certain occasions), but certainly have a long pre-history. I find it difficult, however, to see this concept confirmed at the end of the Second Temple period. In any case the Markan discussion makes an analogy with the *qorban* tradition, which is *not* among the seven. At the time of Jesus I would rather understand the washing of hands before eating *chullin* as an expansionist halakic practice that was questioned as to its legitimacy and antiquity.

[58] Berger 1998, 5, 159, n. 15, referring to Alon, Gilat, Neusner, Jaffee and Kraemer.

[59] Avemarie 2010, quote from p. 267.

marie takes Jesus' answer in an *absolute* rather than a relative sense,[60] claiming that here Jesus upholds Scripture against *halakah*.[61]

Many exegetes consider the saying in Mark 7:15 (οὐδέν ἐστιν ἔξωθεν τοῦ ἀνθρώπου εἰσπορευόμενον εἰς αὐτὸν ὃ δύναται κοινῶσαι αὐτόν, ἀλλὰ τὰ ἐκ τοῦ ἀνθρώπου ἐκπορευόμενά ἐστιν τὰ κοινοῦντα τὸν ἄνθρωπον) as originating with the historical Jesus, but then assuming a *relative* reading, i.e., taking the οὐ ... ἀλλά construction as reflecting a Semitic dialectic negation, meaning "not so much as," or "rather."[62] The meaning would correspond to Israelite prophetic criticism (cf. Hos 6:6), which was meant to emphasize the *priority* of humanitarian concerns, not the abrogation of the cult. Jesus would thus have meant that inner (im)purity takes priority over outer.

In the past, the main problem with taking Mark 7:15 as originating with Jesus was seen in its lack of *Wirkungsgeschichte*; subsequent conflicts around food laws in the early Church were difficult to understand if a clear saying of Jesus to this effect would have been known. Such views, however, presupposed an absolute reading from an anti-Torah perspective. A relative reading greatly diminishes the problem, as the saying originally would not have been understood as questioning food or purity laws, only relativizing them. Alternatively, the lack of *Wirkungsgeschichte* can be explained by an absolute reading like that of Avemarie, restricting the issue to hand-washing. Although Crossley speaks of not taking the saying "literally," he comes close to Avemarie in similarly restricting its scope to defilement through hand-washing, thus understanding it to criticize halakic tradition.[63]

Impurity from within

Restricting the scope of 7:15 to the issue of hand-washing is, however, not without problems. It is this general statement concerning that which goes in and out, which gives occasion to the "in-house" explanation (vv. 17–23) that represents Markan present-day application, as suggested above. This elaboration on moral purity for the benefit of the Markan audience is based on a *non-literal* understanding of the saying in v. 15; what comes out of a person is taken in an ethical sense. If, however, the saying in 7:15 is to be taken in a restricted sense, we would expect this to be valid not only for its first half but also for the second. If οὐδέν ἐστιν ἔξωθεν τοῦ ἀνθρώπου εἰσπορευόμενον εἰς αὐτὸν ὃ δύναται

---

[60] In spite of conceding that a relative sense is consistent with Markan Greek; cf. Mark 9:37.

[61] In v. 19 Mark goes one step further, shifting focus from eater to food, denying the impurity of food altogether, i.e., denying Scriptural law. This is not, however, part of Jesus' argument.

[62] E.g. Westerholm 1978, 83; Booth 1986, 69–71.

[63] Crossley 2004, 193.

κοινῶσαι αὐτόν is taken absolutely and literally, i.e., meaning that no contagion, no impurity, can enter the human person through the intake of common food (since contamination via hands is unscriptural and thus invalid), then what does the following ἀλλὰ τὰ ἐκ τοῦ ἀνθρώπου ἐκπορευόμενά ἐστιν τὰ κοινοῦντα τὸν ἄνθρωπον mean?

One possibility is that it refers to bodily impurities. Avemarie suggests this, but immediately retreats: genital discharge does come from within and is a biblical source of impurity, but this reasoning does not fit with other sources.[64] However, the possibility should at least be tried out. Corpse impurity was understood as some kind of death "ooze," a quasi-physical miasma, coming out of dead bodies, with the ability to, among other things, fill enclosed spaces. "Leprosy," i.e., the skin diseases subsumed under the heading *tzara'at*, seem to have involved scales and cracking of the skin. Jesus' saying would then have expressed that body substances (death "ooze," genital discharges, and "leprosy-stuff" breaching the body envelope) transmit impurity, while food does not. Even with this interpretation, a relative reading is more reasonable; the saying would then have declared these impure "substances" as more aggressive impurity transmitters than food. The idea is interesting, because it would represent one more stance, in addition to the various non-compatible ideas of impurity transmission found in the *Mishnah* (R. Eliezer: connection; R. Joshua: interposition of liquid; R. Aqiva: hands unclean in the first degree; standard view: hands unclean only in the second degree; categorizing according to the concepts of "unclean" and "unfit").[65] And it could claim Scriptural support.

In a recent article, Yair Furstenberg has suggested a somewhat similar interpretation. Taking hand-washing before eating as an originally Graeco-Roman custom, adopted by the Pharisees and integrated into the purity system, Furstenberg argues that the rabbinic system, originating in the Second Temple period, reverses the direction of contamination. Instead of people and vessels contaminating food and liquids as in the biblical system, we find food and liquids contaminating people and vessels. Jesus would then have reacted against these innovations, favouring a view of humans as the *source* of impurity rather than its target.[66]

While these suggestions should be seriously considered, I find it unlikely that the impurity of human beings and their contaminating power should have been the *focus* of the historical Jesus, explaining his motives for defending his disciples' neglect to wash their hands. Narrative traditions elsewhere do not

---

[64] Avemarie 2010, 269.

[65] *m. Yad.* 3:1–2; *m. Ṭehar.* 2:2–7; cf. *m. Ḥag.* 2:5–7; *m. 'Ohal.* 1:1–3.

[66] Furstenberg 2008, 192–198.

suggest that Jesus took a strict view on defilement from the main "fathers of impurity." Moreover, subsequent early Christian development would not make sense had the historical Jesus taken a clear stance, emphasizing the human body as the primary source of impurity and transmitter of bodily contact-contagion. A moral interpretation fits a "continuity perspective" much better.[67] While the Markan exposition is located *eis oikon*, and thus represents early Christian elaboration, the *impetus* for a moral interpretation is likely to have come from the Jesus tradition, as Mark 7:15 suggests.[68]

Moreover, the separation of biblical law from *halakah* is difficult. The idea of separate hand impurity seems to be derived from Scriptural rules concerning the *zav* and hand-washing (Lev 15:11–12). As we have already mentioned, the idea of hand-washing before meals may be seen as a counterpart of this provision with regard to *secondary* impurities. The idea of unclean foods contaminating the eater has some Scriptural support, too. According to Lev 11, various types of "swarmers" are considered disgusting and may not be eaten, but the dead bodies of "ground swarmers" are also said to contaminate by contact, rendering not only clothes and utensils unclean, but also liquids and foodstuff (Lev 11:29–38). The implicit supposition is that unclean food that has somehow come into contact with dead "land swarmers" should be discarded. When Lev 11:45 warns against making oneself disgusting and unclean through these land swarmers, a systemic reading would understand this to include a prohibition against eating such food, since it would make the eater unclean.[69] As purity rules were homogenized, this rule seems to have been applied to all sorts of ritual impurities, to the effect that they contaminated foodstuff by contact and that such food made the eater unclean. This logic is visible in *m. Ṭehar.* 2 where R. Eliezer argues from an idea of connection, and would easily have been understood as scriptural law.

However, the attempt to read Mark 7:15 as referring to the body as a source of impurity should not be dismissed too readily. Some such view could be seen as part of an ongoing inner-Jewish discussion. It is possible to think of the saying behind Mark 7:15 as a kind of slogan, an argument against "expansionists" like Pharisees and Essenes, from "non-expansionists," perhaps Sadducees or people representing an old-fashioned Galilean type of piety, who did not accept

---

[67] For a definition of a continuity or continuum perspective, see Holmén 2007, 1–13.

[68] Furstenberg does acknowledge that "the force of Jesus' statement lies in its ability simultaneously to rise to a moral level" (2008, 197–198).

[69] Most of these examples are mentioned by other interpreters, too, but with differing interpretations. See for example Furstenberg 2008, 195; Crossley 2004, 193–197; Sanders 1990, 199–205, 228–236. For a discussion of Lev 11, see Kazen 2008, 55–57, expanded in Kazen 2011b, forthcoming.

recent "innovations." This does not necessarily mean that some accepted human traditions in addition to biblical law while others did not.[70] Interpretative activity, i.e., halakic development, was necessary for anyone trying to apply ancient law within the bounds of changing historical circumstances. This did not prevent one group from accusing another of transgressing the Torah when the issues at stake depended on differing hermeneutics, as some contemporary texts suggest.[71] Jesus would then have used a current argument against the requirement of hand-washing that was neither his own, nor unknown to his opponents, but at the same time given it his own slant.

The main reason for taking Jesus' saying in a wider sense is that the paradigm of "inner" and "outer" fits with other parts of the Jesus tradition, which is evident when we look at Q.[72] In Q 11:44 Jesus complains that the Pharisees are like unmarked graves. The point in the Lukan version is not, as in Matthew, that they are whitewashed (hypocrites), but that they are unmarked and thus their impurity is invisible.[73] The saying could be taken to indicate that Jesus acknowledged corpse impurity and worked with a basic purity paradigm like any Jew in the Second Temple period, but it says nothing about what significance he attributed to it. In the context, however, the saying is associated with a discussion about inside and outside, emphasizing the *relative priority of inside* over against the outside.

A similar interpretation is reasonable for the cup saying (Q 11:39–41), which reads in Luke's version: "Now you Pharisees, you purify the outside (τὸ ἔξωθεν) of the cup and the plate, but your inside (τὸ δὲ ἔσωθεν) is full of greed and evil. Fools, did not he who made the outside also make the inside? Rather give the contents (τὰ ἐνόντα) as alms, and lo, all is clean to you." For the last sentence, Matthew instead has "Blind Pharisee, purify first the inside (τὸ ἐντὸς) of the cup, so that also its outside (τὸ ἐκτὸς) may become pure."

A number of scholars have related this saying to the rabbinic tradition about the Schools of Hillel and Shammai concerning the order of hand-washing and blessing the cup at a meal.[74] This tradition, like Mark 7, presupposes the separate impurity of hands, based on the assumptions mentioned above. The Q-saying is given a moral interpretation with the point that the inside is just as important, or even *more* important, than the outside. The bottom line is thus the *relative priority of moral issues* over against ritual purity concerns. The subse-

---

[70] Cf. n. 54 above.
[71] Cf. *Pss. Sol.* 2:3, 8:11–13; CD-A IV–V; 4QMMT B 49–72.
[72] For a fuller discussion than the one provided below, see Kazen 2002, 223–228.
[73] For a number of reasons Matthew must be seen as responsible for more redactional changes than Luke. Kazen 2002, 223–228.
[74] *m. Ber.* 8:2–3; cf. *t. Ber.* 6 (5):2–3.

quent saying on tithing (Q 11:42), concluding that "you should have done this without neglecting the other," also suggests a relative interpretation. In the Lukan version, this priority of the inside is motivated by concern for the poor, and almsgiving seems to have a purificatory effect (Luke 11:41). This may be read as a focus on the restoration of the people and a concern for the marginalized that is made difficult by expansionist interpretations, which in the case of purity would have affected social fellowship and food supply. Against such interpretation Jesus is portrayed as giving priority to moral issues for social reasons.

While the narrative context of the Lukan version is provided by Luke (11:37–38),[75] it conspicuously places traditional sayings about inside and outside in a setting that concerns ritual purification, and where Jesus' practice of purification is questioned by a Pharisee, just as his disciples' behaviour is questioned in Mark 7. Outside of the canon, we find *P.Oxy. 840* similarly locating a discussion of inside and outside, interpreted in moral terms, in a setting where the purificatory practice of Jesus and his disciples are questioned by a representative of expansionist interpretation.[76] An inside-outside discourse is thus clearly associated with ritual purification in the Jesus tradition outside of Mark, too.

Conclusions

In this chapter I have suggested that hand-washing before eating ordinary food developed towards the end of the Second Temple period as one of several strategies to maintain a high degree of purity in general life, with no special regard to temple visits. Together with the practice of *tevul yom* and probably also the increased use of stone vessels, hand-washing had a similar function for dealing with secondary (one-day) impurities as initial purificatory rites, such as a first-day ablution, had for primary impurity bearers, i.e., corpse-impure, "lepers" and dischargers entering their purificatory period.

Hand-washing was never a particularly priestly practice, but developed as a means for *non-priests*, who did not generally, like priest or like those adhering to the *Community Rule*, immerse before eating sacred food or ordinary food respectively.

I have argued that hand-washing before ordinary meals depended on presuppositions that were well known and applied during the Second Temple pe-

---

[75] Cf. the Lukan syntax and style; Kazen 2002, 227.

[76] A case can be made for some degree of historical memory behind this tradition; see Kazen 2002, 256–260. For a recent full-length study of *P. Oxy. 840*, judging it an early second century Jewish-Christian text, using memories of canonical stories but *not* earlier sources, see Kruger 2005.

riod, and that it is reasonable to regard it as a first-century practice, advocated by expansionist groups, although not to the extent that Mark's exaggerations suggest.

I have also tried to demonstrate that texts that have been understood to outline various degrees of scrupulousness rather give evidence for advanced ideas of graded purity and impurity, and that our categories of primary fathers of impurity with secondary impurities in four removes, although based on rabbinic texts, are both simplified and more systematized than the diverse and at times contradictory outlines found in the texts themselves. I have suggested that the impurity of hands and the impurity of a *tevul yom* were basically considered as being on the same level (something like a second remove one-day impurity), but that the two categories differed slightly on minute points as to their contamination potential. Both were extremely complicated and intermediate categories. Within such a context, the separate washing of hands before meals can be understood as a meaningful practice.

Turning to Mark 7, the *locus classicus* of the hand-washing debate, I hope to have shown that an early dating of Mark must be based on a disregard for pre-Markan sources and that Mark's own agenda concerns gentile freedom from Jewish food restrictions, although not necessarily referring to unclean meat. By applying the initial hand-washing narrative to moral issues in the subsequent "in-house" section, Mark invites his readers or hearers to recontextualize the Jesus tradition in their own world.

The question of hand-washing *per se* was an issue at a pre-Markan stage and the opposition of divine law against human tradition, although endorsed by Mark, was more relevant at a pre-Markan level, too. The initial tradition about hand-washing most probably goes back to a memory from the time of the historical Jesus, since it is not the obvious fit and contains no clear argument for Mark's agenda, and thus cannot have been shaped for that purpose. The saying in Mark 7:15 is best taken in a relative sense, emphasizing the priority of inner purity. Attempts to interpret it in an absolute sense are less plausible. The idea that the saying could reflect an argument for the body as a much more serious source of impurity than foodstuff should be considered, but then I am inclined to think that Jesus would have used a contemporary argument for his own purposes. It is difficult to avoid the impression that Jesus own emphasis was on the priority of inner or moral purity, in view of pieces of evidence from various parts of the tradition.

Chapter 7

The Good Samaritan and a Presumptive Corpse[1]

Introduction

Teaching students about the development of classical exegetical methods for dealing with the Jesus tradition, we traditionally present the idea of *Sitz im Leben* as possible to apply on at least three levels: *Sitz im Leben Jesu, Sitz im Leben der Kirche,* and *Sitz im Evangelium.*

A naïve belief in the possibility of consistently separating these levels from one another, or simply peeling off one redactional layer from the next, is hardly viable today. The image of various levels is, however, both useful and necessary if gospel materials are to be used for historical purposes at all, and not treated synchronically only, as self-sufficient text-worlds.

In the present chapter I wish to discuss the parable of the so-called "good Samaritan" in Luke 10:25–37, asking for its possible reception in an environment different from and prior to the gospel author's own. I will argue that although this parable has a clear function and meaning within the gospel of Luke, it does contain enough of particular traits to suggest a previous history in a Palestinian context, where it inevitably must have addressed first-century Jewish purity concerns. The idea is definitely not new; the purity issue was argued almost a century ago by Jacob Mann, and more recently by Richard Bauckham. In between, scholars have mostly either ignored it or taken it for granted.[2]

Sources and levels

The Lukan context raises questions as to the sources of the passage. The lawyer's question (Luke 10:25–28), which introduces the story of the Samaritan

---

[1] The chapter develops Excursus 2 and surrounding material from Kazen 2002, and was previously published in *Svensk Exegetisk Årsbok* 71 (2006): 131–144. It is only slightly emended.

[2] Mann 1915–1916; Derrett 1964. Jeremias mentions the idea, but regards it as uncertain (1972, 203–205). Some exegetes almost ignore the purity issue (for example Bovon 1996, 79–99), while others take it more or less for granted (cf. Caird 1963, 148; Fitzmyer 1985, 883, 887). Billerbeck (1924, 183) discarded it, since the parable was about helping a living person. Billerbeck's judgement was accepted by, among others, Marshall (1978, 448). The idea should not be dismissed too easily, however, without taking into account a possible history of textual development. The purity issue has been argued more recently by Bauckham 1998.

(vv. 29–35), has synoptic parallels (Matt 22:34–40 // Mark 12:28–34). In Luke's version, the lawyer asks "What shall I do to inherit eternal life?" rather than enquiring about the primary commandment, as in Mark and Matthew. Luke has apparently adapted the text to his own variant of the likewise synoptic tradition about the "rich young man" (Mark 10:17 // Matt 19:16 // Luke 18:18).[3] When we compare with the Markan version of the lawyer's question (Mark 12:28–34), we find that Luke's omissions are similar to Matthew's. The similarities with Matthew are, however, not consistent enough to ensure a common origin from a partly overlapping source, be it written (Q) or oral. To the Lukan variant of the lawyer's question is appended the actual story about the Samaritan, which belongs to Luke's special material. The obvious conclusion is that Luke has modified the concern for grading commandments with a more straightforward imperative, and joined the lawyer's question with an example story. For Luke, the story of the "good Samaritan" has the main function of exemplifying the humanitarian action that should be regarded as typical of a Christian ethos.

The story of the "good Samaritan," however, itself begins with a further question: "Who is my neighbour?" The story does not answer this question directly, but rather inverts it, by giving an example of how to be a neighbour to somebody else. The somewhat awkward joining of question and narrative has been taken as a sign of Lukan redaction.[4] But the opposite case could also be argued. Since the story does not directly answer the question, Luke would not have joined them had they not been found as a unit before.[5] The latter line of reasoning seems, however, somewhat strained. Joining a question with a parable or exemplary narrative, and turning a question or statement upside-down, is elsewhere found to be a trait of Luke's style.[6]

If Luke is seen as responsible for the redaction here too, he could be suspected of having created the story himself. This is unlikely, however, in view of the apparent discrepancies between question and narrative;[7] it is one thing to join these two but another to create an illustration that does not quite fit. In style and vocabulary, the story has at times been regarded as "exceptional even in

---

[3] This is evident in the initial question of the man, which in both cases in Luke is identical: τί ποιήσας ζωὴν αἰώνιον κληρονομήσω;

[4] Cf. Fitzmyer 1985, 882–883.

[5] Cf. Marshall 1978, 445–446. This line of thought is not convincing, and is necessary only if one presupposes that the present application of the story must have belonged to its original form.

[6] Cf. the narrative about Simon, the Pharisee, the woman who anointed Jesus' feet, and the parable about the two debtors in Luke 7:36–50. The silent question of the Pharisee is not exactly what is answered by the parable. Furthermore, the point of that parable is that forgiveness creates love, while the application amounts to love causing forgiveness.

[7] Evans 1990, 467.

Luke,"[8] but this is somewhat exaggerated. The quality of language is high, just as in other major passages stemming from what is usually considered as Luke's special source.[9] This could alternatively be taken as reflecting Luke's literary ability and ambition to shape such material as he found in oral form. The observation will, however, better serve as an argument for the "L" material having a written pre-history. It is likely that Luke found the story of the "good Samaritan" in written form and joined it to the lawyer's question.

While the narrative's *Sitz im Evangelium* can be argued cogently from the extant text, the *Sitz im Leben der Kirche* of the "good Samaritan" is much more a matter of speculation. If the story reached Luke in a "Hellenistic" form (i.e., written in good Greek), we also have to assume a Hellenistic stage. Without Luke's inverted question as an introduction ("Who is my neighbour?"), the narrative exemplifies two types of action toward a needy person. The first attitude is represented by the priest and the Levite. The second and obviously appropriate attitude is found with the Samaritan. Without introduction and commentary, this story displays a critical stance towards the religious leadership, or perhaps, against Jewish representatives, while the action of the Samaritan is portrayed as exemplary. The old tensions between Jews and Samaritans would not have been unknown in the Hellenistic world, at least not in nearby Syria. In an early Christian Greek-speaking environment, this story would have been understood as critical towards the Jewish establishment. It could also have been taken as applauding Samaritan acceptance of the Jesus movement. We have some evidence for the Samaritans being more prone than the Judeans to join the early Christian movement. The story of the "good Samaritan" could thus be understood as an early piece of pro-Samaritan propaganda.

Such an *origin* for the story is not very likely, however. Arguments from source and style of language are not decisive in this respect. The traits pointing to an early Palestinian-Jewish setting are far too many to be ignored. While signs of "Palestinian provenance" are uncertain as criteria of "authenticity" such signs do give clues as to the context and function of a tradition. We simply have to ask for a *Sitz im Leben Jesu*, not meaning that Jesus *must* have said this – such claims can never be proved – but in the sense of a plausible context and function at the time when, and in the environment in which Jesus lived.

A number of details in the story should be noted. The dangers on the road between Jerusalem and Jericho are historically known.[10] Banditry was an increasing problem during the first century CE.[11] The careful wording

---

[8] Evans 1990, 467.
[9] Bovon 1996, 84, especially n.10.
[10] Bovon 1996, 89, with references to Strabo (16.2.41) and Josephus (*J. W.* 4:474).
[11] Cf. Freyne 1988) 50–68.

(καταβαίνειν is used for going *down* from Jerusalem to Jericho) betrays an awareness of geographical conditions. The identities of the role figures in the story (priest, Levite, Samaritan) are not necessary for the general point of compassion and neighbourly love, which the narrative serves in its Lukan setting. While possibly having a function in an early Christian setting with, or aware of Samaritan converts, these identities gain more detailed relevance in a Palestinian-Jewish setting, with its particular social and ethno-religious tensions.

A purity issue?

In a Palestinian-Jewish setting, this narrative of the "good Samaritan," even in its present form, cannot have failed to address the question of purity.[12] The priest and the Levite are both represented as avoiding the half-dead (ἡμιθανῆ) traveller, by passing by on the other side of the road (ἀντιπαρῆλθεν). This may be understood as due to legal concerns; the man was seemingly dead and both of them wanted to avoid becoming corpse-contaminated. Jesper Svartvik has pointed at a problem with such a line of interpretation: Jewish law is seen as the cause of merciless behaviour.[13] However, an anti-Jewish connotation is not necessarily attached to the question of purity. This is clear from Billerbeck, who denies a purity issue in the text, but nevertheless focuses on the heartlessness of the priest.[14] Whether the parable is read as having an anti-halakic or anti-clerical stance, the interpreter can always add an anti-Jewish flavour.[15]

There are good arguments for seeing a purity issue in the text. As I have argued elsewhere and as we have seen all through this book, purity was a widespread concern in Second Temple Judaism, not only among minor groups, but also to an increasing degree for the Jewish population in general. A comparison of various sources – rabbinic, Qumran, Josephus, Philo and the New Testament – indicates that questions about how to handle *terumah* and *chullin*, how to purify and when, how to regard the role of liquids as transmitters of impurity, how to deal with the possible defilement of hands, and how to relate to others who were not as consistent about purity customs as oneself, were regularly discussed during the first century CE. Archaeological findings of *miqvaot* as well as of stone vessels, point to the influence of an "expansionist" current in Second Temple Judaism.[16]

---

[12] Bauckham 1998, 477–480.
[13] Svartvik 2000, 5, especially the examples in n.12.
[14] Strack and Billerbeck 1924, 183.
[15] Whether this is done already by Luke is a question that will not be discussed here, since our primary interest concerns earlier levels.
[16] For further discussion and references, see Kazen 2002, especially 67–88.

At the bottom of these purity concerns we find an idea of impurity originating with and being transmitted by three basic sources: the corpse, genital discharges and "leprosy," or rather certain scaly skin conditions. Corpses were understood as transmitting a seven-day impurity to anyone by touch, but also without any physical contact to people being present within the same room or house, or finding themselves right above a corpse. The latter meant that not only contact with a human bone but the mere walking over a grave, as well as leaning over a dead body, made a person contract corpse impurity.[17]

It has been questioned whether people in general avoided corpse impurity to any significant degree. E. P. Sanders has even argued that contracting corpse impurity was considered "on the whole, *positively good*, or at least so much a part of nature as to raise no possible objection."[18] While it is true that the burial of relatives was a religious duty and that joining a funeral procession was regarded as pious behaviour,[19] there is evidence for a general avoidance of corpse impurity in Second Temple Judaism. Since it was "a transgression to bring any impurity into the presence of what is holy,"[20] many pilgrims came to Jerusalem a week before Passover in order to undergo purification rites for corpse impurity. This could be interpreted as if people from the countryside and the *diaspora* were considered to be constantly corpse-impure, having no or little access to ashes from the red cow. But apocryphal literature (Tobit) as well as the Temple Scroll and Philo give witness to the fact that people at a distance from Jerusalem actually made every effort to purify immediately after having come into contact with a corpse. As I have argued in previous publications and in the chapters above, a wide-spread practice of first-day ablutions had developed by the first century CE, in spite of not being required by the regulations in Num 19, with the purpose to somewhat mitigate the defiling power of corpse impurity. Although being an inevitable part of life, corpse impurity was taken seriously and was still possible to handle according to an expansionist practice, by first-day ablutions and with the help of the numerous *miqvaot* that we now know existed.[21] This general concern is exemplified by the difficulty Herod Antipas had in settling Tiberias, which was built on an old burial ground.

---

[17] Cf. Kazen 2002, 89–198.

[18] Sanders 1990, 142. For a critical discussion of Sanders' argument, see Kazen 2002, 181–184.

[19] *Ag. Ap.* 2:205.

[20] Sanders 1990, 146.

[21] For a discussion and references, see Kazen 2002, 53–54, 74–76, 259, 281, although the discussion about how to interpret the stepped pools, whether they all served ritual functions, and the possible significance of whether they follow "rabbinic" standards or not, has continued through the last decade, and has received further nuances. Stuart Miller warns against too readily assigning different types of pools to specific groups and drawing too sharp a line between ritual pools and pools used for other purposes, allowing for multiple uses, arguing from an

While corpse impurity was avoided as far as possible by ordinary people, the priests were expressly forbidden by Scripture to contract it, except in the case of close relatives (Lev 21:1–4). As for the high priest and the nazirite, they could not even bury their own parents (Lev 21:11; Num 6:6–7). In the story of the "good Samaritan" the priest avoids what appears to be a corpse. While the purity issue would probably not have been apparent to Luke's Hellenistic readers, it is difficult to see how it could have been ignored or absent in a Palestinian Jewish setting.

Objections and answers

There are three possible objections to such a claim. The most important counter-argument deals with the fact that the traveller is described as "half-dead" (ἡμιθανῆ, Luke 10:30). He is thus not a corpse yet. A second argument against a purity issue in the text focuses on the fact that only priests but not Levites were to avoid corpse impurity according to biblical law.[22] A third argument would emphasize that the priest and Levite were on their way *from* Jerusalem (v. 31, κατέβαινεν), and thus would not need to worry about contracting impurity, since it would not hinder them in their temple service.[23]

As for this last argument, it has little or no validity in view of how seriously corpse impurity was looked upon generally. As we have seen, it seems not only to have been generally avoided, but some sort of purification was undertaken, regardless of whether or not a temple visit was at hands. This view has been strengthened by findings of *miqvaot* adjacent to burial grounds, suggesting that mourners performed an immediate first-day ablution after having taken part in a burial.[24] Furthermore, according to Leviticus (21:1–4), priests were not allowed

---

analogy with the development of the synagogue. We should not "think of the ritual bath as a monolithic institution with a single application or form" (Miller 2007, 217). The point is that whether or not originally intended for ritual purposes, the stepped pools could be *used* for this. Miller also argues from rabbinic evidence that the practice of immersion was continued long after the fall of the Temple not only for menstruating women but for a number of purposes, and suggests that the large number of pools in domestic settings in Sepphoris points to the home as the focus of purity rather than the Temple (Miller 2003; 2007; 2010). Cf. the similar arguments of Galor 2007, that the finds at Sepphoris, together with a number of stepped pools from post-Temple times in other parts of the country disprove ideas of a sharp decline in the practice of immersion. Miller also claims that the fear of corpse impurity hardly disappeared with the fall of the Temple, pointing to rabbinic evidence for the continued use of the ashes of the red cow (Miller 2003, 412).

[22] Maccoby 1999, 150–151.

[23] While κατέβαινεν is used about the priest only, it could be inferred that the Levite is assumed by the narrative to travel in the same direction.

[24] Archaeological evidence for *miqvaot* as part of a burial compound have been found in Jerusalem (near the "Tomb of the Kings"), in Jericho, at Beth She'arim, and others close to tombs of various kinds. For a recent list with references, see Adler 2009, 57–60. These findings fit with

to contract corpse impurity except in case of close relatives and these biblical prohibitions were general, not conditioned by temple service. There is, however, a possible exception, to which we will return below.

As for the second argument, it is formally correct. Levites were, however, to join the priests and may well have appropriated the same rules for themselves. During the latter part of the Second Temple period, their status increased, and they appropriated some priestly functions.[25] This argument is thus of dubious value.

The first argument needs more space. Does the fact that the man is not "really" dead but ἡμιθανής have any bearing upon our issue as such? Here we must be aware of various levels of interpretation. I would like to suggest that *within the story world*, the man is *perceived as dead*, or possibly dead, *by some of the other characters*, i.e. the priest and the Levite. This is implied in the use of the term ἡμιθανής and would apply both to an underlying Palestinian-Jewish story and, although perhaps not obvious at first sight, at the level of the Greek text, as will be argued below.

The term ἡμιθανής is a *hapax* in the NT and an unusual term in any Greek writing.[26] It is at times used for persons who are pictured as far from unconscious.[27] In the Hellenistic Jewish romance *Joseph and Aseneth*, however, the term is used with the meaning of "almost dead" or "seemingly dead." In an attempt to kidnap Aseneth, Pharaoh's son is hindered by Benjamin, who throws a stone, which strikes his left temple, leaving him seriously wounded. "And Pharaoh's son fell down from his horse on the ground, being half dead" (ἡμιθανής τυγχάνων).[28] The wounded prince is pictured as seemingly dead or unconscious, since only later in the narrative does he move.[29]

---

an understanding of first-day ablutions to mitigate the defiling force of corpse impurity. An alternative interpretation has been offered recently by Yonatan Adler, who suggests that these *miqvaot* were rather used for purification from the lesser one-day impurity contracted by contact with corpse-impure people. Adler's argument, however, builds on the presupposition that first-day ablutions for corpse impurity were a sectarian development only, thereby disregarding much of the evidence for such a practice becoming increasingly common towards the end of the Second Temple period (Adler 2009). See the discussion in chapter 4 above.

[25] Cf. Lev 21:1–3; Num 18:2–4; Neh 10:37–38. Sanders 1990, 41–42. Cf. Milgrom 1978, 501–506; Fitzmyer 1985, 883, 887, n.32; Schaper 2000.

[26] ἡμιθανής first in Dionysius of Halicarnassus (10.7); Diodoros of Sicily (12.62.5); and Strabo (2.3.4) instead of the classical ἡμιθνής. Cf. Liddell and Scott[9] 1940, *s.v.* ἡμιθανής.

[27] Cf. *4 Macc.* 4:11.

[28] *Jos. Asen.* 27:3. This is the reading of most Greek manuscripts. Burchard 1983, 714, n. 3.

[29] *Jos. Asen.* 29:1 "And Pharaoh's son rose from the ground and sat up and spat blood from his mouth…" That ἡμιθανής was understood as seemingly dead is clear from several early translations of this work. The influential Latin manuscript tradition (L1) reads "quasi mortuum," and the Armenian version reads "ew elew nman mereloy" (and was like a dead). Cf. Burchard 1983, 714, n. 3.

Levi attempts to save his life, but Pharaoh's son dies on the third day. The description of Levi's action, however, contains several motifs, also found in the parable of the "good Samaritan."

> And Levi raised Pharaoh's son from the ground and washed the blood off his face and tied a bandage to his wound, and put him upon his horse, and conducted him to his father Pharaoh, and described to him all these things.[30]

Literary dependence in either direction is to be doubted, since (except for ἡμιθανής in the earlier passage) verbal similarities are almost non-existent. Similarities in motifs, however, are striking: taking care of and bandaging the wounds of a seemingly dead person, lifting him onto an animal, and transporting him to another place.

While the date and provenance of *Joseph and Aseneth* have been difficult to determine, some date between 100 BCE and the Second Jewish War (132–135 CE) is probable. Egypt is often suggested as the place of origin, but an underlying Semitic original from Palestine or Syria is possible.[31] The writing probably elaborates on a Jewish popular tale from the end of the Second Temple period. It may well have been known in some form by a Palestinian narrator of the parable of the "good Samaritan." While it is Levi who acts in an appropriate way in *Joseph and Aseneth*, it is not one of his descendents, but a Samaritan, who acts similarly in the gospel parable.

As we have seen above, there are signs of a Palestinian origin for the Lukan tradition. What was conspicuous in a first-century Palestinian environment about Levites and priests was their obligation for a higher degree of purity than ordinary people. As will be seen below, the question of how to balance the requirement for purity with the responsibility to the dead, with regard to such categories of people of whom a higher degree of purity was required, was a current and relevant issue. A parable addressing such a dilemma would fit into a first-century context, and give a plausible and a somewhat defensible explanation for the behaviour of the priest and the Levite in the narrative. Without a purity issue in the story of the "good Samaritan," this tradition would represent a position of crude anti-clericalism, or an unsubtle Christian polemic against Jewish leaders. Such an attitude could possibly be credible on the part of the gospel writer, but it is to be doubted for an earlier underlying Palestinian tradition. The idea of the man being seemingly dead, and purity being the issue, is superior for explaining the function and relevance of the Lukan parable in an

---

[30] *Jos. Asen.* 29:5. Καὶ ἀνέστησε Λευὶς τὸν υἱὸν Φαραὼ καὶ ἀπένιψε τὸ αἷμα ἐκ τοῦ προσώπου αὐτοῦ καὶ ἔδησε τελαμῶνα εἰς τὸ τραῦμα αὐτοῦ καὶ ἐπέθηκεν αὐτὸν ἐπὶ τὸν ἵππον αὐτοῦ καὶ ἐκόμισεν αὐτὸν πρὸς τὸν πατέρα αὐτοῦ. Καὶ διηγήσαντο αὐτῷ Λευὶς ἅπαντα τὰ παρακολουθήσαντα.
[31] Burchard 1983, 181, 187.

earlier Palestinian context. While the story would probably not be seen from a purity perspective in Luke's Hellenistic context, this would be natural in a Palestinian environment. *Joseph and Aseneth* shows us that other popular tales were told at the time, in which attempts were made to rescue an unconscious or seemingly dead person, and when such a tale was put into Greek writing, ἡμιθανής was deemed a suitable term to use, just as in the case of the "good Samaritan." There is no point here to argue for a particular underlying Aramaic expression. The point is to argue that the underlying narrative was understood to concern a seemingly dead person, and that the Greek expression used was appropriate for expressing this idea.

Priestly purity and priority

It has been questioned whether the situation pictured in the story of the good Samaritan is realistic, since there were exceptions in the legal tradition for extreme cases. The case in question here is the duty to bury an unburied corpse (מֵת מִצְוָה).[32] Hyam Maccoby points out that a priest is "not only permitted, but obliged, to lay aside his purity" in such a situation, and that the duty to give a corpse a decent burial "far transcends ritual purity considerations."[33] Referring to *m. Naz.* 7:1, Maccoby argues that even a High Priest was obliged to contract corpse impurity if he found a corpse by the road.[34] While this is certainly supposed by the text, it is not self-evident as a statement about historical conditions during the first century CE. The mishnaic passage in question is structured as a discussion between R. Eliezer and the sages. After an initial statement, confirming the general rule that neither a high priest nor a nazirite should contract corpse impurity even on account of close relatives, there is a discussion about the case of a neglected corpse by the road; this case overrules purity concerns but the question is who should rather become contaminated if there is a choice between the two. R. Eliezer argues for a high priest rather than a nazirite contracting corpse impurity, while the sages argue the opposite.

> [If] they were going along the way and found a neglected corpse –
> R. Eliezer says, "Let a high priest contract corpse uncleanness, but let a Nazir not contract corpse uncleanness."
>
> And sages say, "Let a Nazir contract corpse uncleanness, but let a high priest not contract corpse uncleanness."

---

[32] *m. Naz.* 6:5; 7:1.
[33] Maccoby 1999, 150–151. Cf. Derrett 1964, 27.
[34] Maccoby 1999, 27. Cf. Svartvik 2000, 5, n.13. For a discussion on the מֵת מִצְוָה, see Mann 1915–1916, 417–419. Cf. *b. Naz.* 47b, 48a-b.

> Said to them R. Eliezer, "Let a priest contract corpse uncleanness, for he does not have to bring an offering on account of his uncleanness. But let a Nazir not contract corpse uncleanness, for he does have to bring an offering on account of his uncleanness."

> They said to him, "Let a Nazir contract corpse uncleanness, for his sanctification is not a permanent sanctification, but let a priest not contract corpse uncleanness, for his sanctification is a permanent sanctification."[35]

Eliezer's argument is primarily economic, while the sages reason in theological terms. This mishnaic passage gives evidence for the general rule, and for an amount of discussion. We cannot from this, however, draw definite conclusions as to the legal situation during the Second Temple period, and this rabbinic passage can hardly be used as an argument against the presence of a purity issue in the narrative of the "good Samaritan." The opposite should rather be the case. The appropriate action of a priest finding a corpse by the road was apparently not self-evident, but was discussed by the Tannaim in the period following Yavneh.[36] This gives us good reason to believe that the question would have been raised some decades earlier. When the parable of the "good Samaritan" is seen in such a context, it becomes an implicit but pointed comment on the debate.[37]

The discussion in *m. Naz.* 7:1 is interesting, since it gives evidence for different opinions, and the possibility of different types of behaviour. Arguments such as respect for the dead or compassionate behaviour are not explicitly appealed to in the rabbinic text as overruling purity concerns, although the presupposition is that extraordinary conditions must be treated extraordinarily. A rabbinic anecdote from the *Tosefta* (*t. Yoma* 1:12), with several parallels, might also be relevant to our investigation. The context is the daily clearing of ashes from the altar.[38]

---

[35] *m. Naz.* 7:1. Translation from Neusner 1988.

[36] The discussion in *m. Naz.* 7:1 is attributed to R. Eliezer (b. Hyrcanus), a second generation Tanna.

[37] Cf. Bauckham 1998, 480–485, 489.

[38] In *m. Yoma* 2:1–4, which forms an appendix, commenting on *m. Yoma* 1:8 (cf. Neusner 1982, 76), it is stated that whoever reached the altar first was allowed to take up the ashes. However, because of an incident, the court decided that the right to clear off the ashes should be distributed by lot only. The incident is found in the example story in *m. Yoma* 2:2: Two priests got to the altar simultaneously, and one pushed the other so that he fell and broke his foot or leg. In *Tosefta*'s variant (*t. Yoma* 1:12), which is also found in *Sifre* to Num 35:34, the quarrel is a matter of outright murder, and occasions a problem of purity. The narrative ends with a comment on the departure of the *Shekinah* and the sanctuary made unclean. In the *Babylonian Talmud*, however, this endnote is missing. Instead there is a discussion on how to reconcile the two traditions (broken leg and murder). Which incident took place before the other? If the broken leg, the ensuing rule should have prevented the later incident of murder. If the murder, why was no rule about lots issued at once, but only after the less serious incident with a broken leg? The case is solved by regarding the murder as the first incident, but considered so exceptional that no rule was issued (*b. Yoma* 23a).

M'ŚH B: *There were two who got there at the same time, running up the ramp. One shoved the other* [M. Yoma 2:2A-B],[39] within the four cubits [of the altar]. The other then took out a knife and stabbed him in the heart. R. Ṣadoq came and stood on the steps of the porch and said, "Hear me, O brethren of the House of Israel! Lo, Scripture says, *If in the land which the Lord your God gives you to possess, any one is found slain, lying in the open country, and it is not known who killed him, then your elders and your judges shall come forth, and they shall measure the distance to the cities which are around him that is slain* (Deut. 21:1–2). "Come so let us measure to find out for what area it is appropriate to bring the calf, for the sanctuary, or for the courts!" All of them moaned after his speech. And afterward the father of the youngster came to them, saying, "O brethren of ours! I am your atonement. His [my] son is still writhing, so the knife has not yet been made unclean." This teaches you that the uncleanness of a knife is more grievous to Israelites than murder. And so it says, *Moreover Manasseh shed very much innocent blood, till he had filled Jerusalem from one end to the other* (II Kings 21:16). On this basis they have said, "Because of the sin of murder the Presence of God was raised up, and the sanctuary was made unclean."[40]

The critical note, which is even more transparent in the variant of the *Palestinian Talmud*,[41] should be registered. The comment about the uncleanness of the knife being more important than murder is evidently a gloss, expressing a redactor's judgement on what was perceived as earlier conditions.[42] It seems as if the attitude displayed in the example story was deemed unsuitable, because it implied priorities that were considered faulty. We should thus take the comments around this tradition as evidence for an intra-Jewish critical discussion about priorities, and the somewhat relative value of purity in comparison to matters of life and death. Later rabbinic generations expressed elsewhere the idea that the emphasis on purity during the late Second Temple period was disproportionately high.[43] While this opinion should not be accepted without reservations, the material discussed above (*m. Naz.* 7:1; *t. Yoma* 1:12) reveals that questions about priority and the relative value of purity were open to debate, and related to earlier conditions. This is not to claim that "ritual rigidity" dominated the Second Temple period, but only to give evidence for the existence of a discursive context in which the story of the "good Samaritan" would fit very well.

When we consider that *m. Naz.* 7:1 presupposes that the מֵת מִצְוָה applied to *both* a High Priest *and* a nazirite, and that the discussion concerns only cases in which there was a *choice* between the two,[44] the discrepancy between the atti-

---

[39] This far the *Tosefta* follows *m. Yoma* 2:2.

[40] Translation from Neusner 1997–1986, 2:188–189.

[41] "Dies (lehrt), daß ihnen Unreinheit schwerer wog als Blutvergießen—zu (ihrer) Schande" (*y. Yoma* 2:2 in Avemarie 1995, 49). The last word (לגנאי in Ed. princ. Venedig, לגניי in MS Leiden) is missing in Neusner's translation. Compare *y. Yoma* 2:2 in Neusner 1990 with the readings in Schäfer and Becker 2001.

[42] Cf. Kuhn's comment in his translation of *Sifre* to Num 35:34 (Kuhn 1933–1955, 9: 687, n.54).

[43] "Purity broke out in Israel" (פרצה טהרה בישראל), *t. Šabb.* 1:14; cf. *b. Šabb.* 13a; *y. Šabb.* 1:3.

[44] Cf. Mann 1915–1916, 418.

tude of the Tannaim and that, which is implicitly criticized in *t. Yoma* 1:12, becomes the more visible. Although the earlier tendency to indiscriminately ascribe Tannaitic material to the Pharisees must be avoided, the nearly century-old suggestion of Jacob Mann that the parable of the "good Samaritan" contained an attack on Sadducean positions should be seriously considered. As Mann points out, the מֵת מִצְוָה went against the explicit commands of biblical law (Lev 21:1–4, 11; Num 6:7), and rabbinic attempts at exegetical justification were never very successful, and would not have been readily accepted by Sadducees during the Second Temple period.[45] A strict view on corpse impurity with regard to a priest or a nazirite may be understood as a Sadducean position. This would fit the Lukan narrative, since priests and Levites were often identified with the Sadducees. A critical view on legal priority and an anti-clerical stance could thus be seen to coincide in the story. Whether first-century Pharisees would generally applaud the legal stance implicit in the narrative of the "good Samaritan" is another question. We do not know to what extent the מֵת מִצְוָה was an accepted interpretation among Pharisees at the end of the Second Temple period. If any clue should be taken from *m. Naz.* 7:1, it would be that opinions were divided.

Concluding reflections

We have found that the story of the "good Samaritan" can be read at various levels. For the author of the gospel of Luke it exemplifies the moral attitude and humanitarian action that ought to be typical of a Christian ethos. As a Hellenistic piece of Jesus tradition it expresses a critical stance towards the religious leadership, or perhaps, against Jewish representatives, while the exemplary actions of the Samaritan might suggest an environment aware of the relative success of the Christian movement in Samaria in comparison to Judea. In an early Palestinian context, however, the narrative can easily be seen to address contemporary purity concerns. Its implicit view on the relative value of other humanitarian concerns over against purity does not represent a unique position within contemporary Judaism. However, the priorities advocated were not uncontroversial, but in direct conflict with some other Jewish opinions. The story of the "good Samaritan" thus represents an early voice, criticizing certain Jewish authorities for setting false priorities in their application of corpse impurity rules. There is no reason why the gist of the story should not go back to Jesus.

---

[45] Mann 1915–1916, 418–419. Cf. *Sifra* to Lev 21:1 [Parashat Emor Parashah 1]; *b. Naz.* 47b, 48a-b; *b. Zebaḥ.* 100a. Bauckham (1998, 482, n.13) doubts Mann's arguments.

As defilement from corpses was a general idea in Antiquity, not only among Jews but in neighbouring cultures,[46] there is no reason to imagine that Jesus operated without this concept, or ignored it totally. Some gospel traditions, such as the Lukan tradition about the widow's son in Nain (Luke 7:11–17) and the Markan tradition about Jairus and his daughter (Mark 5:21–24, 35–43) suggest, however, a behaviour that would easily have been interpreted as a careless or indifferent attitude, especially when seen against the fact that corpse impurity was generally avoided not only in view of temple visits.[47]

A *rationale* for such a "lenient" attitude might be drawn from the Lukan tradition of the good Samaritan (Luke 10:30–35). In this narrative we find *similarities* with later rabbinic discussions about the priority between the obligation towards the dead and the demand for purity, but Jesus seems to have gone further, and at an earlier time. We also find *differences*, since the rabbis at least formally defended the מֵת מִצְוָה by exegesis. We should assume that practical considerations were important both for Jesus and later rabbis, so that rules about corpse impurity in certain cases were deemed as having less priority than other issues. However, Jesus' somewhat "unqualified" way of setting priorities in an area, in which biblical legislation was clear, and at a time when strictness dominated, must have evoked opposition.[48]

---

[46] For references, see Kazen 2002, 177.

[47] The problems and possibilities of interpreting these two traditions from a purity perspective are discussed in detail in Kazen 2002, 164–189.

[48] Kazen 2002, 197–198.

Chapter 8

Meier on Jesus and Purity[1]

Introduction

While John P. Meier's series *A Marginal Jew: Rethinking the Historical Jesus* was originally planned as a trilogy, it now comprises four volumes, with a fifth and final to come – although I find it unbelievable that one volume would suffice for all that remains, considering Meier's careful, comprehensive and painstakingly meticulous scholarship. For my own part, I have been waiting long for the fourth volume, since it is mostly deals with halakic issues. The volume, *Law and Love*,[2] is indeed a thorough discussion in 700 pages of all the areas of halakic discussion that are relevant to the Jesus tradition; the note in the chapter on divorce, listing only "a sample of representative works," stretches over almost 12 pages. The 35th chapter, "Jesus and Purity Laws," consists of 136 pages, of which 62 are endnotes.[3]

In spite of such an unparalleled mastery of research history and subject matter, the text itself is a relatively easy read, much due to the fact that almost every discussion with other scholars in the field is excluded from the main text and limited to the notes. This is for good and for bad; it gives the reader a clearer picture of Meier's own train of thought, but also makes it possible for him to avoid some major obstacles and even at times to disregard alternative interpretations that would perhaps be disturbing to Meier's preferred views.

In this chapter I wish to discuss Meier's interpretation of purity *halakah* at the end of the Second Temple period, as he relates it to the views and behaviours of that particular marginal Jew who constitutes the focus for the whole endeavour. As will become clear, there are points of both agreement and disagreement, and disagreements concern not only details of halakic interpretation and of Jesus' actions or attitudes, but also the overall view on the reasons for and the motives behind Jesus' particular stance.[4]

---

[1] This chapter is a revised and longer version of my response to John P. Meier at a review session during the SBL Annual Meeting in New Orleans, November 2009.

[2] Meier 2009.

[3] Meier 2009, 342–477.

[4] I will discuss questions of motives and the interpretative framework for understanding the halakic behaviour and attitude of the historical Jesus in more detail in a forthcoming book un-

Three programmatic statements?

As a starting point for discussing Meier's chapter on Jesus and purity law, I wish to focus on three important statements, two in the introduction to the volume and one in the first chapter on Jesus and the law, which I find programmatic, or at least of uttermost importance for Meier's stance in general. The first statement, from the introduction, concerns the use of comparative material for mapping out the state of halakic interpretation at the time of Jesus. Meier says: "A treatment of Jesus and the Law that does not seriously engage the Dead Sea material is in essence flawed."[5] This is an important point, since it acknowledges that the texts from Qumran cannot be bracketed and ignored as if expressing narrow sectarian viewpoints, but must be allowed in reconstructing the larger picture of plausible trajectories along which halakic discussion and expansion evolved during the Second Temple period. We are thus in a much better situation now compared to a time when the Rabbinic corpus was our (almost) only source for understanding legal development.

The second statement comes from the chapter on Jesus and the law, where Meier questions the opposition between ritual and moral/ethical elements in law as anachronistic and reflecting modern evaluations and individualistic thinking. "We moderns can easily be led astray by the fiery rhetoric of the prophets who engaged in what scholars of Semitic languages call 'dialectical negation',"[6] Meier says, exemplifying with the well-known passage from Hos 6:6 ("I desire mercy and not sacrifice"). He emphasizes that this is a highly rhetorical way of phrasing "a relative statement, expressing priorities in a comparison," in the Hebrew language, which lacks comparative forms.[7] This way of speech, then, must not be misunderstood as outright rejection of outer or visible forms of religious practice.

For the third statement we turn back to the introduction. Discussing the conditions for and presuppositions behind a truly historical endeavour, Meier points to the ever-recurring problem of construing an historical image that suits our preferences.

> Perhaps the common mistake of so much of the quest for the historical Jesus in the last two centuries was that it was not a truly historical quest at all. More often than not, it was an attempt at a more modern form of christology masquerading as a historical quest.[8]

---

der preparation: *Scripture, Interpretation or Authority? Tracing Motives in Jesus' Conflicts on Legal Issues* (2011 or 2012).
[5] Meier 2009, 4.
[6] Meier 2009, 44.
[7] Meier 2009, 44.
[8] Meier 2009, 6.

Referring to the heritage of Sanders and Vermes, Meier emphasizes the main lesson from the so-called third quest: that of Jesus' Jewishness. While christology might need to be re-articulated and there is a Christian need for making Jesus relevant to our age, not least in the realm of ethics, this must never be mixed up (although it is frequently done) with the purely historical quest for what kind of Jew he was and exactly where he fitted into a variegated first-century Judaism.[9]

These are statements with which I basically agree. I begin to get worried, however, when I tend to see that neither of them is really adhered to in the chapter on purity. First, I find that Qumran texts are at times dismissed as being too sectarian, fragmentary or ambiguous to be taken into account, when Jesus traditions are being discussed, with the result that they are given no real role in Meier's interpretations. Secondly, the interpretation of oppositions as dialectical negations or relative statements is again dismissed as not relevant for the material on purity, in spite of fact that Meier does employ such interpretations elsewhere. Thirdly, in his conclusions, Meier suggests that for Jesus the whole system of purity does not exist because he has immediate access to the divine will. I would understand such a statement to say that rather than being primarily related to his kingdom vision, Jesus' view of impurity was dependent on his inherent personal and charismatic authority. Let it be clear that I do not suggest that Meier has a crypto-christological agenda. But I think we must ask ourselves if such a view as Meier's cannot at least be *read* and *interpreted* as one type of "modern christology masquerading as historical quest"? These three points that I find troublesome will become clearer below. As we will also see, they are tied to the problems involved with a historical approach that is heavily dependent on traditional criteria of authenticity.

The purity laws

In his chapter on purity, Meier begins with an outline of various types of purity laws. The first category is ritual impurity, which usually refers to temporary conditions that have to do with the normal cycle of human life: birth, disease, sex and death. Meier understands these as liminal experiences of crossing a threshold. They are energy-charged activities that need to be kept away from the divine sphere, and are opposite to what is holy, which means that they must be kept separate from the temple. Impurity is, according to Meier, not sinful, but highly contagious, and most often transmitted by physical contact.

---

[9] Meier 2009, 5–8.

Moral impurity is the second category, referring to certain heinous sins, for which the term *to'evah* is often used. Here Meier relies heavily on the research of Jonathan Klawans.[10]

Meier's third category is genealogical impurity. This type of impurity is not found in the Pentateuch, but is an idea developing after the exile (Ezra, Nehemiah, Jubilees). Here Meier relies on Christine Hayes.[11]

The laws concerning prohibited food constitute a fourth category. They also use to term *to'evah*, which is found in the discourse on moral impurity.[12] This type of impurity is both similar and different from ritual impurity, but also from moral impurity. It is simply unthinkable to eat unclean animals, and there are no rules for purification after having eaten such forbidden meat. These rules fall in between the other categories.[13]

Meier does not believe that these various types of purity laws can be satisfactorily explained by one single model.[14] Personally, I am hesitant to place the third category, genealogical impurity, on the same level as the rest.[15] It seems to me a very special case, with less of a legal base, but rather to be understood as an example of an extended use of purity language in view of particular historical and social circumstances. For the other three categories, the idea of all sorts of liminal experiences probably works, at least as a partial explanation. We would, however, expect other partial explanations, too. Meier mentions very briefly a number of anthropological, sociological and psychological suggestions, but never follows up on any of them, since "it is doubtful that any one hypothesis or model can explain the whole range of purity laws."[16] With this I agree, but nevertheless think that some models may be more useful than others. Meier does mention terms for disgust dealing with the second and fourth category and he also talks of food laws as "gut religion."[17] I regret that he does not try this out further. Although no wholesale explanation is available, emotional disgust could be *one* possible common denominator for all three basic types of impurity, as I have argued in chapter 2.

---

[10] Klawans 2000.

[11] Hayes 2002.

[12] Note that this is true of the food laws only in Deut 14:3–21. The term *to'evah* is not employed for ritual impurities in the P laws, but is used to characterize certain "moral impurities" in the Holiness Code. Elsewhere it is found in Deuteronomy in addition to some other books. See chapter 2 above and Kazen 2008..

[13] The "intermediate" status of the food laws is a classical problem. See Kazen 2008.

[14] Meier 2009, 349.

[15] This is not to deny the role that concepts of the impurity of Gentiles played especially for questions of intermarriage through and beyond the Second Temple period; see Hayes 2002.

[16] Meier 2009, 349.

[17] Meier 2009, 350.

As already mentioned, Meier questions the opposition or dichotomy between ritual and ethical/moral elements of law. There is a certain contradiction, however, in first questioning such a dichotomy and then accepting a classification of ritual and moral impurity. I may myself be guilty of similar contradictions, because we are all badly in need of categories to facilitate discussion. These concepts are convenient shorthands, but is it really true that Philo clearly distinguished, that Qumranites conflated, while rabbis compartmentalized the two?[18] Such an interpretation of Philo is questionable, I think, because Philo's emphasis rather lies on a dichotomy between soul and body, or mind and senses (*Spec. Laws* 1:257–272). This is clear even from a cursory reading of Philo. The soul is itself purified by ritual means, i.e., animal sacrifice, although Philo naturally awards the sacrifice an allegorical meaning. If there is an opposition here, it is between reason and sense-perception (258–259).[19]

I am also more hesitant than before to interpret moral impurity in Qumran as defiling in a ritual sense, i.e., through bodily contact, although ritual purity language is used. The evidence is rather flimsy. Klawans' interpretation in this respect was challenged immediately by Himmelfarb, who suggests that impurity has no moral significance in a non-sectarian text like 4QD, and although sectarian texts (1QS and 4Q512) do associate impurity and sin by using priestly terminology for describing human imperfection and restoration, sins are not understood as ritually defiling, but purity language is being used in a poetic or an evocative way.[20]

Finally, there are signs of "moral" aspects to ritual impurity even in some rabbinic texts, as I have discussed elsewhere, although I do agree that in general the rabbis tried to deal with impurity as a somewhat morally neutral concept.[21] The question is whether that was ever fully possible. Meier's suggestion that already the Pharisees began to compartmentalize ritual and moral impurity is also borrowed from Klawans, but not even Klawans himself finds clear evidence for this, which he admits.[22]

I see an obvious interaction between discussions of impurity and purification on the one hand and purity jargon being used for discourse on sinful behaviour on the other – an interaction that is visible in various forms and to different degrees throughout Early Judaism with all its variant expressions. I remain unconvinced, however, by ideas of total conflation as well as of complete com-

---

[18] Meier 2009, 350–351.
[19] ἐὰν γὰρ μὴ τοῖς ὀφθαλμοῖς μᾶλλον ἢ τῷ λογισμῷ τοῦτο κατίδῃς, ἐκνύψῃ τὰ ἁμαρτήματα... (*Spec. Laws* 1:259). For further details, see Kazen 2002, 220.
[20] Himmelfarb 2001.
[21] Kazen 2002,
[22] Klawans 2000, 150.

partmentalization. Certain impurities like "leprosy" and pathological discharges were associated with sinful behaviour and punishment from an early time.[23] Even menstruation cannot have failed to have become somehow associated with immorality in view of how the term *niddah* is used in some of the prophets, the most obvious examples being the express parallelism between *chattat* and *niddah* in Zech 13:1 and the likening of sinful behaviour with menstrual impurity in Ezek 36:17. These are of course examples of evocative language, which is something quite different from certain impurities being regarded as punishment for sin. Language is nevertheless a powerful tool, and popular conceptions together with prophetic discourse might explain the persistence of views and expressions associating sin and impurity through time, something that is evidenced even in late rabbinic texts.[24]

Meier concludes that there were clashing tendencies in Second Temple Judaism, and that some groups pressed for an extension of purity rules to new areas of life, while others tried to modify them, adapting them to practical demands. Groups with different opinions may well have competed for adherents among ordinary Palestinian Jews. This is a fair and reasonable picture with which I concur. However, in the subsequent discussion we find that Meier does not always allow for this general picture of diversity to play any substantial role, particularly not when interpreting Mark 7.

Mark 7

Most of the remaining pages are devoted to a discussion of the hand-washing narrative in Mark 7. Meier first discusses the literary structure of Mark 7:1–23, including verbal and thematic links.[25] This is thorough work and enjoyable reading – nothing much to comment on but rather to commend. He concludes that "we are dealing with a multilayered Christian composition, not a videotaped replay of what Jesus said and did."[26] This is a self-evident point of departure when doing historical exegesis in the first place. It is true not only of this text, but of *any* text in the gospels, and this shapes our methodology.

Following a structured translation of Mark 7:1–23, Meier then has a section in which he identifies the hand(s) of the Christian author(s).[27] Both in the text and in a note he claims that it is unnecessary for his purpose to discuss whether particular formulations come from Mark or from some pre-Markan level: "Since

---

[23] Cf. 2 Sam 3:29; Num 12:9; 2 Kgs 5:52; 2 Chr 26:20–21. See Kazen 2002, 116–117.
[24] For further discussion and references, see Kazen 2002, 217–219.
[25] Meier 2009, 353–360.
[26] Meier 2009, 360.
[27] Meier 2009, 363–369.

my concern is solely the question of what if anything comes from the historical Jesus, I do not bother to distinguish different levels of Christian redaction."[28] Such a stance, however, is only possible from the vantage point of a particular methodology. Meier's methodology is heavily criteria-based, fairly close to that of the "new quest," with its focus on the words of Jesus, and its belief that behind the gospel traditions we can isolate "genuine" or "original" sayings and thus more or less retrieve Jesus' own words, or better, voice. Such a methodology suggests that the text can be peeled and freed from the redactional overlay, i.e., early Christian interpretations (in Meier's case all the layers could just as well be peeled off together), until either a pure kernel or nothing emerges. This also implies that a thoroughly redacted text is unlikely to contain any historical reminiscences whatsoever.

The third phase[29] has partly questioned a criteria-based approach. There is a risk of replacing this with no real methodology at all, and that is probably what Meier thinks about when he criticizes those scholars who do not bother with criteria but "prefer to 'muddle through'."[30] I fully agree that there is no defence for credulity, or uncritical acceptance of anything that suits. This is one of the reasons why redaction criticism should never be avoided or played down. Even if redaction criticism never brings history back to life it is still just as important as before in sorting out the material before us. But we need a consciousness of the nature of this material. There are hardly any "words" of Jesus to be retrieved at all. We only have Christian sermons. Sometimes, however, these are based on memories of the historical Jesus. Time and again Meier asks for genuine or original sayings, but we only have authors' traditions and elaborations based on earlier traditions based on earlier memories and elaborations. If we are looking for the historical Jesus we should not be primarily looking for original sayings, but for hypotheses about possible traditions and memories *behind* sayings and narratives that have a superior explanatory value for the shape, function and interpretation of the present form of the saying or narrative, i.e., we must look for reasonable suggestions that may satisfactorily explain the development and elaboration of the Jesus tradition, taking the socio-religious and historical context into account. I am referring to something like Theissen & Winter's programme of historical plausibility.[31] The problems involved here in relation to Meier's discussion will become clearer below.

---

[28] Meier 2009, 442 n. 65, cf. 364.
[29] I have always been hesitant to talk of a Third Quest, because historical Jesus research since the 1970's has shown so many faces while still retaining fundamental traits from the so-called New Quest.
[30] Meier 2009, 16–17.
[31] Theissen and Winter 2002.

Meier's next section, by far the longest one, deals with the subunits of Mark 7 more in detail.[32] Meier goes through these subunits one by one, but makes an interesting move by beginning with vv. 6 ff, saving vv. 1–5 until the end. He shows convincingly that the first reply (vv. 6–8), referring to Isaiah, represents early Christian polemics, based on the LXX. The arguments are mostly well known and I think that the majority will agree. The second reply, about *qorban* (vv. 9–13), *could*, according to Meier, contain a core tradition originating with the historical Jesus, although its use as an argument in the hand-washing incident would then come as a result of Markan redaction only. Again, this is a fairly common interpretation that many will agree with. What I do note is that Meier bases his arguments for a *qorban* practice contemporary with Jesus on the combined witnesses from texts associated with Qumran (CD, especially column 16) and the *Mishnah* (*m. Ned.*, especially 5:6), with a nod to Philo and Josephus, and thinks that the fact that this tradition is woven into the narrative by Mark shows that the core tradition must be earlier than 70 CE. This is very much analogous to what others would claim about the hand-washing tradition, which Meier however thinks is unhistorical, as we shall see below.

The next subunit to be treated is vv. 14–23, i.e., the rest, although Meier divides it up somewhat in the course of the discussion. The crucial point is v. 15: "There is nothing outside of a man that, by entering into him, can defile him; but those things that come out of a man are the things that defile him."[33] Meier does not believe this saying to be genuine, although he notes arguments both for and against its authenticity. Discontinuity from Judaism and coherence in style with other sayings can be considered as arguments *for* historicity. But discontinuity from Judaism – how could a Jewish teacher have annulled all food laws? – as well as from early Christianity – how could this radical stance have been forgotten so quickly? – can also be understood as arguments *against* authenticity. Meier also mentions coherence (he presumably means *in*coherence) with Jesus' own sense of being a prophet to Israel – not to the gentiles – as an argument against. I am puzzled, however, by what Meier wishes to show with all this, except for the flaws of a too rigidly criterion-based approach, because any judgement depends on what Jesus actually *said* behind the Markan saying, and what he *meant* by what he said, which in turn depends on the historical context that would be most plausible. In my mind, there are no shortcuts; we have to suggest various possibilities, hypotheses, and try them out. And I guess this is why Meier immediately turns to a discussion of a possible "relative" reading of the saying, i.e., interpreting the idea that "nothing entering can defile, but those

---

[32] Meier 2009, 369–405.
[33] Meier's translation; Meier 2009, 385.

things that come out defile" as a rhetorical way of saying: "nothing entering can defile as much as those things that come out."

While I agree with Meier that Jeremias' idea of "end stress" (emphasis falling on the second part of a statement) is not applicable here, I find it strange that Meier, with so little discussion, rejects the idea of "dialectical negation" that he has argued for as so important in the introduction, and also employed elsewhere in the book. Most of the discussion is devoted to disproving the ideas of end stress and the priority of Matt 15:11. While I used to agree with Dunn and others that Matt 15:11 and *Gos. Thom.* 14 could represent a more original form of the saying, more prone to a relative interpretation,[34] I have changed my mind on that and found, just like Meier, this to be unlikely. Matthew is clearly redacting Mark here, and Matthew's emphasis on "mouth," which is not found in Mark but in *Thomas*, too, is definitely a secondary redaction, most probably Matthew's own as Meier argues, which is then followed up in Matthew's explanation, where the mouth recurs and stays in focus.

A relative interpretation is, however, in no way dependent on arguments about an original "weaker" saying in Matthew. Meier's examples of other antithetical sayings that cannot be interpreted relatively as dialectical negations do not necessarily prove anything for Mark 7:15 – if they did, they would disprove *all* other relative sayings, too. The context must decide in every single case. I agree that Matthew felt the need to soften Mark, but that does not mean that an original saying from Jesus must have had an absolute sense, it only implies something about Matthew's interpretation of Mark. Of course, the saying in *Mark's* sense – which must be deduced from his literary context – is incredible in the mouth of the historical Jesus. But it almost seems as if Meier supposes that there are only two choices here: the saying is either not genuine or it is literally from Jesus. Greek logia in Markan garb are never credible on Jesus' lips and that is all we have in Mark! However, if we are asking for what might lie *behind* Mark, which we have to do if we intend to study the historical Jesus, then we have to set up hypotheses. My questions are: What would the result of a relative saying be? How much would it explain, compared to what other hypotheses can explain? This is an examination I would have liked Meier to do.

Meier argues that there is a clear difference compared to Jesus' revocation of divorce.[35] On this issue there is multiple attestation of sources and forms in Mark, Q and Paul. Moreover, Jesus' prohibition of divorce did not impact his own behaviour, while a revocation of food laws would have done that. On the

---

[34] Dunn 1990, 44; Kazen 2002, 66–67, 228–229. I have modified my stance in the corrected reprint edition (Kazen 2010b, same pages).
[35] For Meier's discussion of divorce, see 2009, 74–181.

issue of purity, however, Paul (Rom 14:14) is seen as a possible *origin* for Mark 7:15 rather than as an independent attestation of an original Jesus tradition.

Meier is in effect excluding evidence for an alternative interpretation by refusing to test a hypothesis of a relative saying behind the Markan text. Many of his strong arguments are directed against the implausible idea of Jesus revoking the food laws in general, and thus become a battle with a straw man. If we, however, *allow* for the possibility of the historical Jesus having said something about impurity from within being more serious than impurity as a contact-contagion, this would have been a saying about *priorities*. Such sayings are also found in Q, in the sayings about cleansing cups and plates, about tithing and about graves (Luke 11:39–44).[36] We could thus speak of multiple attestation for sayings about priorities with regard to purity, even with regard to contact-contagion, vessels and eating specifically. Such sayings would not have involved food laws at all. They would have related to eating, although not from the perspective of unclean foods, but rather from the perspective of bodily transferable impurity, i.e., impurity as a contact-contagion that, even via food and liquid, could defile people in certain instances. Such sayings fit perfectly in an intra-Jewish discussion and would not immediately occur to early Christians as arguments in their quite different struggles about sacrificial meat or food laws, but could in due time become re-interpreted both by Paul and Mark and applied to their differing circumstances. The hypothesis of an original relative saying behind Mark 7:15 could explain much, and definitely needs to be properly tested before it is dismissed.

If a relative saying intent on priorities is presupposed, Meier's arguments and conclusions about Mark 7:15 lose their validity. Meier builds a chain of arguments (if this is inauthentic, this is too…) and by this device quickly dismisses vv. 17–23 because of the purported inauthenticity of v. 15. There are other good reasons for ascribing most of this section to Markan redaction or authorship; it is an "in-house" section (εἰς οἶκον), which is Mark's typical way of expounding the meaning and contemporary relevance of the Jesus tradition for his present audience.[37] The method of chain-building is risky, however, because the whole case is no stronger than its weakest link.

When Meier finally turns to the initial scene in vv. 1–5, there is no room for it, since everything subsequent has been deemed inauthentic; there is no historical Jesus tradition left for which it can serve as an introduction. Hence Meier says that "there is no need to probe vv. 1–5 in great detail." This is to me a hazardous way of treating text. Fortunately, Meier does discuss vv. 1–5 in *some*

---

[36] Meier discusses these but without relating them to Mark 7.
[37] Cf. Mark 2:1; 3:20; 9:28, and the similar ἐν τῇ οἰκίᾳ in 9:33 and 10:10.

detail. His arguments include the common observation that Mark's words about "all the Jews" cannot be true. Meier does not, however, seem to accept them as an exaggeration, but dismisses all evidence for pre-70 hand-washing by lay-people before eating, and follows Sanders in finding its origin in the diaspora.[38] He also argues against the possible unity of vv. 2, 5, and 15 by pointing to the discrepancy between a question regarding ritual impurity being answered by a statement about food laws, again excluding the possibility of an original relative saying emphasizing impurity from within as more serious than contact-contagion.

As far as I am concerned, the case for hand-washing in the context of ordinary meals as a developing expansionist practice towards the end of the Second Temple period is tightly argued by an increasing number of scholars. I think that some of the arguments and evidence presented by for example Tomson, Deines, Poirier, Regev, Crossley, and recently by Furstenberg are too lightly dismissed; in some cases I cannot even find any interaction.[39] We do not have to accept a view of the pre-70 Pharisees as embodying a "normative Judaism" for this; it is quite enough if we find them part of an influential expansionist tendency, and competing with the early Jesus movement for influence in Galilee. We do not need to appeal to stone vessels from Cana in Galilee – or to any references in the gospel of John at all, least of all any "core event";[40] it is quite enough to note that these vessels were widespread in Galilee as well as in Judea, in fact wherever there have been excavations. We do not depend on speculative reconstructions about hand-washing as one of the eighteen decrees passed in the upper room of Hananiah, and the possible dating of such an event.[41] The necessary presuppositions concerning hands and liquids making *terumah* unfit, are found in *m. Zabim* 5:12, the core of which some claim belongs to the oldest layer of the *Mishnah* and originates before 70 CE in Pharisaic tradition. The prerequisites for the problematic impurity of liquids becoming a much-discussed issue are corroborated by Qumran texts.[42]

While it is true that the frequent use of stone vessels at the end of the Second Temple period and their disuse after 70 CE cannot be explained *only* by their insusceptibility to impurity,[43] and that the smaller vessels popularly called

[38] Cf. Sanders 1990.

[39] Tomson 1988; Deines 1993; Poirier 1996, 2003; Regev 2000; Crossley 2004; Furstenberg 2008. The total absence of interaction with for example Crossley is remarkable. For further discussion of hand-washing, see above, chapter 6.

[40] Cf. Meier's discussion with Deines 1993 in Meier 2009, 469–470, n. 180.

[41] Booth 1986, 161–173. Cf. Meier's discussion with Booth in Meier 2009, 402–403.

[42] See further above, chapter 6.

[43] Stone vessels were, together with dung and unbaked clay vessels, regarded as unsusceptible to impurity according to rabbinic sources, cf. *b. Šabb.* 58a; *y. Šabb.* 8, 11c. This also seems to be

"measuring cups" and "cream pitchers" do not have a uniform capacity corresponding to a *log* or the mishnaic requirement for hand-washing as once supposed,[44] a high concern for eating in purity, is still a superior explanation for their popularity and spread, and hand-washing belongs to this paradigm.[45] Meier makes a point of the fact that hand-washing before meals is not an issue in texts from Qumran. However, the relevant texts from Qumran presuppose full *immersion* before meals,[46] which made separate hand-washing superfluous; hand-washing rather belongs to the same context in which the concept of *tevul yom* developed. Both are treated together in the *Mishnah* and the latter is explicitly rejected by Qumran texts, which shows that the concept of *tevul yom* was present at the time of Jesus.[47] What about hand-washing? The fact that hand-washing before ordinary meals is missing from some diaspora texts cannot decide the issue.

Let us turn the problem on its head. Why would Mark make up a conflict setting concerning hand-washing in order to draw conclusions about the validity of food laws in the early church? This must be the result of Meier's conclusions and the most unbelievable of all scenarios. With regard to Mark's argument, the setting is an obvious misfit and begs for an explanation. In this respect it is somewhat analogous to the subsequent story of the Syro-Phoenician woman (Mark 7:24–30). That narrative is given no explanation or conclusion, but almost everyone believes that Mark intended it as a justification for gentile inclusion. It just barely serves its purpose. But you have to do the best you can with

---

presupposed in the *Mishnah* and the *Tosefta*, although not stated so clearly (but see *m. Beşah* 2:3). Stone vessels are, however, repeatedly mentioned together with vessels of dung and of unbaked clay, as subject to the same conditions, and insusceptibility to impurity seems to be taken for granted (*m. 'Ohal.* 5:5; 6:1; *m. Parah* 5:5; *m. Miqw.* 4:1; *m. Yad.* 1:2; *t. Kelim (BM)* 7:4; *t. Kelim (BQ)* 6:5). For a discussion, also including references to the *Midrashim*, see Deines 1993, 192–205. From this we cannot, however, conclude that the property of stone vessels necessarily was the main reason of their frequency at the end of the Second Temple period. The dangers of assuming this are pointed out by Miller 2003. The common explanation is that their demise coincides in time with the destruction of the Temple, but this was also the time when *Tannaitic* elaboration of purity rules increased and the interest in purity did not come to a close with the fall of the Temple. Miller suggests that the reason for stone vessels falling into disuse after 70 CE also had to do with the decline of the stone building industry, to which their production was connected, and that their insusceptibility to impurity increased their popularity, although this was secondary. Similarly, stone ossuaries also went out of use not necessarily because of a change in general views on after-life (Miller 2003, 414–415; cf. Fine 2000).
[44] Reed 2003, 387–389; cf. Miller 2003, 416.
[45] Deines 1993; Magen 2002, 138–147; Regev 2000; Poirier 2003. See further above, chapter 6.
[46] Cf. Booth 1986, 161. Essene immersion before meals is described explicitly by Josephus (*J. W.* 2:129–132). In the texts from Qumran this is one of the issues that is assumed and taken for granted and admittedly never fully explicated. In 1QS V, 13–14, however, it is clearly indicated, and other texts from Qumran suggest that even unclean or purifying persons had to immerse before eating their own food in some intermediate state of purity (cf. 4Q274 1; 4Q514).
[47] For further discussion and references, see above, chapter 6.

those traditions that are available. An invented story would hardly have been that ambiguous. Similarly here: Mark could have invented a much better introduction, but he used what tradition had to offer and squeezed the maximum potential out of it.

I cannot believe that Mark created this "tradition" for the sake of an argument about food laws. The only way to defend or save the setting as a *Markan* creation would be to suggest that it was designed to fit a *relative* version of v. 15. The point served by the setting would then at least bear some resemblance to the setting itself. However, a lesson merely about relative priority is hardly *Mark's* intention. It might, however, have been the intention at a *pre-Markan* stage. I thus find it likely that the setting in vv. 2, 5 and a *relative* saying behind v. 15 *belonged together at a pre-Markan stage*. Whether they belonged together at the level of the historical Jesus is another question. Meier unfortunately thinks it somewhat unnecessary to bother with different levels of redaction, because a criteria-based analysis does the job. Of this I am not sure.

It is interesting to note that the Q sayings about relative priority of the inside against the outside (11:39b–41, 44) are situated by Luke in a similar setting in which Jesus is questioned concerning his neglect to purify before a meal – although here the issue is immersion, not hand-washing (Luke 11:37–38). The setting is most likely due to Lukan redaction, but a meal setting would have naturally suggested itself for a saying about cups and plates.[48] While Luke had a precedent for a meal setting in Mark, Mark might have used a traditional *chreia*-like saying with a setting attached, as a spring-board for his elaborations in chapter 7.[49]

That Mark would have created the setting together with the saying and its interpretation is unbelievable from another point of view, too. He goes out of his way to explain the hand-washing practice to his ignorant gentile hearers/readers. Why create a setting that not only is a misfit, but is also impossible for the addressees to understand without a lengthy parenthesis?

Finally, Meier's historical scepticism regarding hand-washing practice causes great problems for a redaction-critical analysis. If such a practice popped up close to the year 70 CE, via diaspora practice, as Meier seems to argue, are we to believe that Mark readily grabbed this recent innovation that his readers apparently did not know about or understand, pretending that it was ancient Palestinian tradition, in order to construe an invented setting for building an argument in favour of a contested gentile Christian practice that had little if

---

[48] Cf. Kazen 2002, 223–227.

[49] For recent discussions on the role of *chreia* in the Jesus tradition, see Byrskog 2007; 2009; Hägerland 2009. Cf. Gowler 2006.

anything to do with that setting? This is simply asking too much of both Mark and his recipients.

To me, the only reasonable conclusion is that Mark interprets traditional material, in spite of the difficulties involved and the obvious misfit, in order to lend authority to gentile Christian practice and interpretation of his own day. Whether this was his idea or a move already made by others is a different question. As far as I can tell, a hypothesis allowing for hand-washing before meals, not as a general practice but as an increasing expansionist trend at the time of Jesus, and an underlying Jesus tradition expressing the relative importance of impurity from the inside compared to impurity as contact-contagion, explains more and in a simpler way.

Other possible references

After discussing Mark 7, Meier uses eight pages to discuss all other possible references to purity issues in the gospels. As for corpse impurity, he thinks that ordinary Palestinian Jews might have waited until their next pilgrimage to be cleansed from it. In view of all the evidence for how seriously corpse impurity was regarded during the Second Temple period – evidence from a wide variety of sources and discussed in previous chapters – I find Meier's suggestion very unlikely. It is made nearly impossible by all the recent finds and discussions of ritual baths both in towns and adjacent to burial sites throughout the country.[50] Not accepting the idea of a first-day ablution for a seven-day corpse impurity being common practice, Adler has suggested that these *miqvaot* were used for secondary one-day impurities acquired through contact with corpse-impure people during burials. I have argued against such a restricted interpretation in chapter 4 above, but if Adler is right about these stepped pools being used (also) by mourners purifying from a one-day impurity, any room for negligence of a seven-day corpse impurity vanishes.

Concerning impurity from discharges, Meier thinks that neither the bleeding woman, nor Jesus, would have thought that impurity was being communicated through touching her clothes, since Galilean peasants did not observe Essene rules and rabbinic rules were not yet available. One has to ask, however, how ordinary Jews would have understood the purpose of the restrictive rules in Lev 15. I have argued in chapter 3 above that clothes were naturally considered part of the body with regard to contamination by touch. If this were not the case, contact-contagion could have been much more easily dealt with but nowhere do we find such suggestions.

---

[50] See Adler 2009, 57–60, for the sites and further references.

Meier points to the silence of the Jesus tradition with regard to semen emission or menstruation, in view of Jesus' travelling company of celibate men and women. The conclusion is that "for Jesus the whole system of purity does not seem to exist – at least as an object of reflection and teaching," hence his "lack of concern" or "studied indifference."[51] I think, however, that this is drawing too far-reaching conclusions from little evidence. The Jesus tradition preserves traces of Jesus' stance on purity issues to the extent that the material was relevant and useful for later Christian internal discussions and polemics against Jews. Meier himself quotes Neusner elsewhere: What you cannot show you do not know.

Turning to skin disease, Meier says that Lev 13 does not forbid a so-called "leper" to touch a clean person and does not state that touching a "leper" renders a person impure. Moreover, he finds it inconceivable that a priest could examine a "leper" if by touching him the priest would be rendered impure by contact. The latter argument is strange; examination is done before impurity is declared or at the cessation of symptoms in order to declare a person clean or unclean. This must be regarded as a special case, not least since it is commanded by the law.

Meier goes out of his way to explain away Josephus' statements about impurity by touching a "leper" and argues that since Josephus in *Against Apion* is engaged in a polemic against Manetho, who accused Moses of being a "leper," we should perhaps not take him at his word. According to Josephus, Moses states that one who touches a "leper" or lives under the same roof is considered unclean, but this is not explicit in Leviticus. Meier then compares with Josephus' statement in *Antiquities* where he makes no claim about a defiling touch.[52] The latter text, however, also carries polemics against Manetho, and says expressly that Moses banished "lepers" from the city in order to avoid intercourse/fellowship/close living together with anyone, being regarded just like a corpse.[53] The whole idea of "lepers" not conveying impurity by contact is based on a reading that disregards the context. The reason why touch is not an issue in Lev 13 is precisely because "lepers" are supposed to be expelled. Impurity through contact is simply presupposed from the very beginning and need not be addressed, since "lepers" do not live together with others. This explains the warning call and why there are no rules for purification after contact in Leviticus – it was not supposed to happen, but by all means to be avoided. What distinguishes "ritual" impurity from other uses of purity language is exactly that

---

[51] Meier 2009, 411.

[52] *Ag. Ap.* 1:281–282; *Ant.* 3:262, 261, 264–268. Meier (2009, 412).

[53] τοὺς δὲ λεπροὺς ... ἐξήλασε τῆς πόλεως μηδενὶ συνδιαιτωμένους καὶ νεκροῦ μηδὲν διαφέροντας·

it is a matter of *contact*-contagion. Josephus gives evidence for the way Leviticus was read and understood at the end of the Second Temple period: "lepers" were thought to contaminate in ways similar to corpses, both by touch and by "overhang."[54]

For some peculiar reason, however, Meier is suspicious of all evidence for "lepers" contaminating by touch. This includes the bracketing of Qumran texts like 4Q274, that otherwise would fit into the pattern generated by a comparison between Leviticus, the New Testament, Josephus and later rabbinic texts. Qumran texts are dismissed because they are supposed to be too fragmentary or ambiguous.[55] They are indeed often both fragmentary and difficult to interpret, but as I have tried to show in chapter 4, 4Q274 makes perfect sense within a general pattern of expansionist development of rules concerning contamination by touch. Moreover, 4QMMT B 64–72 is not so ambiguous. Like 4Q274 this passage also deals with "lepers" during their purification period, but the focus is not only on the "leper" staying out of his house, but also on avoiding the eating of pure food until the end of the period. This is apparently a question of dissent. The reason touch is not discussed is simply that it out of question and everyone agrees. If restrictions like these concerned purifying "lepers" one cannot possibly think that contact was assumed to take place freely between "full lepers" and pure people, during the time when "lepers" stayed out of cities.

Meier suggests that contamination by touch is a later rabbinic development. This would require an increasing stringency. When we scrutinize rabbinic texts, however, we rather find a tendency to *minimize* the impurity of leprosy as time goes by, and this is done *not by a lenient attitude to touch* but by *restricting the symptoms*[56] *and the type of settlements* from which "lepers" were excluded.[57]

Result

In the end Meier concludes that purity was no issue for Jesus at all. The conclusion is in a sense a natural result of his method. The relevant logion in Mark 7 is deemed inauthentic. Other possible traditions are understood as silent. But since the other traditions are *narratives*, can we really expect them to address the issue explicitly? The gospel authors naturally shape these traditions and use them for their own purposes. Would we not rather have to look for historical remains

---

[54] Cf. Kazen 2002, 112–115.

[55] Meier 2009, 412.

[56] *m. Neg.* 6:8 (only certain parts of the body are susceptible); *m. Neg.* 7:4 (the affected area must be of a certain size); etc. See further Harrington 1993, 198–202, 212.

[57] *m. Kelim* 1:7 ("lepers" only excluded from walled cities); *m. 'Arak.* 9:6 (only walled cities from the time of Joshua). Such restrictions are definitely not known by Josephus in *Ag. Ap.* 1:281 (μήτε μένειν ἐν πόλει μήτ' ἐν κώμῃ κατοικεῖν).

behind them if we wish to retrieve any such information? Such *implicit* information can occasionally be found. Meier, however, ignores the obvious linguistic allusions to Lev 15 in the narrative of the woman with a blood flow, which must have played a role at a pre-Markan level, to mention one example.

Mark 7, on the other hand, contains *sayings*, and here the purity issue is *explicit*, as we could expect, although commented on by Mark, again with his own purposes in mind. Since Meier, however, regards all of this unhistorical, we are left with a lengthy introduction by Mark, based on ideas of ritual purity in which he is otherwise uninterested, in order to argue for the abolition of food laws in a gentile setting. A different use of criteria of authenticity within a framework of testing the explanatory value of various hypotheses, with a view to historical plausibility, could have given a different outcome.

What I once described as Jesus' *"seeming* indifference" is for Meier a *"studied* indifference."[58] Meier explains Jesus' lack of concern from an *incoherent* approach to the law, since he could not have been indifferent to questions of Jewish law in general. Although we cannot expect any human being to be totally consistent in his or her outlook, I would have preferred a more coherent explanation, and I wonder what this implies for the so-called criterion of coherence, not to speak of the criterion of dissimilarity? Do these criteria of authenticity provide a valid methodology for incoherent historical figures?

I would also have preferred an explanation, that does not in the end resort to Jesus' charismatic and intuitive knowledge, "a direct pipeline to God's will."[59] While I agree that Jesus can at least in part be described both as a charismatic and as an "end time" prophet, I think that a concept of relative priority within a prophetic trajectory is a most important key for understanding the behaviour and attitude of this particular marginal Jew, and that this priority concerns the core of the message that the historical Jesus was remembered for: the kingdom. I would thus suggest Jesus' *kingdom vision* as the crucial factor also for Jesus' attitude to halakic issues, such as questions of purity and impurity, rather than his own personal or inherent authority. This suggestion has the advantage of being possible to cast into a hypothesis that can be tried and tested against the available evidence, and when this is done I think it explains more.[60]

---

[58] Meier 2009, 411, italics supplied.
[59] Meier 2009, 415.
[60] I hope to pursue this line of reasoning further in *Scripture, Interpretation or Authority?* (forthcoming, 2011 or 2012, see note 4 above).

Appendix: Standard chart

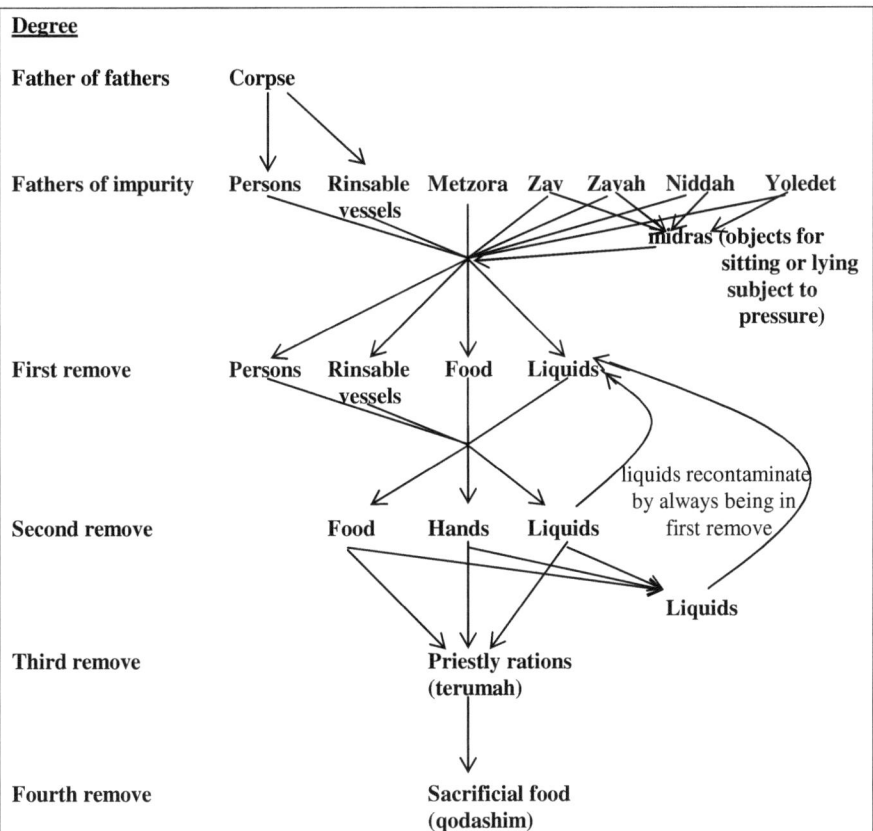

Degree	
Father of fathers	Corpse
Fathers of impurity	Persons Rinsable Metzora Zav Zavah Niddah Yoledet vessels
	midras (objects for sitting or lying subject to pressure)
First remove	Persons Rinsable Food Liquids vessels
Second remove	Food Hands Liquids
	liquids recontaminate by always being in first remove
	Liquids
Third remove	Priestly rations (terumah)
Fourth remove	Sacrificial food (qodashim)

This chart is based on a systemic reading of early Jewish texts, including both biblical and rabbinic material, but is at the same time a gross simplification and generalization of continuously evolving practices that were governed by diverse traditions and rationalized and further developed and differentiated in various circles according to competing and at times incompatible principles, as argued above. It represents contours that emerge to an outsider and late observer bent on systematization. Special cases as intercourse and the saddle are left out. As repeatedly indicated in the main text, a simple "system" like this was never applied exactly in this way, and purity paradigms were in reality immensely more complex. Still, this kind of chart provides a point of departure for discussion. Cf. Wright 1987, Milgrom 1991 and Harrington 1993.

Bibliography

Achenbach, Reinhard, 2003. *Die Vollendung der Tora: Studien zur Redaktions-geschichte des Numeribuches im Kontext von Hexateuch und Pentateuch.* Wiesbaden: Harrassowitz.

Achenbach, Reinhard, 2009. "Verunreinigung durch die Berührung Toter: Zum Ursprung ainer altisraelitischen Vorstellung." Angelika Berlejung and Bernd Janowski (eds.), *Tod und Jenseits im alten Israel und in seiner Umwelt: Theologische, religionsgeschichtliche, archäologische und ikonographische Aspekte.* Forschungen zum Alten Testament 64. Tübingen: Mohr Siebeck. Pp. 347–369.

Adler, Yonatan, 2008. "Second Temple Period Ritual Baths Adjacent to Agricultural Installations: The Archaeological Evidence in Light of the Halakhic Sources." *Journal of Jewish Studies* 59: 62–72.

Adler, Yonatan, 2009. "Ritual Baths Adjacent to Tombs: An Analysis of the Archaeological Evidence in Light of the Halakhic Sources." *Journal for the Study of Judaism* 40: 55–73.

Albertz, Rainer, 2001, "KPR: Kultische Sühne und politische und gesellschaftliche Versöhnung." R. Albertz (ed.), *Kult, Konflikt und Versöhnung: Beiträge zur kultischen Sühne in religiösen, sozialen und politischen Auseinandersetzungen des antiken Mittelmeerraumes.* Veröffentlichungen des AZERKAVO / SFB 493: 2. Münster: Ugarit-Verlag. Pp. 135–149.

Alon, Gedalyahu, 1977. *Jews, Judaism and the Classical World: Studies in Jewish History in the Times of the Second Temple and Talmud.* Jerusalem: The Magnes Press.

Angyal, Andras, 1941. "Disgust and Related Aversions." *Journal of Abnormal Psychology* 36: 393–412.

Aureli, Filippo and Colleen Schaffner, 2006. "Causes, Consequences and Mechanisms of Reconciliation: The Role of Cooperation." Peter M. Kappeler (ed.), *Cooperation in Primates and Humans: Mechanisms and Evolution.* Berlin/Heidelberg: Springer-Verlag. Pp. 121–136.

Avemarie, Friedrich, 1995. *Yoma: Versöhnungstag.* Übersetzung des Talmud Yerushalmi. Edited by H.-J. Becker et.al. Band II:4. Tübingen: Mohr Siebeck.

Avemarie, Friedrich, 2010. "Jesus and Purity." Reimund Bieringer et. al. (eds.), *The New Testament and Rabbinic Literature.* SupJSJ 136. Leiden and Boston: Brill. Pp. 255–279.

Avigad, Nahman, 1984. *Discovering Jerusalem.* Oxford: Basil Blackwell.

Bandura, Albert, 1999. "Moral Disengagement in the Perpetration of Inhumanities." *Personality and Social Psychology Review* 3: 193–209.

Bauckham, Richard, 1998. "The Scrupulous Priest and the Good Samaritan: Jesus' Parabolic Interpretation of the Law of Moses." *New Testament Studies* 44: 475–489.

Baumgarten, Joseph M., 1980. "The Pharisaic-Sadducean Controversies about Purity and the Qumran Texts." *Journal of Jewish Studies* 31: 157–170.

Baumgarten, Joseph M., 1992. "The Purification Rituals in *DJD 7*." D. Dimant and U. Rappaport (eds.), *The Dead Sea Scrolls: Forty Years of Research*. Studies on the Texts of the Deserts of Judah 10. Leiden: Brill. Pp. 199–209.

Baumgarten, Joseph M., 1995a. "The Laws about Fluxes in 4QTohora^a (4Q274)." D. Dimant and L. Schiffman (eds.), *Time to Prepare the Way in the Wilderness*. Studies on the Texts of the Deserts of Judah 16. Leiden: Brill. Pp. 1–8.

Baumgarten, Joseph M., 1995b. "The Red Cow Purification Rites in Qumran Texts." *Journal of Jewish Studies* 46: 112–119.

Baumgarten, Joseph M., 1999. "D. Tohorot." Joseph Baumgarten et al. (eds.), *Qumran Cave 4, XXV: Halakhic Texts*. Discoveries in the Judaean Desert 35. Oxford: Clarendon Press. Pp. 79–122.

Baumgarten, Joseph M., 2000. "The Use of מי נדה for General Purification." L. H. Schiffman, E. Tov and J. C. VanderKam (eds.), *The Dead Sea Scrolls Fifty Years after Their Discovery: Proceedings of the Jerusalem Congress, July 20-25, 1997*. Jerusalem: Israel Exploration Society/The Shrine of the Book, Israel Museum. Pp. 481–485.

Bekoff, Marc, 2004. "Wild Justice and Fair Play: Cooperation, Forgiveness and Morality in Animals." *Biology and Philosophy* 19: 489–520.

Berger, Michael S., 1998. *Rabbinic Authority*. New York: Oxford University Press.

Berkowitz, Leonard, 1999. "Anger." Tim Dalgleish & Mick J. Power (eds.), *Handbook of Cognition and Emotion*. Chichester et al.: John Wiley & Sons. Pp. 411–428.

Blau, Joel, 1916. "Lex Talionis." *Yearbook of the Central Conference of American Rabbis* 26: 336–366.

Bóid, I. Ruairidh M., 1989a. *Principles of Samaritan Halachah*. Studies in Judaism in Late Antiquity 38. Leiden: Brill.

Bóid, I. Ruairidh M., 1989b. "The Samaritan Halachah." Alan D. Crown (ed.), *The Samaritans*. Tübingen: J. C. B. Mohr (Paul Siebeck). Pp. 624–649.

Bóid, I. Ruairidh M., 1997. "L'Antiquité des Racines du Karaïsme." *Jaarbericht van het Vooraziatisch-Egyptisch Genootshap: Ex Oriente Lux*, No. 34 (1995–1996). Pp. 101–115.

Booth, Roger P., 1986. *Jesus and the Laws of Purity: Tradition History and Legal History in Mark 7*. Journal for the Study of the New Testament Supplement Series 13. Sheffield: JSOT Press.

Bovon, Francois, 1996. *Das Evangelium nach Lukas*. Vol. II: *Lk 9,51-14,35*. Evangelisch-katolischer Kommentar zum Neuen Testament 3:2. Zürich: Benziger.

Bowker, John, 1973. *Jesus and the Pharisees*. Cambridge: Cambridge University Press.

Boyce, Mary, 1982. *A History of Zoroastrianism*, vol. 2. Handbuch der Orientalistik 1.8.1.2.2A. Leiden: Brill.

Boyce, Mary, 1992. *Zoroastrianism: Its Antiquity and Constant Vigour*. Columbia Lectures on Iranian Studies 7. Costa Mesa, California and New York: Mazda Publishers/Bibliotheca Persica.

Boyce, Mary, 1996. *A History of Zoroastrianism*, vol. 1. Third impression with corrections. First impression 1975. Handbuch der Orientalistik 1.8.1.2.2A. Leiden: Brill.

Brennan, Tad, 1998. "The Old Stoic Theory of Emotions." Juha Sihvola and Troels Engberg-Pedersen (eds.), *The Emotions in Hellenistic Philosophy*. The New Synthese Historical Library 46. Dordrecht/Boston/London: Kluwer Academic Publishers. Pp. 21–70.

Broshi, Magen, 1974. "The Expansion of Jerusalem in the Reigns of Hezekiah and Manasseh." *Israel Exploration Journal* 24: 21–26.

Brosnan, Sarah F. and Frans B. M. de Waal, 2003. "Monkeys Reject Unequal Pay." *Nature* 425: 297–299.

Brosnan, Sarah F. and Frans B. M. de Waal, 2004. "Fair Refusal by Capuchin Monkeys." *Nature* 428: 140.

Brosnan, Sarah F., 2006. "Nonhuman Species' Reactions to Inequity and their Implications for Fairness." *Social Justice Research* 19: 153–185.

Büchler, Adolf, 1906. *Der galiläische 'Am-ha'areṣ des zweiten Jahrhunderts: Beiträge zur innern Geschichte des palästinischen Judentums in den ersten zwei Jahrhunderten*. Wien: Alfred Höhler.

Büchler, Adolph, 1928. *Studies in Sin and Atonement in the Rabbinic Literature of the First Century*. London: Oxford University Press.

Burchard, Christoph, (ed.), 1983. *Joseph und Aseneth: Unterweisung in erzählender Form*. Jüdische Schriften aus hellenistisch-römischer Zeit II:4. Gütersloh: Gütersloher Verlagshaus Gerd Mohn.

Byrskog, Samuel, 2007. "The Early Church as a Narrative Fellowship: An Exploratory Study of the Performance of the *Chreia*." *Tidsskrift for Teologi og Kirke* 78: 207–226.

Byrskog, Samuel, 2009. "When Eyewitness Testimony and Oral Tradition Become Written Text." *Svensk Exegetisk Årsbok* 74: 41–53.

Caird, G. B., 1963. *Saint Luke*. Harmondsworth: Penguin.

Chankin-Gould, J. D'ror, Derek Hutchinson, David Hilton Jackson, Tyler D. Mayfield, Leah Rediger Schulte, Tammi J. Schneider and E. Winkelman, 2008. "The Sanctified 'Adulteress' and her Circumstantial Clause: Bathsheba's Bath and Self-Consecration in 2 Samuel 11." *Journal for the Study of the Old Testament* 32: 339–352.

Chilton, Bruce, Darrell Bock, Daniel M. Gurtner, Jacob Neusner, Lawrence H. Schiffman and Daniel Oden, 2010. *A Comparative Handbook to the Gospel of Mark: Comparisons with Pseudepigrapha, the Qumran Scrolls, and Rabbinic Literature*. The New Testament Gospels in their Judaic Contexts 1. Leiden and Boston: Brill.

Choksy, Jamsheed K., 1989. *Purity and Pollution in Zoroastrianism: Triumph over Evil*. Austin: University of Texas.

Cohen, Shaye J. D., 1991. "Menstruants and the Sacred in Judaism and Christianity." Sarah B. Pomeroy (ed.), *Woman's History and Ancient History*. Chapel Hill: University of North Carolina. Pp. 273–299.

Collins, Billie Jean, 2002. "Necromancy, Fertility and the Dark Earth: The Use of Ritual Pits in Hittite Cult." Paul Mirecki and Marvin Mayer (eds.), *Magic and Ritual in the Ancient World*. Leiden: Brill. Pp. 224–241.

Colpe, Carsten, 1995. "Priesterschrift und Videvdad: Ritualistische Gesetzgebung für Israeliten und Iranier." M. Weippert and S. Timm (eds.), *Meilenstein: Festgabe für Herbert Donner*. Ägypten und altes Testament 30. Wiesbaden: Harrassowitz. Pp. 9–18.

Colpe, Carsten, 2003. *Iranier – Aramäer – Hebräer – Hellenen*. Wissenschaftliche Untersuchungen zum Neuen Testament 154. Tübingen: Mohr Siebeck.

Crawford, Sidnie White, 2000. *The Temple Scroll and Related Texts*. Companion to the Qumran Scrolls 2. Sheffield: Sheffield Academic Press.

Crawford, Sidnie White, 2008. *Rewriting Scripture in Second Temple Times*. Grand Rapids, Michigan: Eerdmans.

Crossley, James G., 2004. *The Date of Mark's Gospel: Insights from the Law in Earliest Christianity*. Journal for the Study of the New Testament Supplement Series 266. London and New York: T & T Clark.

D'Angelo, Mary Rose, 1999. "Gender and Power in the Gospel of Mark: The Daughter of Jairus and the Woman with the Flow of Blood." John C. Cavadini (ed.), *Miracles in Jewish and Christian Antiquity: Imagining Truth*. Notre Dame Studies in Theology 3. Notre Dame, In.: University of Notre Dame Press. Pp. 83–109.

Damasio, Antonio R., 1994. *Descartes' Error: Emotion, Reason and the Human Brain*. New York: Grosset/Putnam.

Damasio, Antonio R., 1999. *The Feeling of What Happens: Body and Emotion in the Making of Consciousness*. New York: Harcourt Brace.

Damasio, Antonio R., 2003. *Looking for Spinoza: Joy, Sorrow, and the Human Brain*. Orlando: Harcourt.

Darwin, Charles, 1989b [1890, 1st ed. 1872]. *The Expression of the Emotions in Man and Animals*. The Works of Charles Darwin, vol. 23. New York: University Press.

De Troyer, Kristin, 2003. "Blood: A Threat to Holiness or toward (Another) Holiness?" Kristin de Troyer et. al. (eds.), *Wholly Woman, Holy Blood: A Feminist Critique of Purity and Impurity*. Harrisburg: Trinity. Pp. 45–64.

de Vaux, Roland, 1964. *Les sacrifices de l'ancien testament*. Les cahiers de la Revue Biblique 1. Paris: Gabalda.

de Waal, Frans B. M. and A. van Roosmalen, 1979. "Reconciliation and Consolation Among Chimpanzees." *Behavioral Ecology and Sociobiology* 5: 55–66.

de Waal, Frans B. M. and Filippo Aureli, 2000. "Shared Principles and Unanswered Questions." Filippo Aureli and Frans B. M. de Waal (eds.), *Natural Conflict Resolution*. Berkeley/Los Angeles/London: University of California Press. Pp. 375–379.

de Waal, Frans B. M., 1989. *Peacemaking among Primates*. Cambridge, Ma./London: Harvard University Press.

de Waal, Frans B. M., 1996. *Good Natured: The Origins of Right and Wrong in Humans and Other Animals*. Cambridge, Ma./London: Harvard University Press.

de Waal, Frans B. M., 2000. "The First Kiss: Foundations of Conflict Resolution Research in Animals." Filippo Aureli and Frans B. M. de Waal (eds.), *Natural Con-*

flict Resolution. Berkeley/Los Angeles/London: University of California Press. Pp. 15–33.

de Waal, Frans B. M., 2007 [1982]. *Chimpanzee Politics: Power and Sex among Apes.* 25th anniversary ed. Baltimore: John Hopkins University Press.

Dead Sea Scrolls Electronic Library. Revised ed. 2006, version 7.0.24. Leiden: Brill, 2006 / Provo, Utah: Brigham Young University, 1991–2006.

Deines, Roland, 1993. *Jüdische Steingefässe und pharisäische Frömmigkeit: Ein archäologisch-historischer Beitrag zum Verständnis von Joh 2,6 und der jüdischen Reinheitshalacha zur Zeit Jesu.* Wissenschaftliche Untersuchungen zum Neuen Testament 2:52. Tübingen: J. C. B. Mohr (Paul Siebeck).

Deines, Roland, 1997. *Die Pharisäer: Ihr Verständnis im Spiegel der christlichen und jüdischen Forschung seit Wellhausen und Graetz.* Wissenschaftliche Untersuchungen zum Neuen Testament 101. Tübingen: J. C. B. Mohr (Paul Siebeck).

Derrett, Duncan M., 1964. "Law in the New Testament: Fresh Light on the Parable of the Good Samaritan." *New Testament Studies* 10: 24–28.

Dietrich, Jan, 2009. *Kollektive Schuld und Haftung: Religions- und rechtsgeschichtliche Studien zum Sündenkuhritus des Deuteronomiums und zu verwandten Texten.* Orientalische Religionen in der Antike 4. Tübingen: Mohr Siebeck.

Douglas, Mary, 1966. *Purity and Danger: An Analysis of the Concepts of Pollution and Taboo.* London and Henley: Routledge and Kegan Paul.

Douglas, Mary, 1999. *Leviticus as Literature.* Oxford: University Press.

Douglas, Mary, 2003. "The Go-away Goat." Rolf Rendtorff and Robert A. Kugler (eds.), *The Book of Leviticus: Composition and Reception.* Leiden: Brill. Pp. 121–141.

Dunbar, Robin I. M., 1987. "Sociobiological Explanations and the Evolution of Ethnocentrism." V. Reynolds, Vincent Falger and Ian Vine (eds.), *The Sociobiology of Ethnocentrism.* London: Croom Helm. Pp. 48–59.

Dunn, James D. G., 1990. *Jesus, Paul and the Law: Studies in Mark and Galatians.* London: SPCK.

East, Martin P. and Fraser N. Watts, 1999. "Jealousy and Envy." Tim Dalgleish and Mick J. Power (eds.), *Handbook of Cognition and Emotion.* Chichester et al.: John Wiley & Sons. Pp. 569–588.

Eisenman, Robert H. and Michael Wise, 1992. *The Dead Sea Scrolls Uncovered: The First Complete Translation and Interpretation of 50 Key Documents Withheld for Over 35 Years.* Shaftesbury, Dorset: Element, 1992.

Ellens, Deborah L., 2003. "Menstrual Impurity and Innovation in Leviticus 15." Kristin de Troyer et. al. (eds.), *Wholly Woman, Holy Blood: A Feminist Critique of Purity and Impurity.* Harrisburg: Trinity. Pp. 29–43.

Ellens, Deborah L., 2008. *Women in the Sex Texts of Leviticus and Deuteronomy: A Comparative Conceptual Analysis.* Library of Hebrew Bible/Old Testament Studies 458. New York, London: T & T Clark.

Elliger, Karl, 1966. *Leviticus.* Handbuch zum alten Testament. Tübingen: Mohr Siebeck.

Engberg-Pedersen, Troels, 1998. "Marcus Aurelius on Emotions." Juha Sihvola and Troels Engberg-Pedersen (eds.), *The Emotions in Hellenistic Philosophy.* The

New Synthese Historical Library 46. Dordrecht/Boston/London: Kluwer Academic Publishers. Pp. 305–337.

Eshel, Esther, 1997. "4Q414 Fragment 2: Purification of a Corpse-Contaminated Person." Moshe Bernstein, Florentino García Martínez and John Kampen (eds.), *Legal Texts and Legal Issues: Proceedings of the Second Meeting of the International Organization for Qumran Studies, Cambridge 1995*. Leiden: Brill. Pp. 3–10.

Eshel, Esther, 1999. "4QRitual of Purification A." J. M. Baumgarten et al. (eds. and tr.), *Qumran Cave 4, XXV: Halakhic Texts*. Discoveries in the Judaean Desert 35. Oxford: Clarendon. Pp. 135–153.

Eshel, Hanan, 2000. "CD 12:15–17 and the Stone Vessels found at Qumran." Joseph M. Baumgarten et al. (eds.), *The Damascus Document: A Centennial of Discovery*. Leiden: Brill. Pp. 45–52.

Evans, Christopher Francis, 1990. *Saint Luke*. London: SCM.

Faulkner, Jason, Mark Schaller, Justin H. Park and Lesley A. Duncan, 2004. "Evolved Disease-Avoidance Mechanisms and Contemporary Xenophobic Attitudes." *Group Processes & Intergroup Relations* 7: 333–353.

Fine, Steven, 2000. "A Note on Ossuary Burial and the Resurrection of the Dead in First Century Jerusalem." *Journal of Jewish Studies* 51: 69–76.

Finkelstein, Jacob J., 1973. "The Goring Ox: Some Historical Perspectives on Deodands, Forfeitures, Wrongful Death and the Western Notion of Sovereignty." *Temple Law Quarterly* 46: 169–290.

Finkelstein, Louis, 1938. *The Pharisees: The Sociological Background of their Faith*. 2 vols. Philadelphia: The Jewish Publication Society of America.

Fitzmyer, Joseph A., 1985. *The Gospel According to Luke*. Vol. 2. 2nd ed. Anchor Bible 28A. New York: Doubleday.

Fonrobert, Charlotte E., 1997. "The Woman with a Blood Flow (Mark 5.24–34) Revisited: Menstrual Laws and Jewish Culture in Christian Feminist Hermeneutics." C. A. Evans and J. A. Sanders (eds.), *Early Christian Interpretation of the Scriptures of Israel: Investigations and Proposals*. Journal for the Study of the New Testament Supplement Series 48. Studies in Scripture in Early Judaism and Christianity 5. Sheffield: JSOT Press. Pp. 121–140.

Freyne, Seán, 1988. "Bandits in Galilee: A Contribution to the Study of Social Conditions in First-Century Palestine." J. Neusner et. al. (eds.), *The Social World of Formative Christianity and Judaism: Essays in Tribute to Howard Clark Kee*. Philadelphia: Fortress.

Fry, Douglas P., 2000. "Conflict Managment in Cross-Cultural Perspective." Filippo Aureli and Frans B. M. de Waal (eds.), *Natural Conflict Resolution*. Berkeley/Los Angeles/London: University of California Press. Pp. 334–351.

Furstenberg, Yair, 2008. "Defilement Penetrating the Body: A New Understanding of Contamination in Mark 7.15." *New Testament Studies* 54: 176–200.

Galor, Katharina, 2007. "The Stepped Water Installations of the Sepphoris Acropolis." Douglas R. Edwards and C. Thomas McCollough (eds.), *The Archaeology of Difference: Gender, Ethnicity, Class and the "Other" in Antiquity: Studies in Honor of Eric M. Meyers*. The Annual of the American Schools of Oriental Research 60/61. Boston: American Schools of Oriental Research. Pp. 201–213.

García Martínez, Florentino, 1994. *The Dead Sea Scrolls Translated: The Qumran Texts in English*. Leiden: Brill. 2nd ed. 1996. Leiden: Brill/Grand Rapids: Eerdmans.

García Martínez, Florentino and Eibert J. C. Tigchelaar, 1997–1998. *The Dead Sea Scrolls Study Edition*. 2 vols. Leiden: Brill. Pbk ed. 2000. Grand Rapids: Eerdmans.

Gärdenfors, Peter, 2005. *Tankens vindlar: Om språk, minne och berättande*. Nora: Nya Doxa.

Gerstenberger, Erhard S., 1993. *Das dritte Buch Mose: Leviticus*. Das Alte Testament Deutsch 6. Göttingen: Vandenhoeck & Ruprecht.

Gilders, William K., 2004. *Blood Ritual in the Hebrew Bible: Meaning and Power*. Baltimore/London: John Hopkins University Press.

Gowler, David B., 2006. "The *Chreia*." Amy-Jill Levine, Dale C. Allison Jr., and John Dominic Crossan (eds.), *The Historical Jesus in Context*. Princeton Readings in Religion. Princeton and Oxford: Princeton University Press. Pp. 132–148.

Grabbe, Lester L., 2004. *A History of the Jews and Judaism in the Second Temple Period*. Volume 1: *Yehud: A History of the Persian Province of Judah*. Library of Second Temple Studies 47. London and New York: T&T Clark.

Gruber, Mayer I., 1987. "Women in the Cult According to the Priestly Code." J. Neusner, B. A. Levine and E. S. Frerichs (eds.), *Judaic Perspectives on Ancient Israel*. Philadelphia: Fortress. Pp. 35–48.

Haber, Susan, 2003. "A Woman's Touch: Feminist Encounters with the Hemorrhaging Woman in Mark 5.24–34." *Journal for the Study of the New Testament* 26: 171–192.

Haber, Susan, 2008. *"They Shall Purify Themselves": Essays on Purity in Early Judaism*. Edited by Adele Reinhartz. Early Judaism and Its Literature 24. Atlanta: Society of Biblical Literature.

Hägerland, Tobias, 2009. *Jesus and the Forgiveness of Sins: An Aspect of his Prophetic Mission*. Skrifter utgivna vid Institutionen för litteratur, idéhistoria och religion, Göteborgs universitet 33. Göteborg: Göteborgs universitet.

Haidt, Jonathan, 2003. "The Moral Emotions." R. J. Davidson, K. R. Scherer and H. H. Goldsmith (eds.), *Handbook of Affective Sciences*. Oxford: Oxford University Press. Pp. 852–870.

Harrington, Hannah K., 1993. *The Impurity Systems of Qumran and the Rabbis: Biblical Foundations*. SBL Dissertation Series 143; Atlanta: Scholars Press.

Harrington, Hannah K., 2004. *The Purity Texts*. Companion to the Qumran Scrolls. London: T & T Clark.

Hayes, Christine E., 2002. *Gentile Impurities and Jewish Identities: Intermarriage and Conversion from the Bible to the Talmud*. Oxford: University Press.

Hempel, Charlotte, 2000. *The Damascus Texts*. Companion to the Qumran Scrolls 1. Sheffield: Sheffield Academic Press.

Himmelfarb, Martha, 2001. "Impurity and Sin in 4QD, 1QS, and 4Q512." *Dead Sea Discoveries* 8: 9–37.

Himmelfarb, Martha, 2004. "The Purity Laws of 4QD: Exegesis and Sectarianism." Esther G. Chazon et. al. (eds.), *Things Revealed: Studies in Early Jewish and Christian Literature in Honor of Michael E. Stone*. Leiden: Brill. Pp. 155–169.

Hofer, Heribert and Marion L. East, 2000. "Conflict Management in Female-Dominated Spotted Hyenas." Filippo Aureli and Frans B. M. de Waal (eds.), *Natural Conflict Resolution*. Berkeley/Los Angeles/London: University of California Press. Pp. 232–234.

Hoffmann, David Z., 1905–1906. *Das Buch Leviticus übersetzt und erklärt*. 2 vols. Berlin: M. Poppelauer.

Holmén, Tom, 2007. "An Introduction to the Continuum Approach." Tom Holmén (ed.), *Jesus from Judaism to Christianity: Continuum Approaches to the Historical Jesus*. ESCO; LNTS 352. London: T & T Clark. Pp. 1–16.

Hooker, Morna D., 1991. *The Gospel according to Saint Mark*. Black's New Testament Commentaries. London: A & C Black [Reprint: Hendrickson].

Houston, Walter, 1993. *Purity and Monotheism: Clean and Unclean Animals in Biblical Law*. Journal for the Study of the Old Testament Supplement Series 140. Sheffield: JSOT Press.

Hübner, Hans, 1986. *Das Gesetz in der synoptischen Tradition: Studien zur These einer progressiven Qumranisierung und Judaisiering innerhalb der synoptischen Tradition*. 2nd ed. Göttingen: Vandenhoeck & Ruprecht.

Hulse, E. V., 1975. "The Nature of Biblical 'Leprosy' and the Use of Alternative Medical Terms in Modern Translations of the Bible." *Palestinian Exploration Quarterly* 107: 87–105

Humbert, Paul, 1960. "Le substantif *to'ēbā* et le verbe *t'b* dans l'Ancien Testament." *Zeitschrift für die Alttestamentliche Wissenschaft* 72: 217–237.

Instone-Brewer, David, 2004. *Traditions of the Rabbis from the Era of the New Testament*. Vol. 1: *Prayer and Agriculture*. Grand Rapids: Eerdmans.

Instone-Brewer, David, 2010, forthcoming. *Traditions of the Rabbis from the Era of the New Testament*. Vol. 2A: *Feasts and Sabbaths: Passover and Atonement*. Grand Rapids: Eerdmans.

Jackson, Bernard S., 2002. "Models in Legal History: The Case of Biblical Law." *Journal of Law and Religion* 18: 1–30.

Jackson, Bernard S., 2006. *Wisdom-Laws: A Study of the* Mishpatim *of Exodus 21:1–22:16*. Oxford: University Press.

Jaffee, Martin S., 2001. *Torah in the Mouth: Writing and Oral Tradition in Palestinian Judaism, 200 BCE–400 CE*. Oxford: Oxford University Press.

Jastrow, Marcus, 1926. *A Dictionary of the Targumim, the Talmud Babli and Yerushalmi, and the Midrashic Literature*. Vol. 1–2. New York / Berlin: Verlag Choreb; London: Shapiro, Vallentine & Co.

Jeremias, Joachim, 1972 [1962]. *The Parables of Jesus*. 3rd ed. London: SCM.

Kahl, Brigitte, 1996. "Jairus und die verlorenen Töchter Israels: Sozioliterarische Überlegungen zum Problem der Grenzüberschreitung in Mk 5, 21–43." L. Schottroff and M.-T. Wacker (eds.), *Von der Wurzel getragen: Christlich-feministische Exegese in Auseinandersetzung mit Antijudaismus*. Biblical Interpretation Series 17. Leiden: Brill. Pp. 61–78.

Kaufmann, Yehezkel, 1960 [1937–1948]. *The Religion of Israel: From Its Beginnings to the Babylonian Exile.* Translated and abridged by Moshe Greenberg. Chicago: The University of Chicago Press.

Kazen, Thomas, 2002. *Jesus and Purity* Halakhah*: Was Jesus Indifferent to Impurity?* ConBNT, 38. Stockholm: Almqvist & Wiksell International.

Kazen, Thomas, 2007. "Explaining Discrepancies in the Purity Laws on Discharges." *Revue Biblique* 114: 348–371.

Kazen, Thomas, 2008. "Dirt and Disgust: Body and Morality in Biblical Purity Laws." Baruch J. Schwartz, David P. Wright, Jeffrey Stackert and Naphtali S. Meshel (eds.), *Perspectives on Purity and Purification in the Bible.* Library of Hebrew Bible/Old Testament Studies 474. New York: T & T Clark. Pp. 43–64.

Kazen, Thomas, 2010a. "4Q274, Fragment 1 Revisited – or Who Touched Whom? Further Evidence for Ideas of Graded Impurity and Graded Purifications." *Dead Sea Discoveries* 17: 53–87.

Kazen, Thomas, 2010b. *Jesus and Purity* Halakhah*: Was Jesus Indifferent to Impurity?* ConBNT, 38. Corrected reprint edition. Winona Lake, In.: Eisenbrauns.

Kazen, Thomas, 2010c. "Jesus, Scripture and *Paradosis*: Response to Friedrich Avemarie." Reimund Bieringer et. al. (eds.), *The New Testament and Rabbinic Literature.* SupJSJ 136. Leiden and Boston: Brill. Pp. 281–288.

Kazen, Thomas, 2011a [forthcoming]. "Concern, Custom and Common Sense: Discharge, Hand-washing and Graded Purification." Robert Webb and Marc Goodacre (eds.), *Jesus as Restoration Prophet: Engaging the Work of E. P. Sanders.* LNTS 372. London and New York: T & T Clark, 2011.

Kazen, Thomas, 2011b [forthcoming]. *Emotions in Biblical Law: A Cognitive Science Approach to Some Moral and Ritual Issues in Pentateuchal Legal Collections.*

Kazen, Thomas, 2011c [forthcoming]. "Jesus and the *Zavah*: Implications for interpreting Mark." Carl Ehrlich et al. (eds.), *Purity and Holiness in Ancient Judaism and Early Christianity: Essays in Memory of Susan Haber.* Wissenschaftliche Untersuchungen zum Neuen Testament. Tübingen: Mohr Siebeck.

Kekes, John, 1992. "Disgust and Moral Taboos." *Philosophy* 67: 431–46.

Klawans, Jonathan, 2000. *Impurity and Sin in Ancient Judaism.* New York: Oxford University Press.

Knohl, Israel, 1995. *The Sanctuary of Silence: The Priestly Torah and the Holiness School.* Minneapolis: Fortress.

Knowles, Melody D., 2006. *Centrality Practiced: Jerusalem in the Religious Practice of Yehud and the Diaspora in the Persian Period.* Archaeology and Biblical Studies 16. Atlanta: Society of Biblical Literature.

Knuuttila, Simo and Juha Sihvola, 1998. "How the Philosophical Analysis of Emotions was Introduced." Juha Sihvola and Troels Engberg-Pedersen (eds.), *The Emotions in Hellenistic Philosophy.* The New Synthese Historical Library 46. Dordrecht/Boston/London: Kluwer Academic Publishers. Pp. 1–19.

Kolnai, Aurel, 2004 [1929]. *On Disgust.* Edited by Barry Smith and Carolyn Korsmeyer. Chicago/La Salle, Il.: Open Court.

Krebs, Dennis L., 2008. "The Evolution of a Sense of Justice." Joshua Dutley and Todd K. Shackleford (eds.), *Evolutionary Forensic Psychology: Darwinian Foundations of Crime and Law*. New York: Oxford University Press.

Kruger, Michael J., 2005. *The Gospel of the Savior: An Analysis of P. Oxy. 840 an its Place in the Gospel Traditions of Early Christianity*. Texts and Editions for New Testament Study 1. Leiden: Brill.

Kuhn, Karl Georg, 1933-1955. *Tannaitische Midraschim: Sifre zu Numeri*. Rabbinische Texte, Zweite Reihe, Band 2, Heft 1–9. Stuttgart: W. Kohlhammer.

Lakoff, George and Mark Johnson, 1999. *Philosophy in the Flesh: The Embodied Mind and Its Challenge to Western Thought*. New York: Basic Books.

Lawrence, Jonathan D., 2006. *Washing in Water: Trajectories of Ritual Bathing in the Hebrew Bible and Second Temple Literature*. SBL Academia Biblica 23. Atlanta: Society of Biblical Literature.

Lemerise, Elizabeth A. and Kenneth A. Dodge, 2004. "The Development of Anger and Hostile Interactions." Michael Lewis and Jeanette M. Haviland-Jones (eds.), *Handbook of Emotions*. 2nd edn. New York: Guildford. Pp. 594–607.

Lemos, Tracy M., 2008. "Where There Is Dirt, Is There System? Revisiting Biblical Purity Constructions." Paper presented at the SBL Annual Meeting, Boston, November 2008.

Lemos, Tracy M., 2009. "The Universal and the Particular: Mary Douglas and the Politics of Impurity." *The Journal of Religion* 89: 236–251.

Levine, Baruch A., 1974. *In the Presence of the Lord: A Study of Cult and Some Cultic Terms in Ancient Israel*. Studies in Judaism in Late Antiquity 5. Leiden: Brill.

Liddell, Henry George and Robert Scott, 1940. *A Greek-English Lexicon*. 9th ed., revised by H. S. Jones. Oxford: Clarendon.

Lightstone, Jack N., 2007. "The Pharisees and the Sadducees in the Earliest Rabbinic Documents." Jacob Neusner and Bruce D. Chilton (eds.), *In Quest of the Historical Pharisees*. Waco, Tx.: Baylor. Pp. 255–295.

Lockett, Darian R., 2008. *Purity and Worldview in the Epistle of James*. Library of New Testament Studies 366. London and New York: T & & Clark.

Looy, Heather, 2004. "Embodied and Embedded Morality: Divinity, Identity, and Disgust." *Zygon* 39: 219–235.

Luomanen, Petri, Ilkka Pyysiäinen and Risto Uro, 2008. "Introduction: Social and Cognitive Perspectives in the Study of Christian Origins and Early Judaism." Luomanen, Petri, Ilkka Pyysiäinen and Risto Uro (eds.), *Explaining Christian Origins and Early Judaism: Contributions from Cognitive and Social Sciences*. Biblical Interpretation Series 89. Leiden/Boston: Brill.

Maccoby, Hyam, 1999. *Ritual and Morality: The Ritual Purity System and its Place in Judaism*. Cambridge: Cambridge University Press.

Magen, Yitzshak, 2002. *The Stone Vessel Industry in the Second Temple Period: Excavations at Ḥizma and the Jerusalem Temple Mount*. Judea and Samaria Publications 1. Jerusalem: Israel Exploration Society and Staff Officer of Archaeology.

Malandra, William W., 1983. *An Introduction to Ancient Iranian Religion: Readings from the Avesta and the Achaemenid Inscriptions*. Minnesota: Minnesota University Press.

Mann, Jacob, 1915-1916. "Jesus and the Sadducean Priests: Luke 10. 25-37." *Jewish Quarterly Review* 6: 415-422.

Marshall, I. H., 1978. *The Gospel of Luke: A Commentary on the Greek Text.* New International Greek Testament Commentary. Exeter: Paternoster.

Maul, Stefan M., 1994. *Zukunftsbewältigung: Eine Untersuchung altorientalischen Denkens anhand der babylonisch-assyrischen Löserituale (Namburbi).* Baghdader Forschungen 18. Mainz am Rhein: Verlag Philipp von Zabern.

Mazar, Benjamin, 1975. *The Mountain of the Lord.* Garden City, N.Y.: Doubleday.

McEvoy, Chad Joseph, 2002. "A Consideration of Human Xenophobia and Ethnocentrism from a Sociobiological Perspective." *Human Rights Review*, April-June 2002: 39–49.

Meacham (leBeit Yoreh), Tirẓa, 1999a. "An Abbreviated History of the Development of the Jewish Menstrual Laws." R. R. Wasserfall (ed.), *Women and Water: Menstruation in Jewish Life and Law.* Hanover, New Hampshire: Brandeis University Press. Pp. 23–39.

Meacham (leBeit Yoreh), Tirẓa, 1999b. "Appendix." R. R. Wasserfall (ed.), *Women and Water: Menstruation in Jewish Life and Law.* Hanover, New Hampshire: Brandeis University Press. Pp. 255–260.

Meier, John P., 2009. *A Marginal Jew: Rethinking the Historical Jesus.* Vol. 4: *Law and Love.* Anchor Yale Bible Reference Library. New Haven and London: Yale University Press.

Menninghaus, Winfried, 1999. *Ekel: Theorie und Geschichte einer starken Empfindung.* Frankfurt am Main: Suhrkampf.

Milgrom, Jacob, 1972. " 'Eglah 'Arufah." *Encyclopaedia Judaica.* Vol. 6.Jerusalem: Keter Publishing House. Col. 475–477.

Milgrom, Jacob, 1978. "Studies in the Temple Scroll." *Journal of Biblical Literature* 97: 501–523.

Milgrom, Jacob, 1981. "The Paradox of the Red Cow (Num. xix)." *Vetus Testamentum* 31: 62–72.

Milgrom, Jacob, 1990. "The Scriptural Foundations and Deviations in the Laws of Purity of the *Temple Scroll.*" L. H. Schiffman (ed.), *Archaeology and History in the Dead Sea Scrolls: The New York University Conference in Memory of Yigael Yadin.* Journal for the Study of the Pseudepigrapha Supplement Series 8. Journal for the Study of the Old Testament / American Schools of Oriental Research Monographs 2. Sheffield: JSOT Press. Pp. 83–99.

Milgrom, Jacob, 1991. *Leviticus, 1–16: A New Translation with Introduction and Commentary.* Anchor Bible 3; Garden City, N.Y.: Doubleday.

Milgrom, Jacob, 1992. "First Day Ablutions in Qumran." Julio Trebolle Barrera and Luis Vegas Montaner (eds.), *The Madrid Qumran Congress: Proceedings of the International Congress on the Dead Sea Scrolls: Madrid 18–21 March 1991.* Vol. 2. Leiden: Brill. Pp. 561–570.

Milgrom, Jacob, 1995. "4QTohora[a]: An Unpublished Qumran Text on Purities." D. Dimant and L. Schiffman (eds.), *Time to Prepare the Way in the Wilderness.* Studies on the Texts of the Deserts of Judah 16. Leiden: Brill. Pp. 59–68.

Milgrom, Jacob, 2000a. *Leviticus, 17–22: A New Translation with Introduction and Commentary.* Anchor Bible 3a; Garden City, N.Y.: Doubleday.

Milgrom, Jacob, 2000b. *Leviticus, 23–27: A New Translation with Introduction and Commentary.* Anchor Bible 3b; Garden City, N.Y.: Doubleday.

Miller, Stuart S., 2003. "Some Observations on Stone Vessel Finds and Ritual Purity in Light of Talmudic Sources." Stefan Alkier and Jürgen Zangenberg (eds.), *Zeichen aus Text und Stein: Studien auf dem Weg zu einer Archäologie des Neuen Testaments.* TANZ 42. Tübingen and Basel: Francke Verlag. Pp. 402–419.

Miller, Stuart S., 2006. *Sages and Commoners in Late Anique 'Erez Israel: A Philological Inquiry into Local Traditions in Talmud Yerushalmi.* TSAJ 111. Tübingen: Mohr Siebeck.

Miller, Stuart S., 2007. "Stepped Pools and the Non-Existent Monolithic 'Miqveh'." Douglas R. Edwards and C. Thomas McCollough (eds.), *The Archaeology of Difference: Gender, Ethnicity, Class and the "Other" in Antiquity: Studies in Honor of Eric M. Meyers.* The Annual of the American Schools of Oriental Research 60/61. Boston: American Schools of Oriental Research. Pp. 215–234.

Miller, Stuart S., 2010. "Stepped Pools, Stone Vessels, and other Identity Markers of Complex Common Judaism." *Journal for the Study of Judaism in the Persian, Hellenistic and Roman Periods* 41: 214–243.

Miller, Susan B., 2004. *Disgust: The Gatekeeper Emotion.* Hillsdale, N.J./London: The Analytic Press.

Miller, William Ian, 1997. *The Anatomy of Disgust.* Cambridge, Mass.: Harvard University Press.

Navarrete, Carlos David and Daniel M. T. Fessler, 2006. "Disease Avoidance and Ethnocentrism: The Effects of Disease Vulnerability and Disgust Sensitivity on Intergroup Attitudes." *Evolution and Human Behavior* 27: 270–282.

Neusner, Jacob, 1971. *The Rabbinic Traditions about the Pharisees before 70.* 3 vols. Leiden: Brill.

Neusner, Jacob, 1977. *A History of the Mishnaic Law of Purities.* Vol. XVIII. Studies in Judaism in Late Antiquity 6:18. Leiden: Brill.

Neusner, Jacob, 1977. *A History of the Mishnaic Law of Purities.* Vol. XXII. Studies in Judaism in Late Antiquity 6:22. Leiden: Brill.

Neusner, Jacob, 1977–1986. *The Tosefta: Translated from the Hebrew.* 6 vols. New York: KTAV Publishing House.

Neusner, Jacob, 1979 [2nd ed. 1979]. *From Politics to Piety: The Emergence of Pharisaic Judaism.* New York: KTAV.

Neusner, Jacob, 1982. *A History of the Mishnaic Law of Appointed Times.* Vol. III: *Sheqalim, Yoma, Sukkah:Ttranslation and Explanation.* Studies in Judaism in Late Antiquity 34:3. Leiden: Brill.

Neusner, Jacob, 1988. *The Mishnah: A New Translation.* New Haven/London: Yale University Press.

Neusner, Jacob, 1990. *The Talmud of the Land of Israel: A Preliminary Translation and Explanation.* Vol. XIV: *Yoma.* Chicago Studies in the History of Judaism. Chicago: University Press.

Neusner, Jacob, 2007a. "The Rabbinic Traditions about the Pharisees before 70 CE: An Overview." Jacob Neusner and Bruce D. Chilton (eds.), *In Quest of the Historical Pharisees*. Waco, Tx: Baylor. Pp. 297–311.

Neusner, Jacob, 2007b. "The Pharisaic Agenda: Laws Attributed in the Mishnah and the Tosefta to Pre-70 Pharisees." Jacob Neusner and Bruce D. Chilton (eds.), *In Quest of the Historical Pharisees*. Waco, Tx.: Baylor. Pp. 313–327.

Neusner, Jacob, 2007c. "The Debate with E. P. Sanders since 1970." Jacob Neusner and Bruce D. Chilton (eds.), *In Quest of the Historical Pharisees*. Waco, Tx.: Baylor. Pp. 395–405.

Nihan, Christophe, 2004. "The Holiness Code between D and P: Some Comments on the Function and Significance of Leviticus 17–26 in the Composition of the Torah." Eckart Otto and Reinhard Achenbach (eds.), *Das Deuteronomium zwischen Pentateuch und Deuteronomistischen Geschichtswerk*. Forschungen zur Religion und Literatur des Alten und Neuen Testaments 206. Göttingen: Vandenhoeck & Ruprecht. Pp. 81–122.

Nihan, Christophe, 2007. *From Priestly Torah to Pentateuch: A Study of the Composition of the Book of Leviticus*. Forschungen zum Alten Testament 2:25. Tübingen: Mohr Siebeck.

Nihan, Christophe, 2009. "Foreigners, Resident Aliens and Natives in the Holiness Code: Semantic and Legal Issues." Paper presented at the SBL International Meeting, Rome, July 2009.

Noam, Vered, 2008. "The Dual Strategy of Rabbinic Purity Legislation." *Journal for the Study of Judaism in the Persian, Hellenistic and Roman Periods* 39: 471–512.

Noam, Vered, 2009. "Impurity and Sanctity in Josephus and in Rabbinic Halakhah: The Exclusion of Impure Persons from Holy Precincts." Paper presented at the SBL Annual Meeting, Boston, November 2009.

Noam, Vered, 2010. "Ritual Impurity in Tannaitic Literature: Two Opposing Perspectives." *Journal of Ancient Judaism* 1: 65–103.

Nogalski, James, 1993. *Literary Precursors to the Book of the Twelve*. Beihefte zur Zeitschrift für die alttestamentliche Wissenschaft 217. Berlin and New York: Walter de Gruyter.

Nussbaum, Martha, 2004. *Hiding from Humanity: Disgust, Shame, and the Law*. Princeton: University Press.

Nyberg, H. S., 1937. *Irans forntida religioner: Olaus-Petri-föreläsningar vid Uppsala Universitet*. Stockholm: Svenska kyrkans diakonistyrelses bokförlag.

O'Grady, Kathleen, 2003. "The Semantics of Taboo: Menstrual Prohibitions in the Hebrew Bible." Kristin de Troyer et. al. (eds.), *Wholly Woman, Holy Blood: A Feminist Critique of Purity and Impurity*. Harrisburg: Trinity. Pp. 1–28.

Öhman, Arne, 2000. "Fear and Anxiety: Evolutionary, Cognitive, and Clinical Perspectives." Michael Lewis and Jeanette M. Haviland-Jones (eds.), *Handbook of Emotions*. 2nd edn. New York/London: Guildford. Pp. 573–593.

Oppenheimer, Aharon, 1977. *The 'Am Ha-Aretz: A Study in the Social History of the Jewish People in the Hellenistic-Roman Period*. Arbeiten zur Literatur und Geschichte des Hellenistischen Judentums 8. Leiden: Brill.

Otto, Eckart, 1999. *Das Deuteronomium: Politische Theologie und Rechtsreform in Juda und Assyrien.* BZAW 284. Berlin, New York: Walter de Gruyter.

Pardee, Dennis, 2002. *Ritual and Cult at Ugarit.* Writings from the Ancient World 10. Atlanta: Society of Biblical Literature.

Parisi, F., 2001. "The Genesis of Liability in Ancient Law." *American Law and Economics Review* 3: 82–124.

Park, Seung-Ryong and Robert D. Enright, "Forgiveness Across Cultures." Filippo Aureli and Frans B. M. de Waal (eds.), *Natural Conflict Resolution.* Berkeley/Los Angeles/London: University of California Press. Pp. 359–361.

Peterson, Gregory R., 2003. *Minding God: Theology and the Cognitive Sciences.* Theology and the Sciences. Minneapolis: Fortress.

Philip, Tarja S., 2006. *Menstruation and Childbirth in the Bible: Fertility and Impurity.* Studies in Biblical Literature 88. New York: Peter Lang.

Phillips, Anthony, 2004 [2002]. *Essays on Biblical Law.* London/New York: T & T Clark [Journal for the Study of the Old Testament Supplement Series 344. Sheffield: Sheffield Academic Press].

Poirier, John C., 1996. "Why Did the Pharisees Wash Their Hands?" *Journal of Jewish Studies* 46: 217–233.

Poirier, John C., 2003. "Purity Beyond the Temple in the Second Temple Era." *Journal of Biblical Literature* 122: 247–265.

Power, Mick and Tim Dalgleish, 1997. *Cognition and Emotion: From Order to Disorder.* Hove: Psychology Press.

Qumran Cave 4, XXV: Halakhic Texts. Ed. and tr. by Joseph M. Baumgarten et. al. Discoveries in the Judaean Desert 35. Oxford: Clarendon, 1999.

Range, Friederike, Lisa Horn, Zsófia Viranyi and Ludwig Huber, 2009. "The Absence of Reward Induces Inequity Aversion in Dogs." *Proceedings of the National Academy of Sciences* 106: 340–345.

Reed, Jonathan L., 2003. "Stone Vessels and Gospel Texts: Purity and Socio-Economics in John 2." Stefan Alkier and Jürgen Zangenberg (eds.), *Zeichen aus Text und Stein: Studien auf dem Weg zu einer Archäologie des Neuen Testaments.* TANZ 42. Tübingen and Basel: Francke Verlag. Pp. 381–401.

Regev, Eyal, 2000a. "Pure Individualism: The Idea of Non-Priestly Purity in Ancient Judaism." *Journal for the Study of Judaism in the Persian, Hellenistic and Roman Periods* 31: 176–202.

Regev, Eyal, 2000b. "Non-Priestly Purity and its Religious Aspects according to Historical Sources and Archaeological Findings." M. J. H. M. Poorthuis and J. Schwartz (eds.), *Purity and Holiness: The Heritage of Leviticus.* Jewish and Christian Perspectives Series 2. Leiden: Brill. Pp. 223–244.

Reich, Ronny, 1988. "The Hot Bath-House Balneum, the Miqweh and the Jewish Community in the Second Temple Period." *Journal of Jewish Studies* 39: 102–107.

Reich, Ronny, 1989. "Two Possible Miqwā'ōt on the Temple Mount." *Israel Exploration Journal* 39: 63–65.

Reich, Ronny, 1993. "The Great Miqveh Debate." *Biblical Archaeology Review* 19:2, pp. 52–53.

Reich, Ronny, 2000. "Mikwa'ot at Khirbet Qumran and the Jerusalem Connection." L. H. Schiffman, E. Tov, and J. C. VanderKam (eds.), *The Dead Sea Scrolls: Fifty Years after their Discovery*. Jerusalem: Israel Exploration Society / The Shrine of the Book, Israel Museum. Pp. 728–731.

Reich, Ronny, 2002. "They Are Ritual Baths: Immerse Yourself in the Ongoing Sepphoris Mikveh Debate." *Biblical Archaeology Review* 28:2, pp. 50–55.

Reiner, Erica, 1958. *Šurpu: A Collection of Sumerian and Akkadian Incantations*. Archiv für Orientforschung, herausgeben von Ernst Weidner, 11. Im Selbstverlage des Herausgebers: Graz.

Rivkin, Ellis, 1978. *A Hidden Revolution: The Pharisees' Search for a Kingdom Within*. Nashville: Abingdon.

Römer, Thomas C., 2005. *The So-Called Deuteronomistic History: A Sociological, Historical and Literary Introduction*. London: T & T Clark.

Römer, Thomas, 2008. "De la périphérie au centre: les livres du Lévitique et des Nombres dans le débat actuel sur le Pentateuque." Thomas Römer (ed.), *The Books of Leviticus and Numbers*. Bibliotheca ephemeridum theologicarum lovaniensium 215. Leuven: Uitgeverij Peeters. Pp. 3–34.

Roth, Martha T., 2003 [1997]. *Law Collections from Mesopotamia and Asia Minor*. 2nd edn. SBL Writings from the Ancient World 6. Atlanta, Ga.: Scholars Press.

Rottschaefer, William A., 1998. *The Biology and Psychology of Moral Agency*. Cambridge: University Press.

Rozin, Paul, Jonathan Haidt and Clark McCauley, 2000. "Disgust." Michael Lewis and Jeanette M. Haviland-Jones (eds.), *Handbook of Emotions*. 2nd edn. New York: Guildford. Pp. 637–653.

Rozin, Paul, Jonathan Haidt, Clark McCauley and Sumio Imada, 1997. "Disgust: Preadaptation and the Cultural Evolution of a Food-Based Emotion." Helen Macbeth (ed.), *Food Preferences and Taste: Continuity and Change*. Providence: Berghahn. Pp. 65–82.

Sanders, E. P., 1990. *Jewish Law from Jesus to the Mishnah: Five Studies*. London: SCM.

Sanders, E. P., 1992. *Judaism: Practice and Belief, 63 BCE–66 CE*. London: SCM.

Schäfer, P. and H.-J. Becker (eds.), 2001. *Synopse zum Talmud Yerushalmi*. Vol. II:1-4: *Ordnung Mo"ed: Shabbat, "Eruvin, Pesaḥim und Yoma*. Texts and Studies in Ancient Judaism 82. Tübingen: Mohr Siebeck.

Schaper, Joachim, 2000. *Priester und Leviten im achämenidischen Juda*. Forschungen zum Alten Testament 31. Tübingen: Mohr Siebeck.

Schart, Aaron, 2000. "Reconstructing the Redaction History of the Twelve Prophets: Problems and Models." James D. Nogalski and Marvin A. Sweeney (eds.), *Reading and Hearing the Book of the Twelve*. Symposium Series 15. Atlanta: Society of Biblical Literature. Pp. 34–48.

Schiffman, Lawrence H., 1994. "Pharisaic and Sadduceean Halakhah in Light of the Dead Sea Scrolls: The Case of Ṭevul Yom." *Dead Sea Discoveries* 1: 285–299.

Schwartz, Baruch J., 2009. "Introduction: The Strata of the Priestly Writings and the Revised Relative Dating of P and H." Sara Shectman and Joel S. Baden (eds.), *The*

Strata of the Priestly Writings: Contemporary Debate and Future Directions. Zürich: Tehologischer Verlag. Pp. 1–12.

Schweinhorst-Schönberger, Ludger, 1990. *Das Bundesbuch (Ex 20,22–23,33). Studien zu seiner Entstehung und Theologie.* Berlin, New York: Walter de Gruyter.

Scurlock, JoAnn, 2002. "Translating Transfers in Ancient Mesopotamia." Paul Mirecki and Marvin Mayer (eds.), *Magic and Ritual in the Ancient World.* Religions in the Graeco-Roman World 141. Leiden: Brill. Pp. 209–223.

Shweder, Richard A., Nancy C. Much, Manomohan Mahapatra and Lawrence Park, 1997. "The 'Big Three' of Morality (Autonomy, Community, Divinity) and the 'Big Three' Explanations of Suffering." A. Brandt and P. Rozin, (eds.), *Morality and Health.* New York/London: Routledge. Pp. 119–169.

Sievers, Joseph, 1997. "Who Were the Pharisees?" J. H. Charlesworth and L. L. Johns (eds.), *Hillel and Jesus: Comparative Studies of Two Major Religious Leaders.* Minneapolis: Fortress. Pp. 137–155.

Silk, Joan B., 1996. "Why Do Primates Reconcile?" *Evolutionary Anthropology* 5: 39–42.

Silk, Joan B., 2000. "The Function of Peaceful Post-Conflict Interactions: An Alternative View." Filippo Aureli and Frans B. M. de Waal (eds.), *Natural Conflict Resolution.* Berkeley/Los Angeles/London: University of California Press. Pp. 179–181.

Sklar, Jay, 2005. *Sin, Impurity, Sacrifice, Atonement: The Priestly Conceptions.* Hebrew Bible Monographs 2. Sheffield: Sheffield Phoenix Press.

Stackert, Jeffrey, 2007. *Rewriting the Torah: Literary Revision in Deuteronomy and the Holiness Legislation.* Tübingen: Mohr Siebeck.

Stark, Rodney, 2001. "Gods, Rituals, and the Moral Order." *Journal for the Scientific Study of Religion* 40: 619–636.

Stemberger, Günther, 1995 [German 1991]. *Jewish Contemporaries of Jesus: Pharisees, Sadducees, Essenes.* Minneapolis: Fortress.

Stemberger, Günther, 2010. "Dating Rabbinic Traditions." Reimund Bieringer et. al. (eds.), *The New Testament and Rabbinic Literature.* SupJSJ 136. Leiden and Boston: Brill. Pp. 79–96.

Strack, Hermann L. and Paul Billerbeck, 1924. *Kommentar zum Neuen Testament aus Talmud und Midrasch.* Vol. II: *Das Evangelium nach Markus, Lukas und Johannes und die Apostelgeschichte: erläutert aus Talmud und Midrasch.* München: C. H. Beck'sche Verlagsbuchhandlung.

Strange, James F., 2007. "Archaeology and the Pharisees." Jacob Neusner and Bruce D. Chilton (eds.), *In Quest of the Historical Pharisees.* Waco, Tx.: Baylor. Pp. 237–251.

Sulzberger, Mayer, 1914. "The Ancient Hebrew Law of Homicide: I." *Jewish Quarterly Review* 5: 127–161.

Sulzberger, Mayer, 1915a. "The Ancient Hebrew Law of Homicide: II–III." *Jewish Quarterly Review* 5: 289–344.

Sulzberger, Mayer, 1915b. "The Ancient Hebrew Law of Homicide: IV." *Jewish Quarterly Review* 5: 559–614.

Svartvik, Jesper. *Mark and Mission: Mk 7.1–23 in Its Narrative and Historical Contexts*. ConBNT 32. Stockholm: Almqvist & Wiksell International, 2000.

Taylor, Vincent, 1966. *The Gospel according to St. Mark: The Greek Text with Introduction, Notes and Indexes*. 2nd ed. London: Macmillan.

Teehan, John, 2003. "Kantian Ethics: After Darwin." *Zygon* 38: 49–60.

Theissen, Gerd, 1983 [German 1972]. *The Miracle Stories of the Early Christian Tradition*. Edinburgh: T & T Clark.

Theissen, Gerd and Dagmar Winter, 2002 [German 1997]. *The Quest for the Plausible Jesus: The Question of Criteria*. Louisville, London: Westminster John Knox Press.

Tigay, Jeffrey H., 1996. *Deuteronomy*. The JPS Torah Commentary. Philadelphia and Jerusalem: The Jewish Publication Society.

Tomson, Peter, 1988. "Zavim 5:12 – Reflections on Dating Mishnaic Halakha." A. Kuyt and N. A. van Uchelen (ed.), *History and Form: Dutch Studies in the Mishnah: Papers Read at the Workshop "Mishnah"*. Amsterdam: J. Palache Instituut. Pp. 53–69.

Trummer, Peter. 1991. *Die blutende Frau: Wunderheilung im Neuen Testament*. Freiburg: Herder.

Ulrich, Eugene Charles, Jr., 1978. *The Qumran Text of Samuel and Josephus*. Harvard Semitic Monographs 19. Missoula: Scholars.

van der Dennen, Johan M. G, 1987. "Ethnocentrism and In-group/Out-group Differentiation: A Review and Interpretation of the Literature." V. Reynolds, Vincent Falger and Ian Vine (eds.), *The Sociobiology of Ethnocentrism*. London: Croom Helm. Pp. 1–47.

van Wolkenten, Megan, Sarah F. Brosnan and Frans B. M. de Waal, 2007. "Inequity Responses of Monkeys Modified by Effort." *Proceedings of the National Academy of Sciences* 104: 18854–18859.

von Weiher, Egbert, 1998. *Uruk: Spätbabylonische Texte aus dem Planquadrat U 18*, Teil V. Ausgrabungen in Uruk-Warka, Endberichte, Band 13. Mainz am Rhein: Verlag Philipp von Zabern.

Wacholder, Ben Zion, 2007. *The New Damascus Document: The Midrash on the Eschatological Torah of the Dead Sea Scrolls: Reconstruction, Translation and Commentary*. Studies on the Texts of the Deserts of Judah 56. Leiden: Brill.

Wacholder, Ben Zion and Martin G. Abegg, 1995. *A Preliminary Edition of the Unpublished Dead Sea Scrolls: The Hebrew and Aramaic Texts from Cave Four*. Fascicle 3. Washington, D. C.: Biblical Archaeological Society.

Wahlen, Clinton, 2004. *Jesus and the Impurity of Spirits in the Synoptic Gospels*. Wissenschaftliche Untersuchungen zum Neuen Testament 2.185. Tübingen: Mohr Siebeck.

Wassén, Cecilia, 2005. *Women in the Damascus Document*. Atlanta: SBL.

Wassén, Cecilia, 2008. "Jesus and the Hemorrhaging Woman in Mark 5:24–34: Insights from Purity Laws from the Dead Sea Scrolls." A. Voitila and J. Jokiranta (eds.), *Scripture in Transition*. SupJSJ 126. Leiden/Boston: Brill. Pp. 641–660.

Watts, James W., 2003. "The Rhetoric of Ritual Instruction in Leviticus 1–7." R. Rendtorff and R. A. Kugler (eds.), *The Book of Leviticus: Composition and Reception.* Leiden: Brill. Pp. 79–100.

Wegner, Judith Romney, 2003. "'*Coming Before the Lord*': The Exclusion of Women from the Public Domain of the Israelite Priestly Cult." R. Rendtorff and R. A. Kugler (eds.), *The Book of Leviticus: Composition and Reception.* Leiden: Brill. Pp. 451–465.

Wenham, Gordon J., 1979. *The Book of Leviticus.* NICOT. London: Hodder and Stoughton.

Werrett, Ian C., 2007. *Ritual Purity and the Dead Sea Scrolls.* Studies on the Texts of the Deserts of Judah 72. Leiden: Brill.

Westerholm, Stephen, 1978. *Jesus and Scribal Authority.* ConBNT 10. Lund: CWK Gleerup.

Wilson, James Q., 1993. *The Moral Sense.* New York: Free Press.

Wise, Michael, Martin Abegg, Jr. and Edward Cook, 1996. *The Dead Sea Scrolls: A New Translation.* New York: HarperSanFrancisco.

Wöhrle, Jakob, 2006. *Die frühen Sammlungen des Zwölfprophetenbuches: Entstehung und Komposition.* Beihefte zur ZAW 360. Berlin and New York: Walter de Gruyter.

Wright, David P., 1987a. *The Disposal of Impurity: Elimination Rites in the Bible and in Hittite and Mesopotamian Literature.* SBL Dissertation Series 101. Atlanta, Ga.: Scholars Press.

Wright, David P., 1987b. "Deuteronomy 21:1–9 as a Rite of Elimination." *Catholic Biblical Quarterly* 49: 387–403.

Wright, David P., 2003. "The Laws of Hammurabi as a Source for the Covenant Collection (Exodus 20:23–23:19)." *Maarav* 10: 11–87.

Wright, David P., 2007. "Homicide, Talion, Vengeace, and Psycho-Economic Satisfaction in the Covenant Code." David A. Bernat and Jonathan Klawans (eds.), *Religion and Violence: The Biblical Heritage. Proceedings of a Conference Held at Wellesley College and Boston University, February 19–20, 2006.* Recent Research in Biblical Studies 2. Sheffield: Sheffield Phoenix Press. Pp. 57–78.

Wright, David P., 2009. *Inventing God's Law: How the Covenant Code of the Bible Used and Revised the Laws of Hammurabi.* Oxford: University Press.

Yadin, Yigael, 1983. *The Temple Scroll.* Vol. 2: *Text and Commentary.* Jerusalem: The Israel Exploration Society / The Institute of Archaeology of the Hebrew University of Jerusalem / The Shrine of the Book

Yee, Gale A., 1987. *Composition and Tradition in the Book of Hosea: A Redaction Critical Investigation.* SBL Dissertation Series 102. Atlanta: Scholars Press.

Zaehner, R. C., 1961. *The Dawn and Twilight of Zoroastrianism.* London: Weidenfeld and Nicolson.

Zetterholm, Karin Hedner, 2006. "Kontinuitet och förändring i judendomen: Den muntliga Torahs roll." *Svensk Exegetisk Årsbok* 71: 209–230.

Source index

Author index

Word index

Itero

www.ehs.se/itero

1. Åke Viberg, *Symbols of Law: A Contextual Analysis of Legal Symbolic Acts in the Old Testament.* 2021. First published 1992 by Almqvist & Wiksell International.

2. Thomas Kazen, *Jesus and Purity* Halakhah*: Was Jesus Indifferent to Impurity?* 2021. First published 2002 by Almqvist & Wiksell International. Corrected reprint edition published 2010 by Eisenbrauns.

3. Åke Viberg, *Prophets in Action: An Analysis of Prophetic Symbolic Acts in the Old Testament.* 2021. First published 2007 by Almqvist & Wiksell International.

4. Thomas Kazen, *Issues of Impurity in Early Judaism.* 2021. First published 2010 by Eisenbrauns.

5. Rikard Roitto, *Behaving as a Christ-Believer: A Cognitive Perspective on Identity and Behavior Norms in Ephesians.* 2021. First published 2011 by Eisenbrauns.